New Challenges for the American Presidency

New Challenges for the American Presidency

George C. Edwards III
Texas A&M University

Philip John Davies
*The Eccles Centre for American Studies
at the British Library*

PEARSON
Longman

New York Boston San Francisco
London Toronto Sydney Tokyo Singapore Madrid
Mexico City Munich Paris Cape Town Hong Kong Montreal

Vice President and Publisher: Priscilla McGeehon
Executive Editor: Eric Stano
Senior Marketing Manager: Megan Galvin-Fak
Senior Production Manager: Bob Ginsberg
Project Coordination, Text Design, and Electronic Page Makeup: Nesbitt Graphics, Inc.
Senior Cover Design Manager and Cover Designer: Nancy Danahy
Cover Photo: Rick Friedman/Black Star
Manufacturing Manager: Dennis J. Para
Printer and Binder: Courier Corporation, Stoughton
Cover Printer: Lehigh Press, Inc.

Library of Congress Cataloging-in-Publication Data

New challenges for the American presidency / [edited by] George C.
Edwards, Philip John Davies.
    p. cm.
  ISBN 0-321-24381-1
  1. Presidents—United States—Congresses. 2. United States—Politics
and government—1993–2001—Congresses. 3. United States—Politics and
government—2001—Congresses. I. Edwards, George C. II. Davies,
Philip, 1948–
JK516.N49 2004
320.973—dc22

                         2003023025

Please visit our website at http://www.ablongman.com

ISBN 0-321- 24381-1

2 3 4 5 6 7 8 9 10—CRS—06 05 04

Dedication

The editors and contributors dedicate
this volume to the memory of Richard E. Neustadt,
who passed away at the age of 84 in the autumn
of 2003. Dick was a giant in the field of
the American presidency and a loyal friend,
a selfless colleague, and an irreplaceable
intellectual leader. We are especially honored to
include his last written work in this book.

Contents

Introduction   Philip John Davies   1

OVERVIEW

CHAPTER 1   Challenges Created by Contemporary
             Presidents   12
             Richard E. Neustadt

LEADING THE PUBLIC

CHAPTER 2   George W. Bush's Strategic Presidency   23
             George C. Edwards III

CHAPTER 3   The Bully Pulpit and the War on Terror   49
             Marc Landy

MANAGING THE PRESS

CHAPTER 4   News Organizations as a Presidential Resource
             in Governing: Media Opportunities and
             White House Organization   65
             Martha Joynt Kumar

LEADING CONGRESS

CHAPTER 5   Leading and Competing: The President
             and the Polarized Congress   85
             Barbara Sinclair

CHAPTER 6   Bush and Congress: Old Problems and
             New Challenges   101
             Stephen J. Wayne

CHAPTER 7 Challenging (and Acting for) the President: Congressional Leadership in an Era of Partisan Polarization 123
John E. Owens

APPOINTING THE JUDICIARY

CHAPTER 8 Presidential Strategies in the New Politics of Supreme Court Appointments 144
Robert J. McKeever

MAKING DECISIONS

CHAPTER 9 George W. Bush: Policy, Politics, and Personality 161
James P. Pfiffner

CHAPTER 10 The New National Security Strategy and the Old National Security Council 182
John Hart

IMPLEMENTING THE WAR ON TERROR

CHAPTER 11 Old Wars, New Wars, and the American Presidency 195
G. Calvin Mackenzie

CHAPTER 12 Constitutional Prerogatives and Presidential Power 211
Richard M. Pious

CHAPTER 13 The Bush Doctrine 229
John Dumbrell

INTRODUCTION

New Challenges for the American Presidency

◆ ◆ ◆

Philip John Davies

All presidents come under intense scrutiny, but the administration of George W. Bush was always likely to draw particular attention. Part of the reason for this is little more than an accident of timing. The constitutional provision for quadrennial elections means that every new century will open with a presidential election and inauguration. The turn of a century is always likely to imbue the coincident presidential election and administration with a particular significance, or at least to put them under a particularly powerful microscope. Centenaries prompt significant celebrations, and fire more than usual hopes and expectations. It would not be surprising if centennial political leaders felt more than the usual pressure of civic, economic and political aspiration from the public and the polity.

In 1801 President Thomas Jefferson became the second of the "Virginia dynasty" that occupied the executive office from the first presidency for the best part of a generation, challenged before 1828 only by the Massachusetts father and son team of John Adams and John Quincy Adams. The 1800 election was remarkable in many ways. Adams lost, to become the first one-term president. Jefferson and his running mate Burr received exactly the same number of Electoral College votes, throwing the election into the House of Representatives. The House, with one vote per delegation, sat through the night, and took thirty-six ballots before choosing, in Alexander Hamilton's words, "the lesser evil," in Thomas Jefferson. The tie was an unanticipated consequence of the growth of political organization, and the remarkable party discipline that was achieved among Jefferson's supporters. The demonstration of political success was a significant step in the continuing development of political party structures. The tie also caused enough consternation to prompt the Twelfth Amendment to the Constitution, ensuring that a parallel, but separate, elections process would produce future presidents and vice presidents.

Jefferson's administration led the United States into a new century in which national expansion and international recognition became central to the country's

1

being. Having once been concerned about the potential centralization of authority in the new nation's constitution, Jefferson nevertheless grasped the potential that lay in the Executive office to promote the national destiny. The century's first president's commissioning of the Lewis and Clark expedition and execution of the Louisiana Purchase were just part of the momentum from his administration that helped propel the fledgling nation through the century towards national consolidation and international significance.

The turn of the next century did not bring a new president, since in 1901 William McKinley returned to the office he had held first in 1897. This was nonetheless a momentous time in the nation's politics. McKinley's election campaigns featured spending on a scale not matched by any candidate again until Harding's 1920 campaign, and not exceeded consistently by both major party candidates until the 1950s. The expenditure underpinned a centrally managed and strongly organized approach brought to Republican party campaign politics by McKinley's manager, Mark Hanna. Skilled political management and deep pockets notwithstanding, Hanna's warnings that "there's only one life between this madman and the White House" did not succeed in keeping Theodore Roosevelt from the vice presidency, and when McKinley was assassinated in September 1901 the nation moved on from this tragedy with the ebullient Roosevelt at the helm.

The opening administration of the twentieth century, faced by high expectations of economic development, worries about the power of concentrated capital, contentious debates about trade isolationism, controversies about war and intervention in other nations, and concerns about its appropriate place in world affairs, had to tackle these issues both within the party and more broadly on the national scene. The result was not always tidy, but Republican national strength was relatively well maintained for a further generation, and the foundation was set for what was to become labelled the "American Century."

The opening of the twenty-first century was a time when the debate about the nation's role in the world was again paramount, confidence in the economic underpinnings of domestic policy making was again threatened, and the battle between the major U.S. political parties for potential long-term advantage was at its most intense. Coming out of the "American Century" automatically begs the question, who or what symbolizes the century upcoming. Furthermore, the nation was not just celebrating the turn of a century, but the turn of a millennium, and satellite-distributed television made sure that this was a global event.

The first presidential election of the twenty-first century produced a result carrying less clarity and conviction than anyone would have hoped, although the general acceptance of the decision, with all its flaws and imprecision, is, unless it has cynically to be put down to the political apathy of the U.S. public, a testament to a shared belief in the peaceful transfer of power in democracies. It was widely touted that the new president had no mandate, and the fact that his losing opponent had received the support of around half a million more U.S. voters seemed to make this pretty clear. President-elect Bush made a conscious effort to acknowledge the intensity of the contest that had put him in office, and at least in his initial statements after being awarded the victory, to stress his wish to reach out to a broad spectrum of political leaders, and a broad coalition of the politically interested public.

The challenges faced at this time were significant, even in the quiet early days of the presidency. Conducting national politics looking towards a broad-based coalition was always going to be difficult for a national Republican leader at the beginning of the twenty-first century. In the first two years of the Eisenhower presidency the Republican had paper-thin control of both chambers in the national legislature. That apart, the G.O.P. had not occupied both legislative chambers and the presidency since the presidency of Herbert Hoover. Having suffered the overwhelming dominance of the Democrats for one generation, there had been a feeling among many Republican activists that the period since the late 1960s had seen a series of wasted and thwarted opportunities for the Republican party to take control of the agencies of government, and of the policy agenda. The margin of victory in 2000 was modest not just at the executive level, but also in the U.S. House of Representatives, where just a handful of seats separated the parties, and in the U.S. Senate, where the vice president's casting vote gave the Republicans control. All that having been said, the Republican party contained activist groups strongly committed to shifting national policy agendas, who had waited a long time for this opportunity, and who were in no mood to compromise. It would take a skilful leader to negotiate successfully between these pressures.

The broader context presented potential difficulties too. After a Clinton presidency which benefited from economic growth indicators more consistently positive than in any period of U.S. history, there were indications even during the campaign that the boom was not going to turn into a new economics of constant growth. By spring 2001 the stock market was showing distinct weakness, especially in those high-technology industries that some had predicted would become the unbridled engine of a new communications, economic and business revolution. It was already unclear whether the new administration could deliver on its promises of tax cuts without undermining the bipartisan commitment that had emerged in the 1990s to avoid the regular annual budget overspending that had been typical of much of the last half century.

With an apparently modest national electoral foundation, a party coalition that included influential elements pushing for radical changes, and a weakening economic background, the challenge of fulfilling millennial expectations appeared to demand a leader with more than usual political skills and eloquence. Reactions to George W. Bush's early attempts to fill this role were often not generous, suggesting that many critics thought this Texan was not growing to fill the presidential office that he had taken. Judgments were inevitably partisan, as decisions that seemed rational and pragmatic to conservative Republican supporters were received as isolationist and backward-looking by those liberals who had hoped for policy framed within the terms of the bipartisan rhetoric of late 2000. In practice the new administration took firm and partisan political stances that might have been more expected from a president with a substantial electoral victory, than one coming to office amid electoral controversy. The most grievous damage suffered by the Republicans was the loss, within months, of their grip on the U.S. Senate, and Senator Jeffords of Vermont declared himself independent of party affiliation, and returned the tiniest of controlling margins to the Democrats. At this time many in the party, the nation, and the international audience were unconvinced that President Bush was the leader who could successfully face the clear challenges of the new millennium.

All of these challenges pale in the wake of the attacks of September 11, 2001. Although the immediate response of the executive to these attacks was not convincing, it was not long before the presidential team appeared to be assessing the remodelled landscape of challenges, and devising strategy they felt appropriate. The problems that the Bush presidency had formerly faced did not go away. For example, the stock market slide had been well established in the summer, but it steepened in the fall, and continued at various rates of acceleration through 2002 and into 2003. In December 2001 the nation saw its biggest ever bankruptcy centred in Texas, as Enron collapsed. In spring 2002 the bankruptcy record was beaten again by the implosion of WorldCom, and the reputation of the internationally respected accounting firm Arthur Andersen was so tarnished that this icon of U.S. financial probity and power was damaged beyond repair.

These huge commercial failures might have been interpreted as indications of severe and structural economic problems, but in a country increasingly focused on the threat of international terrorism, their political impact was more limited than might otherwise have been the case. The economy was taking a beating on many fronts, and some of this at least could be laid at the door of the attacks. Reconstruction and support were needed certainly in New York City and Washington D.C., but also in the airline industry and other key locations. Reservations about budget deficits fell away in the face of the inevitable and necessary costs of being visibly responsive to perceived threats and consequent public needs. The tight party political balance, especially in the Senate, became less relevant as the agenda shifted to one driven by the nation's reaction to shocking terrorist attack, and led by the executive.

The administration made the case for a "War on Terror." Although this might have captured the American public mood, it created problems for policy makers and practitioners. The enemy in this war is difficult to define, its motivation may not be geopolitical, and its location may not be defined by national borders, or in any way geographically. U.S. arguments linking together elements of military intelligence pinpointed the Taliban regime of Afghanistan for special attention in a way that much of the global community found convincing. The further step of identifying Iraq as a threat so considerable as to justify an invasion found a much smaller level of international support, and leaders in Spain and the United Kingdom who gave support found themselves out of step with their electorates on this issue.

The U.S. electorate had no such difficulty, and the 2002 mid-term election campaign, in which the president took an active part, produced a swing to the Republicans consolidating their majority in the U.S. House of Representatives, and taking clear control of the U.S. Senate. For the first time in seventy-five years the Republicans could anticipate the possibility of more than one congressional term with party control of both legislative chambers and the executive branch. Party activists were again able to polish the vision that this might be the beginning of a long and steady era of Republican success.

That possibility still relies on convincing the electorate that the Republican executive can face the new challenges of this twenty-first century, as remodelled by the national shock prompted by the terrorism of September 11, 2001. The economic pressures on the American economy have increased in the aftermath of the terrorist attacks. An economy that was already weakening has taken further hard knocks in such areas as air travel and aero engineering. Commitments to balanced budgets, and to the inviolability of certain government funds, have weakened in the face of the spending priorities of a re-energized national commitment to militarized defense and pre-emption. The executive relationship with the legislature has been simplified by Republican party gains, but checks, balances, and the debating practices of the U.S. Senate, make sure that the president is still in no position to ignore the courtesy of some negotiation with his legislative colleagues.

Richard Neustadt explores the notion that even within the complex of changing institutional and issue-based challenges that beset them, presidents can themselves create, enlarge or exacerbate challenges for their own and at least the immediately subsequent administrations. The first administration of the new century failed to start smoothly not just because of the weak vote held by the Bush administration, but also by the weakness of character in taking office. The transition period was disfigured by an administration managing to appear "almost paranoid," claims Neustadt. The rhetoric of the War on Terror is potentially mistaken, in landing an American public that hates long wars with one that is by definition lengthy and unsatisfyingly ragged in its definition. The pre-emptive action of that war also places the administration in a difficult position in the long run, especially if, as Neustadt suspects, the dynamic behind the policy is coming from a political group of intense ideology, but of modest size, who will eventually lose the support that they need. Meanwhile Bush's predecessor, still young enough to take an active political role, and still charismatic enough to draw support, remains part of the political landscape. If Neustadt is right, then the next president, as well as the current president, faces challenges based on these factors.

Presidential strategy, George Edwards quotes Richard Neustadt as saying, is "not how he masters Congress in a peculiar instance, but what he does to boost his chance for mastery in any instance." George Bush needed a strategy that would cope with his lack of a popular plurality in the election of 2000. Edwards credits the president with a bold perception that taking his case to the people would succeed, and that successfully going public would bring the legislature along on the major policy aims of the administration. The strategy has not created a string of unalloyed policy victories, but given the limited credibility of the early days of the presidency, the Bush administration's success in setting the policy agenda, pushing the envelope of policy demands, compromising pragmatically on results, and declaring an administration policy victory, draws favourable comment. The percentage results in terms of legislation are good, but the image of success, and of connection with the electorate that is generated by the administration is possibly more powerful even than the actual results. The mid-term elections provided an opportunity for the president to help convert this potential into real muscle, and the resulting Republican victories, while not huge, were enough to add the value of numbers to the pre-existing strategic approach taken by the administration. Strategy notwithstanding, the frustrations of influencing the other branch remain real for the modern presidency, and in the end it may take a larger party majority to change this state of affairs dramatically.

The president has thrust upon him the role of "teacher in charge" claims Marc Landy, and the lessons to be learned about the changed international context and role of America are considerable, and not necessarily welcome. Countries act in their own self-interest, possibly counter to historical precedent, and not necessarily with great universal values as their ultimate end. It is a lesson to be learned that other countries, as well as the U.S.A., choose to take this approach. Landy echoes a point made elsewhere in this volume by Calvin Mackenzie, that when the enemy is real but indistinct, no surrender can be obtained, and the time frame of difficult and unpleasant consequences for the nation can be extended indefinitely—indicating the necessity of further executive-led training for the public to be prepared for the long haul. Understanding of the international context, forces, and peoples is an important part of this learning process, but this understanding is strengthened by the awareness of a presidency willing and able to act decisively in the proclaimed cause of national security. While nineteenth- and twentieth-century presidents have "fed false hopes and impossible dreams" there is a high risk in continuing to use "false sentimentalism" in this educative process. Opponents cannot always be presented as grotesques, military might is not impregnable in every case, victory is rarely complete, and the way that international politics is shaping up in the twenty-first century suggests that the presidency faces a new challenge in educating the American citizenry to a new a understanding of these realities.

Martha Joynt Kumar confirms that President Bush himself interprets his role at least to some degree as Landy has typified it, as a "teacher" to the nation. Kumar reports that the President stated to others his own conviction that post September 11 he now had an important role in "educating the American people about the nature of this conflict." That this event demanded a focused communications strategy is without doubt, and that the White House rallied to the needs of the moment, at least fairly quickly, is also evident. But as Kumar points out, a communications strategy is an essential part of any administration's armory, having one "is not a matter of choice." The tension between political actors and news reporters is centuries old. The essential interplay in which politicians attempt to influence, even control, the distribution of information, and news gatherers attempt to get the information and stories that they need, continues daily. The technological changes of contemporary news gathering have put political administrations everywhere under greater scrutiny, and nowhere is this more than in open and pluralist democracies. No administration wants unpleasant surprises in the news, and all administrations prefer positive coverage. Mass communications provide the executive with an opportunity to connect with a nation of voters, rather than a handful of politicians. But the strategy devised to do this must play to the strengths of the incumbent, acknowledging the potential pitfalls, as well as the concurrent advantages presented by the burgeoning communications business.

Meanwhile, inside the Beltway, partisan polarization in the U.S. Congress continues apace, according to the analysis offered by Barbara Sinclair. The decline in partisanship that was very evident in congressional voting patterns immediately following September 2001 certainly was in part a rallying reaction on all sides to support the nation and the president. But it also reflected the issues that flew up the

agenda in those weeks and months. Terrorism, reactions to terror, budgetary decisions to meet the expense of confronting terror, all came to the fore, and there was
little in the way of strong partisan division on these and other issues directly relating to the perceived threats to the U.S.A. However Sinclair points out that "on issues beyond terrorism, the effect on the level of partisanship was relatively short-
lived," the 107th Congress went on to be "about as partisan as its immediate
predecessors." Voting decisions in the U.S. House and Senate on most issues, and
even on some terror-related issues, followed patterns of behavior and influence well-
established in the legislature. Any president has a careful negotiating job to under-
take in the checked and balanced U.S. system, and this is no less true in the early
twenty-first century. A continuing and substantial shift in party political dominance
in the legislature would make a difference, and Republicans may well be hoping
that there is the potential for this to happen. In that case partisan strength across
institutional boundaries would appear to create presidential opportunities, but
would face the executive with different problems of negotiation with the factions of
his own supporters. In either case, the traditional challenge to gather and use powers of persuasion remains very evident in the modern presidency.

Pointing out that the legislative component of the modern presidency "was not
designed to be easy nor has it been for contemporary presidents," Stephen Wayne
goes on to point out that the twenty-first century presidency started in the conventional way. The challenge of the legislative process was "conditioned by the partisan, political environment, persistent institutional rivalries, and the public and congressional expectations set by the campaign"—factors which themselves change
over time, but which weave through the space where presidential persuasion meets
legislative process. The conventional success that a new president can expect in imposing his agenda on Congress was fulfilled reasonably well, and the disadvantage of
divided government after Senator Jeffords' defection from Republican ranks was
counterbalanced legislatively by the congressional rally to the presidency after September 2001. Challenges remain nonetheless. The partisan shade of Congress will
have substantial effect on the nature of this challenge over time. A president who
can lead the party to dominance in the legislature as well as the executive may be
fortunate enough to become "a prime minister with a partisan majority" while administrations facing divided control of government are tempted to short-circuit the
system, increasing tension. In all cases the skill of the president is in judging correctly all elements of the political etiquette that determines executive-legislative relations inside the Beltway.

Congressional partisanship also plays a major part in John Owens' analysis of
executive-legislative relationships in start-of-the-century Washington. But here the
discussion draws the reader to examine the challenges in terms of the lessons to be
learned from the differing reactions, leadership styles, and strategies of the major
players in Congress during this period—Speaker Dennis Hastert, and Senate Majority Leaders Trent Lott and Bill Frist, and all within the context of the sometimes
startling leadership heritage left by former Speaker Newt Gingrich. Leadership decision-making, Owens clearly demonstrates, is conducted within a web of influences—partisan balance, elections results, public opinion, personal policy agendas

being just a few. Nonetheless the modern leaders are no corks bobbing about in the maelstrom of influences, and nor are they sophisticated calculators, capable of finding and shifting to the balance point of a web whose strands might make the view opaque to the politically less perceptive. They are actors in their own right, and the choices of strategy, timing, and direction that they make are significant independent forces in the Washington decision-making process. Their judgements can make the president's role easier, but will not always do so.

In other arenas too, the domestic scene may be no less problematical after the turn of the century than it was before. Robert McKeever quotes Senator John Cornyn's reference to "the broken judicial confirmation process" in his analysis of the challenge faced by the presidency early in the twenty-first century in making federal judicial appointments. The judicial appointments process has become highly politicized, on ideological lines, over the past generation, as the courts have increasingly become a major location for battles over policies concerning social welfare and cultural behaviour, as well as the ever contentious areas of institutional and political demarcation. Some parallelism in party approaches to developing foreign policy does not suggest any similar bipartisanship of views on the domestic scene where, suggests McKeever, it is partisan politics as usual. The eventual re-emergence of a period of one-party dominance would be one way forward, but failing this, a president wishing to pack the courts might look to McKeever's seven-step plan. A Republican president representing a party containing strongly ideological forces, may find it difficult to follow McKeever's advice.

Presidential personality makes a difference in facing the challenges of the modern presidency, and James Pfiffner detects in George W. Bush leadership skills that have overcome significant disadvantages, and considerable unexpected difficulties. The president's moral certainty provided firmness of direction in the early days of his term, when he appeared to have no electoral mandate, and later, when the administration needed to create a response to the altered shape of international politics. His tendency to action helped create a military response that the U.S. public appeared to find satisfying and appropriate. His personalization of politics created opportunities and problems in international relations. The talents brought by Bush to the executive may have suited the moment, but are not generically beneficial, and do not form an automatically successful strategy for the modern presidency. The personality that the president brings to the executive can itself become part of the challenge.

This personalization in the operation of the executive is significant also in John Hart's examination of the Bush approach to national security policy and policy-making institutions. Hart reports that Bush has asserted that "All of [these institutions] must be transformed," but in Hart's judgement this transformation has not yet proven its adequacy in facing modern challenges. More players are involved in the system, but it is not clear to the author that the re-jigged NSC is constructed in a way that helps the delivery of national security strategies that are being mapped and developed to take the U.S.A. into the twenty-first century. Hart proposes functionally based directorates, a reduced staff, and a more globally focussed approach as being particularly relevant to modern challenges. But he also returns to the notion of presidential individuality, and especially to the strong impression given that President Bush allows his instincts to play an active role in many policy areas, including national security.

As Calvin Mackenzie points out, "no nation is the same at the end of the war as it was at the beginning—nor is any arrangement of authority or power." While he insists, quite rightly, that there are many unknowns when trying to evaluate the impact of the conflict that the Bush administration has nominated as a war on terrorism, he draws inferences both from its parallels to, and its differences with, the last century of wars that have been faced by the U.S.A. The lack of a geopolitical enemy means that unconventional difficulties exist in pinpointing the site of the war, the population who are the enemy, and the methods of attack or defense. The motivations of the enemy are difficult to express in traditional geopolitical terms, and if the precise start of any war can be a matter of debate, the inability to gain a traditional surrender in the absence of a traditional military or political leadership structure, creates the problem of never quite knowing when it is over. The war on terrorism may therefore become intimately integrated into vast areas of American domestic as well as foreign policy. Agency funding in many areas might be affected, as risk and security strategy impact widely on American life. The emergence of this "battleground very close to home" creates potentially "the frame and the rationalization for the greatest enlargement of presidential power in American history," while simultaneously opening the door to political failure if expensive and grand gesture politics gains few results, or, even worse, fails to prevent further terrorist attacks of appalling magnitude. Twenty-first century presidents have to face these challenges as part of the reality of their administrations.

In tackling the unanticipated consequences of these new leaps in policy Richard Pious considers the twenty-first century presidency is in danger of placing an over-reliance on "prerogative power" that is potentially unsustainable over time. Precisely those unintended consequences that concern Calvin Mackenzie can undermine the expansion of presidential authority and legitimacy at home and abroad that Pious sees as necessary underpinnings for the increased presidential prerogative that has already been seen in the early years of the new century. The defense in a war against terrorism cannot be expected to be complete in its coverage, even given measures comprehensive enough to strain America's constitutional boundaries. Crisis could be created by the institutional and policy strains. Backlash could develop, undermining the foundations of growing presidential claims of authority. Countering that, it is possible that the context of the new century is so altered that a newly enhanced presidency can emerge, not forever expanding the prerogatives of executive power, but skilled enough to take on the challenge of compromising the gains that have been made, with the realpolitic of acting within an established network of political relationships at home and abroad.

Responding to a heightened perception of the international threats to the United States with a doctrine of pre-emptive military action would seem, superficially at least, to be a fairly simple and comprehensible reaction. It is not surprising, furthermore, that some observers would consider the rhetoric of pre-emption more destabilizing than comforting. Nevertheless, what John Dumbrell calls the "elemental" quality of the rhetoric is going to strike a chord with listening publics at home and abroad. This apparently simple statement of doctrine, though, does take the presidency into areas ringing with complexity. Dumbrell concludes that the Bush administration has extended presidential foreign policy authority considerably, but as he documents, this has not been a tidal wave of unilateralism signalling a victory for the neoconservative imperialist policy agenda. Rather the pragmatics of policy making and its implementation have had to take account of sometimes disjointed and countervailing interests. Domestically the challenges faced by the president in reconciling competing voices within his own administration, and in gaining the cooperation and support of Congress, did not disappear after the September Al-Quaeda attack, but they became temporarily less relevant. Internationally the reaction was unilateral, but stimulated a greater recognition, at least in rhetorical terms, of the value of multilateral cooperation if national threat is increasingly seen as potentially emerging from all parts of the world, and as being embedded in threats to values in all parts of the world. Not all attacks are as obvious as that of September 11, and not all unilaterally driven reactions are generally acceptable. The challenge of continuing to grapple with this complexity while dealing with competing interests that tend to elemental visions will continue to confront the executive regardless of the apparent growth of its foreign policy authority.

The authors in this volume address the new landscape of challenges faced by the executive in the range of roles that the president performs. In a nation commonly thought of as having political parties of relatively weak ideological commitment, the U.S. president in the early twenty-first century finds himself trying to maintain a leadership role in a national legislature with the tightest party cohesion in decades. The particular skills needed by a party leader and national leader in this context of party tension, division over policy, potential confrontation over court appointments, yet with a bedrock of common commitment to some national needs, form one part of the content of this volume.

A president who was initially identified and criticized by many international observers as isolationist in nature has emerged to take a major and very active international role, but in a way that has proved not without controversy. The altered challenges in the president's roles as chief executive and commander in chief made by the demands of a war on terror provide the focus for several of the authors in this volume. Their multi-faceted coverage of the tasks and the observed and potential executive reaction examine the response to, doctrinal basis for, implementation of, and the implications for the future conduct of a potentially permanent war.

Presidents of character, and presidents living through interesting times, often themselves leave a legacy that forms part of the challenge for succeeding administrations. The administrations of President Bill Clinton and President George W. Bush are both likely to leave stamps of this kind. The construction of challenge becomes to some degree circular, as an administration's response to external and internal challenges, guided by the character and leadership of the incumbent, redefines the way that challenges will be faced in the future. The authors of this volume provide a most valuable examination of the current, new and emerging challenges for the modern presidency.

This volume originated from an idea floated by Professors Gary McDowell, then of the Institute for U.S. Studies (IUSS) at the University of London, and David Nichols of Montclair State University. The IUSS partnered with the Eccles Centre for American Studies at the British Library to host a two-day meeting that brought together the international team of authors who are represented in this collection. The meeting, held at the British Library in London, attracted participants and audience members from political parties, government, journalism, and business, as well as academe. The discussions over those two days informed strongly the final form that this collection took. The thanks of the authors and editors go particularly to the Institute for U.S. Studies, and to the Eccles Centre for American Studies, for their central role in sponsoring the event, and also to everyone who took part, and gave generous support and creative feedback.

These authors have produced a range of discussion, analysis, and argument that encourages the reader to view the modern presidency from a variety of perspectives. The collection shows that the presidency continues to play a central role in American government. The challenges that have faced President George W. Bush have been extraordinary, and understanding these challenges is essential to understanding American politics and public policy. The presidential office carries authority, but not automatic power. The personnel in the executive branch, and the political contexts within which they work, matter fundamentally. Contemporary undergraduate and postgraduate students undertaking courses on the presidency are well aware through their own life experience that the leadership of the United States faces special, and in some cases dramatically new, challenges both at home and abroad. These essays provide the intellectual frameworks through which that experience and knowledge can be most usefully explored. The authors provide the most contemporary analyses of the presidency, all expertly presented to inform and stimulate all students of the modern American presidency.

CHAPTER 1

Challenges Created by Contemporary Presidents

◆◆◆

Richard E. Neustadt

Challenges to presidents come in many types and guises. Some are native to the job and to its place in a separated system. Some arise out of its burgeoning institutionalization. Some are rooted in the current political climate, others in the climates of society and economy. Still others stem from America's emergence after 1989 as the sole super-power, to employ a somewhat misleading cliché.

Just now, I propose to deal with none of these—or not directly—but rather with a very special set, namely challenges that George W. Bush, along with Bill Clinton before him, have created, enlarged, or exacerbated, thus far, for Bush's own presidency and the one that comes after in 2009, or perhaps, though I doubt it, in 2005. To look farther ahead becomes unrealistic. To look farther back begins to poach on the historians—which I don't in the least mind doing, but not here. So I shall stick with what Bush and his predecessor seem to me to have done to him and to whomever follows him, as best I understand it from afar, without the benefit of historians' sources.

In this I intend not to be comprehensive but merely selective, discussing what strikes me as one observer, from the vantage points, mainly, of London, England and Wellfleet, Massachusetts. I shall group the challenges I think I see under four headings: Transition, Prerogative, Preemption, and, for want of better words, "Clintonitis." I should like to have included a fifth, which I might label "Mixed Perceptions," noting what officials think they see, compared with what the press reporting on them sees, and what the public gleans from press reportage. Discrepancies, I think, are widening. But space will not allow, so that awaits another occasion.

TRANSITION

Now to the first of my categories, "Transition." Presidential transitions have concerned me for a long time. The transfer of the Office from an experienced incumbent at the end of his term to an inescapably inexperienced outsider, especially if from the other party, propels the latter into a long course of learning-on-the-job, for which he has prepared himself only catch-as-catch-can during the eleven weeks since his election. He is likely to get many things wrong and to have difficulty setting them right, the more so as his previous experience is in a different sort of polity from Washington. Southern governors, accustomed to a different kind of legislative politics and free from close observance by a national press corps, have had particular troubles in recent years, especially Presidents Carter and Clinton, from Georgia and Arkansas respectively. Yet in the administrative and programmatic realms where they so stumbled, the second George Bush, from Texas, appears to have been notably successful, using senior associates from previous Republican regimes to inject precisely the experience he lacked. So where is the challenge in that—except to do as he did?

The challenge lies in the public relations of dealing with apparent policy commitments by the previous regime. Not since 1933, when Franklin Roosevelt sabotaged the London Economic Conference, in which Herbert Hoover had invested major hopes, have there been such reversals of international obligations undertaken, or at least ostensibly backed, by Clinton but repudiated by Bush. And FDR was cheerful about it, whereas the Bush administration managed to seem angry, scornful, almost paranoid. I refer, in particular to the Kyoto Protocol and the convention on an International Criminal Court, these among others. The Clinton administration had endorsed them all, though calculating that none could get through the Senate's hurdle for treaties, a two-thirds vote, or even be reported out by the then Chairman of the Senate Foreign Relations Committee. Aware of that, the incoming administration, which disliked the substance in these cases, apparently took them all to be traps set by Clinton precisely to catch *them*, and reacted accordingly.

Yet Clinton, it seems, was actually aiming to conciliate constituencies both domestic and foreign, without delivering what they wanted, which he couldn't. His successors couldn't either, and what's more, they didn't want to. But in the public relations of changing course they could have couched their negatives more sorrowfully, less angrily, and could have tried to offer something like alternatives, conceding the importance, not the substance, of the issues. A year later, after they had gauged the unfortunate effects of their abruptness, and still more their language—effects in Europe, among other places—I don't doubt that Bush's White House regretted the tone, though not the substance, and wished they'd focussed early on its consequences abroad. They evidently didn't, and why not? Apparently because their paranoia about Clinton got in the way—a paranoia fueled by many things, most recently by Albert Gore's sustained (and to them outrageous) refusal to concede Florida.

I have written extensively about hazards of transition. But here's a new one not previously identified, not, at least, by me. So add it to the list. Consequences can be serious. I dare say that the caricature of the younger Bush as "cowboy," "stupid," "unilateralist," "right-winger," heard so often on this side of the Atlantic, and affecting serious business like support in the UN Security Council, owes much to the tone on Kyoto and the subsequent series of scorned conventions.

Paranoid reactions against predecessors, which have boomerang effects upon their holder and his policies, are natural accompaniments of hard-fought campaigns in a politics as partisan and personal as ours is now, especially if the predecessor or an intimate associate was the person against whom the campaign had been fought. But the foreign consequences of indulging in those feelings have been quite severe enough so that Bush's successor in '09 (or conceivably '05) ought to take note and endeavor to do differently. And whenever the time comes, Bush, the outgoer, should be as helpful and forbearing as he can be, even in the event, horrid for him, that his successor turns out to be Hillary Clinton!

There's the first challenge.

WAR POWER

My next challenge relates to the War Power, so called, first claimed by Abraham Lincoln. After September 11, last year, Bush showed us it still exists, good as new (although not named). The challenge is this: Can he keep it?

I do not refer to the War Powers Acts of Woodrow Wilson's time, which Democratic Congresses repealed in the 1970s as knee-jerk revenge on Richard Nixon, or to the War Powers Resolution, also of the '70s, which no president since has accepted as constitutional. Rather, I refer to that implicit constitutional authority, drawn from combining the commandership-in-chief with the presidential oath of office—Lincoln's combination—which Edward Corwin, more than 50 years ago, taught my generation to consider the equivalent of the royal prerogative as understood by John Locke in the early eighteenth century. To quote Corwin quoting Locke:

> " . . . this power to act according to discretion for the public good, without the prescription of the law and sometimes against it . . . . whilst employed for the benefit of the community and suitably to the trust and ends of government. . . . is [un]questioned. For the people are very seldom or never scrupulous or nice in the point or questioning of prerogative whilst it is in any tolerable degree employed for the use it was meant—that is the good of the people and not manifestly against it. . . ."

Does that embrace "unlawful combatants" in Guantanamo Bay? Yes—assuming American courts continue to go along (and recognizing that there is no European Court to constrain them). No doubt other instances will follow. A federal system in which public health is principally a state and local function could prompt instant nationalization, for example, on the first authenticated outbreak of chemical or biological warfare.

In the *Youngstown* case of 1952, the United States Supreme Court refused to treat the then-current hostilities as "war" within the meaning of War Power, because Congress had not declared it, which constitutionally only Congress can. In 2001, by contrast, President Bush declared the War on Terrorism and within two weeks he had a Resolution of Support from both Houses of Congress. If the issue ever comes before it, the present Court, I've little doubt, will find that Resolution the full functional equivalent to a congressional declaration of war. The Justices, presumably, saw the twin towers crumble on TV even as you and I did.

Thus I presume the War Power has been Bush's since September 2001. Contemporary lawyers do not read Corwin, let alone Locke, so the term is not currently in use. But the reality is there, and seemingly is broad enough to cover lesser if sharper hostilities, as in Afghanistan and Iraq, which are said to tie in with terrorism. Congressional sanction in advance for the invasion of Iraq lets it also stand on its own, apart from the wider war.

But in this there is one catch which may turn out to be a veritable "Catch 22." By the president's own acknowledgment, reinforced from time to time in statements of his secretaries of Defense and State, the wider War on Terror is to be a conflict of indefinite duration. By its nature it frequently will be ambiguous in its results. By the law of probabilities it will produce more setbacks, perhaps terrible defeats, on the territory of the United States, not to mention Western Europe. Yet historically Americans have never tolerated long wars well. Historically, we have hated them. We begin in blazing patriotism, Jacksonians almost all, brandishing our flintlocks, watchful even of our neighbors. Then we start to criticize, angered at the caution of our leaders or the stubbornness of enemies, or both. And soon enough we splinter into factions of the super-patriotic, the increasingly indifferent, the aroused opponents, and the violent peaceniks, who in their way are Jacksonian too. All in all, we hate it to drag on—but we despise to lose.

The great exception was the Second World War, which began for us with the Japanese attack on Pearl Harbor. Yet it lasted for us only half the time it did for the British, and for us it was a period of unaccustomed high prosperity without physical risk to civilians.

By contrast, in the Revolutionary War, if one combines United Empire Loyalists with the genuinely indifferent, I dare say that three years into the struggle, by 1779, not more than one-third of the country actually supported hostilities. In the Civil War, the North was so disaffected after three years that Lincoln expected to lose the 1864 election to a "peace candidate" he'd fired, General McClellan, and very likely would have done had General Sherman not taken Atlanta and begun his march to the sea.

In World War I, which for us only lasted a year and a half, an almost totalitarian patriotism gave way, after the war's end, to an almost total cynicism about it and its causes, fueling the isolationism of the next twenty years. The Korean War, fought actively for only two and a half years, made Harry Truman more unpopular than even Nixon at the moment of the latter's resignation, because Truman was perceived to be at once unable to make "peace" and unwilling to "win." A similar perception, in the instance of Vietnam, required Lyndon Johnson to retire from the presidency after his first full term. Yet that war then was less than three years old. Four years more and Nixon withdrew our last troops. A year and a half after that, Gerald Ford, constrained by Congress, had to let the Vietnam War be wholly lost, standing by as Saigon fell, with divisive effects in the United States we have not seen the last of yet.

Aside from World War II, only the Spanish-American War and the First Gulf War stand out historically as truly popular from start to finish, the first a matter of months, the second a matter of days. Both were showy, neither costly, whether of lives or dollars. The Second Gulf War may or may not be in that category, depending on how its aftermath plays out and how the whole is then perceived—and also on how it is seen in relation to terrorism. For that war, the War against Terror, the larger encompassing effort, as the president described and still pursues it, has not yet lasted long enough to demonstrate a level of support belying the historically-low norm. When the time comes I doubt that it will. That's where the catch comes in.

It was Bush himself, on September 11 and 12, 2001, who labeled as "war" the attacks on New York and Washington. Given the shock, the pictures, and bin Laden's previous attacks in East Africa, that labeling is understandable. But the Pope, at the same time, labeled the same events "a crime against humanity." By the time he leaves office I suspect that Bush will wish he had done so too.

Nothing up to now suggests that the War on Terrorism will escape American distaste for sustained hostilities. Indeed its punctuation by brief intervals of more conventional warfare is likelier than not to sharpen popular impatience with the underlying conflict. Short-run appearances of relative success will only heighten consciousness of the more basic indeterminacy, and add to irritation about setbacks along the way.

Most people think, and I am one of them, that sooner or later we will witness or be victims of other dramatic attacks on American soil. Coming before the Second Gulf War, I think those would have evoked sympathy for the embattled president, and further rallying around him. Coming after, they are likelier to evoke doubts, dissatisfactions, in proportion to perceptions that successive seizures of Afghanistan and Iraq "ought" to have made us safer, somehow, but didn't. Every year that passes, not to speak of further seizures, should there be any, will enlarge prospects for dissatisfaction while also enlarging likely causes. The situation, of course, is unprecedented, our first war of indefinite duration, so history becomes a still-worse guide than usual. But insofar as it proves relevant, the prognostication is poor. Historically, to repeat, Americans hate long wars.

"Why" is a crucial question in assuming, as I do, that the future in this instance will be something like the past. It is, I think, because long wars accumulate such costs in terms of money, or consumption, rising prices, nervous strain, enforced attention, or, last but not least, blood—any or all of these. This is to say that long wars interfere too much with what we mean by private life, and also pose too many moral ambiguities, which most of us dislike confronting in out lives. Of course, there may be something happening at present, that I cannot see, which will divorce the future from the past. Everyone is free to speculate on that. But as regards the War on Terrorism, I, for one, don't see it. Americans, I think, will come to hate that war too.

Hate undoes the public acquiescence underpinning prerogative—and by the same token, War Power. Coping with that is my second challenge.

PREEMPTION

Now for the third challenge. I have labeled it "Preemption," after the doctrine which the Bush administration elevated into aspiration-policy last September, in a National Security statement, and into action-policy on one carefully chosen occasion, thus far, the Second Gulf War. The doctrine is neither as new as its authors make it sound, nor as universally applicable without pragmatic distinctions. A century ago, the United States "preempted" in the Caribbean often, and indeed in Panama as recently as 1989. In the current Bush administration, Iraq was preferred to North Korea for one very pragmatic reason, perhaps in conjunction with others, that the latter holds a city of 11 million hostage, just across its border, 35 miles away and subject to artillery barrage, whereas Iraq had no comparable deterrent handy— a pragmatic choice indeed.

But some, in this administration, are more ideological than pragmatic. There is a group of what the British would call junior ministers—actually more potent than most of theirs—who are centered in the Pentagon with outriders at State, the NSC, and the vice president's office. They constitute a veritable Cabal within the government, tightknit, like-minded, and reaching out aggressively: Within the last two years they have recruited at least two powerful seniors. Some label the group "Neo-Conservative," which suggests they all have moved from left to right over the years. As to that I cannot say, not knowing the biographies of all. But I do know that for several, the Democratic Party's abandonment of patriotism, so to speak, in the years after 1968 was a molding force.

Now, the Cabal members seem intent on reshaping other countries in the interest of American security and world stability. They have chafed for years at successive failures of previous administrations to use American military supremacy as a tool in the reshaping. They don't deceive themselves that the supremacy is guaranteed forever, so they wish to strike while the iron is hot. The wish is reinforced by their shared interest in security for Israel.

The Cabal is said to have entered this administration with a little list, headed by Iraq. As often in Washington, they had a solution in search of a problem. September 11, last year, offered them terrorism as a problem and they fastened onto it. In time, the Second Gulf War followed. Flushed with success in that quarter, they may well try to continue down their list, if and as they can persuade the President to join them.

How Bush sees them is far from clear; perhaps his heart is with them but his head not, or not consistently. How they see him seems more obvious: As the indispensable lever, necessary to their cause and, if in hand, sufficient. So Iraq seemed to show. In that the Cabal members much remind me of the more ideological New Dealers around Franklin Roosevelt. Like them these "junior ministers" appear to disregard the limits on the presidency embedded in the Constitution, and to take their president's prestige as tantamount to public acquiescence in whatever he proposes. Roosevelt was capable, occasionally, of being equally unrealistic, but not often. That spared him what I think is almost certain to be Bush's fate if he should fall in blindly with the wishes of those juniors.

For the great prospective checks on application of the doctrine of preemption are two, in my opinion, the inwardness of American psychology and the separateness of Congress. These Bush disregards at his peril, as Roosevelt would have done had he yielded to advisers pressing him toward a peacetime planned economy or early intervention in the European war.

To take the psychological factor first, we Americans have been and remain a continental people of diverse regions and origins, absorbed in our occupations, our locales, our widely varied scenes and climates, aware of their diversity and also ours as individuals. Never having known the Welfare State in your terms, most of us are preoccupied, because we have to be, by getting on, coping (or not) with child care, struggling with medical bills, jostling each other for our prospects in life. It is a consuming experience, absorbing energy, narrowing perspective, underscoring individual performance. It makes for mobility too, in physical terms. Something like a fifth of us change cities every year. Perhaps for those reasons, we seem peculiarly intent on the relatively few things that unite us, the flag, the Court, the Constitution, and on our shared, felt distance from all other nations, a distance all our families volunteered for (unless Native- or African-American).

As a mark of that intensity, isolationism in our foreign policy was more than a pragmatic adaptation to our weakness at the end of the eighteenth century. It was, or anyway became, in the course of the nineteenth century, a deeply ingrained expression of our common nationality. Franklin Roosevelt, who strained against it, saw it so, and looking toward its natural resurgence after World War II did everything he could to institutionalize a set of multilateral dimensions in our conduct of foreign affairs. That is why the World Bank and the I.M.F. had to be agreed before the war's end. That is why the United Nations had to be located physically on our side of the oceans. That is why, at Yalta, he accepted three votes for the Soviets in the UN General Assembly. He sought to get them signed up fast.

Roosevelt assumed we would resume our inward-looking course after the war. He hoped that having once adopted multilateral obligations, and embedded them by treaty in our laws, they too would join the narrow number of things that unite us, stretching inwardness as wide as it could be made to reach, legitimating our assumption of external responsibilities. That indeed did happen to a degree; even today the United Nations remains popular with a majority of Americans. But underpinning it from 1947 to 1989 was something else, which Roosevelt, in anticipation, had hoped to avert, the Cold War.

I have often quoted President Truman's comment to me in a conversation after he left office about the chain of actions his administration sponsored in its most creative period, from aid to Greece and Turkey, through the Marshall Plan, to the Berlin Airlift, and NATO. To quote him once again, "Hell, that wasn't Truman's foreign policy, that was Stalin's foreign policy. If it hadn't been for Stalin, I'd never have got those things through Congress." Truman was referring, above all, to the coup d'etat in Prague of 1948 and the attempted isolation of Berlin that year. He could have continued with Moscow's "ok" for the North Korean attack on South Korea two years later, which militarized the Cold War and set it on course for the next two generations.

The Cold War interfered decisively with American inwardness, and while it did so Roosevelt's multilateral institutions took a relative back seat. But that war ended more than a decade ago and now those institutions have to bear the burden he intended them to bear of tempering an innate tendency toward isolation—under the current guise of unilateralism. The Cabal, be it said, consists of idealistic unilateralists, willing, with some disdain, to use those institutions if and as they contribute to their designs, but not otherwise. And rarely, if ever, do they seem to think of using them as Roosevelt hoped to do, to moderate the inwardness of the American public. Instead, they evidently think that they themselves do that, by simply giving inwardness an imperial twist affirmed by anti-terrorism—if only the president will step out front, leading the procession in the way they wish to go.

But I remain impressed with Roosevelt's insights more than theirs, even though theirs are 60 years more "up to date." For the postwar prospect Roosevelt had in view has quite a lot in common with the post-cold war reality. The Cabal's disdain might destroy the multilateral institutions, or cripple their utility, without actually rendering Americans less inward looking than before, not even when faced with terror. Then nothing but the president, together with his "ministers," blocks a drift back toward traditional isolationism. While inward enough, that scarcely suffices to support a worldwide empire, however idealistic. The rest of the world is mostly too far off. Americans and their media, it seems, have already forgotten Afghanistan!

Stalin was real and ever present, a human being with red blood, and troops, and continuity—and after 1949 the Bomb—whereas terror, up to now, is an abstraction (and a memory) most days of most years. Under current conditions, it cannot be expected to exert an equal strength with him in countering our concentration on ourselves. Terrorism is not now, or anyway not yet, in the same class as the Cold War, and I believe it is unlikely to become so, for inherent reasons of its own intrinsic character.

Turning to the separateness of Congress, the first years after September 11, 2001, can give a misleading impression, just as did the first years after the bank crisis of March 1933, when Roosevelt took over and New Dealers got stars in their eyes. We too readily forget that congressional independence of the presidency is rooted in the localism of political-party nominating processes for House and Senate seats, where White House influence is limited and shaky, or non-existent. Above those roots the separateness is nurtured by the different atmospheres and customs of "the Hill" and "Downtown." And it is crowned by constitutional strictures now worked out in practice to require two-thirds of the senators to vote for treaties, three-fifths to close debate on controversial bills and appropriations. Those votes come in a Senate narrowly divided between sharply partisan Republicans and Democrats, a condition unlikely to change any time soon. So party votes cannot produce the needed super-majorities.

Insofar as foreign policy is tied to legislation, bipartisanship becomes a necessity. That is fostered by a sense of crisis leading toward War Power, but it weakens as assent beneath that power wanes. How long can the War on Terrorism foster needed votes for Bush from Democrats? How often can he punctuate that war with bouts of more conventional hostilities, as in Iraq, before one-third-plus-one, or two-fifths-plus-one, of senators from either party form a solid bloc against him—spurred on, as they would be, by the politics of their home states? That is what it would take, but also *all* it would take, to frustrate the intentions of idealist junior ministers. Something comparable happened to idealistic New Dealers, though a number of them never noticed and continued to expect the President to wave a magic wand. He mostly had the good sense to count noses on the Hill and then refrain. How it will be with Bush I do not know.

In that lies the third challenge.

"CLINTONITIS"

The fourth and final challenge I would put before you is of a different order, not a matter of policies and institutions but instead a matter of personalities: one individual, unconstrained by power, with status, charm, and empathy, and romantically recalled good times, all televised. I lack the right term for it. Temporarily, "Clintonitis" will have to do.

Spending time in England, as I do part of each year, I have seen quite a lot of popular reactions to the former president, appearing here in public and speaking out on numerous occasions to groups of various sorts and sizes. He never fails to "wow" them. He never fails to suit his subject to his audience, and to give them what they want to hear. Being out of office makes that easy. He can speak intelligently about anything, and passionately when the subject warrants. He projects sophistication, knowledge, charm—and empathy. For that last he is justly famous. He seems never to forget the name attached to every face he's ever met and to come out with it at just the psychologically right moment, "right" in terms both private and public.

Having supreme status, Clinton now, apparently, goes everywhere he wishes to see any one he likes, and thanks to Lyndon Johnson he is blessed by the perpetual convenience of Secret Service advance-work. Having no powers, he arouses no fresh enemies for what he does, or says, or wishes, or withholds in realms of policy. Indeed he now can speak for liberal constituents, and to them, with no constraints upon him save his history, and neither he nor they are of a mind to hold him to it narrowly. On the lecture circuit his workload seems immense, but what of it? He is still under 60, he adores campaigning, he is paying off his debts and legal fees, and soon will be accumulating capital to supplement his presidential pension and his wife's senatorial salary.

Consider him then, when the next presidential campaign rolls around, a year from now, and the one after that, and the one after that—and so on for twenty or more years! If his wife should be the Democratic candidate on one or more of those occasions, he would have to take a back seat as he did with Albert Gore, lest he blur her image, which, alas, he'd almost surely do. But with anyone else as candidate, Clinton could let it rip, as the candidate would almost certainly want him to, at least until the latter had been president himself.

Never before in American politics will we have seen anything like this. Truman conducted a separate campaign for Adlai Stevenson in 1952, but Truman then was massively unpopular and the undoubted interest in him evidently was historical, to witness one among his final "whistle-stops." John Quincy Adams, who also left office unpopular, had the good sense to withdraw from presidential politics and performed his further service in the House of Representatives. Jack Kennedy would have been young enough to create a precedent for Clinton had he lived, but he didn't. So would Teddy Roosevelt had he not personally chosen his successor, then turned bitterly against him. But he did. So it goes. Clinton will be unprecedented.

I grant that Clinton, as campaigner for somebody else, could well have more effect on Blue than on Red America (TV election reports in the United States reverse the colors that in Britain are assigned Tories and Laborites), thus piling up majorities less likely to affect results in the Electoral College. But what of Florida? What of Texas? And so forth. To be sure, Red America contains large numbers of the one-time Clinton-haters. But with them his power and location were his principal offenses. He's now shed both. And generations change. The haters' children may well find him more an object of curiosity, and then feel the seduction of his empathy—as surely will their Black and Hispanic neighbors.

And not minorities only. In Red America as much as in Blue, or more so, the Clinton years were prosperous years, hopeful years, years of low inflation, high employment, and a rising stock-market, with ample tax returns for states, and federal budget surpluses almost sufficient to eliminate prospective shortfalls in Social Security and Medicare. Such were the years from 1993 to 2001 as they are now remembered. And Clinton's relationship to them was more than coincidental. With some justice he can claim—and no doubt will—that his initial economic judgments and decisions, and his general willingness to stick to them, made it all happen.

In future election years marked by less favorable economic prospects—as next year, for one, seems fated to be—memories of the 1990s cannot help but add to the advantages of a campaigning Clinton.

There were, of course, far less attractive aspects of those years, some of them the president's own doing, some the product of radical Republicanism after the midterm elections in 1994. Others produced by anti-social biases inherent in individualism, still others by sheer greed in the private sector, together with the usual excesses and frivolities of the new rich. But if the 1920s, as recalled a generation later, are a guide, and I think they are, those negatives will dim with time, indeed are already dimming for most voters, while the aura of prosperity sheds an increasingly romantic light over the 1990s—and thus over Clinton too. In that respect, he has nowhere to go but up.

Might Clinton blow it? With his past record of indiscipline and indiscretion that cannot be ruled out, although as an ex-president the troubles he makes for himself should matter less, by far, than when he was in the White House. But he must avoid corruption and he must confine his intimate relations to consenting adults of the opposite sex, preferably not indiscreet. That doesn't sound too hard and probably suffices. Secret Service protection is an asset—and those agents *are* discreet.

So far as I have followed it, the commentary in the spring of 2003 on so-far declared Democratic candidates for 2004, seems very like the comments on their counterparts at the same stage in 1991, a bunch of "midgets," as I recollect the term, an almost unknown Clinton not excluded. But suppose it had been taken as a given, twelve years ago, that the Democratic nominee, no matter who, was virtually assured the lively and sustained support of Clinton as we know him now. How might that have affected calculations about both the nomination and the chances of election? How should it be affecting calculations now? In my view it reduces both the risks of newness and the advantages of current name-recognition. Whoever is the nominee (so long as it's not Hillary), Clinton will be there to run his separate, supportive campaign. That would have given heart to Clinton then. Who will it hearten now? And how will it affect considerations at the White House? Those are interesting questions for 2004.

They become still more interesting for 2008, 2012, and after, when romance about the '90s has entirely taken hold. In 2016, Clinton will still be about the age of Ronald Reagan when the latter *began* his presidency!

Clinton loves campaigning, perhaps much more than governing, and he has managed not to interfere—at least visibly—in his wife's conduct of her Senate office. But until they have experienced the same forbearance, no Democrats elected president with help from the perpetually campaigning Clinton I foresee, will trust that he won't try to look over their shoulders in the White House when they get there. So this Clinton promises to be or seem a challenge, not only to the candidates for Democratic nominations, but also to the sitting presidents of either party. One thing I am sure of: He'll enjoy that.

CONCLUSION

So there are my four man-made challenges, created or enlarged by Clinton and Bush between them and affecting Bush for sure, along with, in all likelihood, whoever is his successor: Transition, Prerogative, Preemption and "Clintonitis." They don't exhaust my list of challenges that Bush has thus far managed to impose upon himself, sometimes with help from Clinton, but they will, I hope, suffice to generate thoughtful discussion.

CHAPTER 2

George W. Bush's Strategic Presidency

◆◆◆

George C. Edwards III
Texas A&M University

Richard Neustadt focused his landmark work on *Presidential Power* on the strategic level of power. As he put it,

> There are two ways to study "presidential power." One way is to focus on the tactics . . . of influencing certain men in given situations. . . . The other way is to step back from tactics on those "givens" and to deal with influence in more strategic terms: what is its nature and what are its sources? . . . Strategically, [for example] the question is not how he masters Congress in a peculiar instance, but what he does to boost his chance for mastery in any instance . . .[1]

This chapter follows Neustadt's lead in focusing on political strategy with particular attention to the George W. Bush administration's relations with Congress and the public. The 43rd president, more than most of his predecessors, has focused on developing and implementing a strategy for governing. In this essay, I devote special attention to the relationship between the White House's core governing strategy, going public, and its success in obtaining support for its initiatives in Congress.

ASSESSING STRATEGIC POSITION

The first step a new administration should take to ensure success is to assess accurately its strategic position so it understands the potential for change and will not overreach or underachieve. Presidents must largely play the hands that the public deals them through its electoral decisions on the presidency and Congress and its evaluations of the chief executive's handling of his job.[2] Presidents are rarely in a position to augment substantially their political capital, especially when just taking office.

George W. Bush took office after one of the closest elections in American history. The highly unusual, protracted denouement of the election and the truncated transition period of only 38 days between the resolution of the election and the inauguration—about half the normal time for a shift in power—had the potential to turn the transition into a circus and undermine the new president's chances of success.

Bush received neither a majority nor even a plurality of the vote, and many (mostly Democrats) saw his victory as illegitimate, because he received more than a half-million fewer votes than Al Gore and because of the peculiar circumstances surrounding the determination of the winner of Florida's electoral votes. A Gallup poll taken just before the inauguration found that 31 percent of Americans thought Bush "won on a technicality" and 24 percent thought he "stole the election," while 45 percent said he "won fair and square." Thirty-eight percent of Americans still considered Gore to be the "real winner of the election."[3]

In light of the election results, the new president could not credibly claim a mandate from the people. Moreover, the Republicans lost seats in both houses of Congress, undermining any claim to presidential coattails. After the election, Republicans found themselves with only a very narrow majority in the House and required the vice president to break a 50-50 split in the Senate.

It is not difficult to imagine a president elected in such circumstances to move cautiously, seeking first to increase his legitimacy with the majority of the public who did not support him for president. Some commentators saw the potential for paralysis in Washington, and others (again, mostly Democrats) urged the president to act as if he were indeed paralyzed, proposing only policies that enjoyed bipartisan support.

Neither the narrowness of his election nor the nature of its resolution intimidated Bush, however. Although his tone was one of reconciliation, he ignored those who urged him to strike a bipartisan posture and hold off on his major initiatives. The White House correctly understood that the one policy that both unified and energized Republicans was tax cuts. Although most congressional Democrats would oppose the cuts, a majority of the public, including Independents and even some Democrats, would support or at least tolerate them. Equally important, tax cuts, unlike most other major policies, could be considered under rules that prohibited a filibuster. Thus, a united, although slender, majority could prevail.

CHOOSING A STRATEGY FOR GOVERNING

Once a president has evaluated his strategic position, the White House must design a strategy for operating within the context in which it finds itself in its efforts to win support in Congress. One approach is to seek to pass legislation through relatively quiet negotiations with congressional leaders. The president's father, George H. W. Bush, provided an example with his administration's efforts regarding environmental, education, and budget policy. An alternative strategy is to take the case to the people, counting on public opinion to move Congress to support the president. The second President Bush, surprisingly to some, chose the latter course.

Going Public

Soon after taking office, the president launched a massive public relations campaign on behalf of his priority initiatives. At the core of this effort was the most extensive domestic travel schedule of any new president in American history.[4] Bush spoke in 29 states by the end of May, often more than once.

The president not only spoke extensively about each initiative, but also went to considerable lengths to focus attention on each proposal in the early weeks of the administration. The faith-based initiative received attention in the week after the inauguration, followed in successive weeks by education, tax cuts, and defense.

The White House employs a "rolling" announcement format in which it alerts the press that it will be making an announcement about a legislative initiative in coming days, sparking stories on the upcoming news. Then it makes the announcement, generating yet additional stories. Finally, the president travels around the country repeating the announcement he just made, obtaining both local and network coverage of his media events.

In her extensive study of the Bush White House communications operation, Martha Kumar found that it is dedicated to making news on the president's terms and is organized to plan and get ahead of events. As Karen Hughes put it about the president, "He'll want to know the plan. What's the plan? How are we rolling this out?" Similarly, Mary Matalin observed that "he's very engaged in the strategic thinking." "He has a feel for when is the right time to give the speech. What is our objective? Are we talking to the Congress, are we talking to America, are we talking to the world? . . . He knows when is the time when the iron's hot, if you will, or carpe diem. He gets those moments in ways that we often don't."[5]

President Bush's interest goes down to the operational level as well. For example, he pushed the staff in terms of making certain events related to the administration's response to the events of September 11 rose to his level. He was furious when he was sent documents regarding freezing financial assets to sign at Camp David. He demanded to know, "Why am I just signing this document and Secretary [Paul] O'Neill is announcing this tomorrow. This is the first strike in this new war against terror. It's not with a missile. It's with a stroke of a pen." The communications operation put together a Rose Garden signing event for the following morning.

The president also placed two strategic thinkers, Karl Rove and Karen Hughes, in top positions in the White House. Karen Hughes was given a broad mandate to think about the White House's message, whether the president's policies were being understood, whether there was support for the president's policies, and how to build more support for them. The elements that might be used in an issue campaign outside of government fell under her supervision: speechwriting, media affairs, television, press secretary, and communications.

There is a daily meeting with the president, including Dick Cheney, Andy Card, Karl Rove, Karen Hughes (now Dan Bartlett), and sometimes Condi Rice where they discuss strategic direction and issues and approaches. Once or twice a month Karl Rove convenes a strategy session to plan several months ahead, focusing on the president's travels, message, and daily themes. The strategy meetings provide them with a direction for the months ahead even if they are blown off course by events outside of their control.

An innovation of the George W. Bush administration is the control it exercises over the publicity officers in the departments. The White House screens the persons named to these positions and the release of information by departments. Controlling departmental public affairs offices allows the president and his staff to avoid the problem many administrations have faced with such units focusing their attention on the departmental secretary and his goals rather than those of the president.

Coordination with the departments has the advantage of making certain everyone has the same version of events and also that each knows what the other is doing. In addition, coordination with the departments has the advantage of making it easier for the White House to leverage off of the resources of the departments. Not only can the department secretaries serve as effective surrogates for the president on issues important to the administration, agencies also have at their disposal resources to send out their message.

In general, the emphasis on strategic planning has aided the president in defining himself and his programs rather than allowing his critics to do so. For example, since early 2001, Democrats have raised the issue of the fairness of the president's proposals for cutting taxes, arguing that most of the immediate benefits of the tax reductions would go to the affluent. However, from the beginning the administration aggressively framed the president's proposals as efforts to benefit much larger segments of the population. Although the public did not necessarily adopt the president's view, the White House's efforts seemed to have blunted the edge of the Democrats' charge and undermined their ability to engage in class warfare.[6]

The White House communications operation was especially impressive during the War in Iraq. The White House plotted appearances by officials in a daily communications grid, ensuring that in the first half of the day there was a news briefing by an administration official every two hours, and that everyone was taking a similar line. The White House, Pentagon, and State Department had a 9:30 A.M. conference call about the theme of day and who was delivering it. Starting at 7 A.M. from the command center in Qatar, a briefing was held so that it could run live on the morning news shows to put the administration's spin on overnight battlefield developments. A former deputy in the White House communications office prepped General Brooks, the chief military briefer. Ari Fleischer, the president's press secretary, held three press conferences per day, and there were additional briefings at the Pentagon and State, and sometimes special sessions for foreign reporters.[7]

The administration also exercised message discipline in its characterizations of people and developments in terms favorable to its policy. U.S. and British troops were "coalition forces." Regime change was "liberation," not "occupation." The paramilitary fedayeen were "death squads." Iraqi troops and fighters were "thugs." The Hussein government was a "regime." These terms became part of the accepted language of describing the war.[8]

Despite its efforts to think strategically and plan ahead, the White House has frequently found itself in a reactive mode. I discuss several instances below, but Martha Kumar cites the example of the administration's reaction to the issue of corporate fraud as an issue the White House did not anticipate and to which it was slow to react. Months of articles in newspapers and pieces on television news appeared detailing the depth of the issues and the connections some of the corporate players had with the White House. By the time the president delivered a speech on the issue on July 9, 2002, the bar representing success had been raised. Although the first day's stories focused on the president's rhetoric, the day two and day three stories focused on the speech's lack of effective enforcement mechanisms. One of the byproducts of a communications operation geared towards action is the difficulty inherent in listening while selling.

Public Relations Techniques

There are less direct ways of going public than the president giving a speech. The White House employs some public relations techniques in ways that it hopes will affect broad perceptions of the Bush presidency or structure thinking about issues. These are some of the characteristic patterns in the Bush White House's public relations efforts.

Control the Venue.　Although the president has gone public actively, he has done so in controlled venues. As the *Washington Post* reported in September 2002, Bush had devoted far more time to golf (15 rounds) than to solo news conferences (six).[9] After holding three news conferences in his first four months, he held only five more in his next 24 months—not counting the question and answer sessions he has had with foreign leaders during this period.[10]

Emphasize the Bright Side.　Another pattern of White House public relations efforts is what one journalist described as "compromise quietly, claim victory loudly." Bush is a pragmatist who makes the best deal he can with Congress and then declares victory. The White House knows that few Americans will notice or care that he did not get all, or even most, of what he wanted. Regarding education policy, for example, the Heritage Foundation complained on July 5, 2001, that "key elements of the president's plan—accountability, choice, flexibility and structural change—have been eliminated or weakened to the point that his design for educational reform is barely recognizable." Two weeks earlier, however, the president projected a more optimistic view. "I'm pleased to say that we're nearing historic reforms in public education," he said. "This is a victory for every child and for every family in America." The administration would rather public commentary focus on the size of the president's victory than on whether there *was* a victory.[11] Naturally, the White House hopes that its claims of victory will be self-fulfilling, improving its reputation and thus the chances for future successes.

The White House serves up its upbeat diagnosis each day and again at week's end. Bush's aides send the talking points throughout the White House, to allies on Capitol Hill, and to Republican opinion leaders around town. Interest groups receive customized talking points, such as a list of Bush victories for Hispanics. In an era of 24-hour cable and Internet news, the administration hopes that its talking points, repeated by administration officials or allies, will be reported by outlets too pressed for time to put the claims in context.

Manage the Image.   The Bush White House is also skilled at using the powers of television and technology to promote the president. "We pay particular attention to not only what the president says but what the American people see," said Office of Communications Director Dan Bartlett. Thus the White House has hired experts in lighting, camera angles, and backdrops from network television to showcase the president in dramatic and perfectly lighted settings. In May 2003, at a speech promoting his economic plan in Indianapolis, White House aides went so far as to ask people in the crowd behind Mr. Bush to take off their ties so they would look more like the ordinary people the president said would benefit from his tax cut. For a speech that the president delivered in the summer of 2002 at Mount Rushmore, the White House positioned the platform for television crews off to one side so that the cameras caught Mr. Bush in profile, his face perfectly aligned with the four presidents chiseled in stone.[12]

Perhaps the most elaborate White House event was Mr. Bush's speech aboard the *Abraham Lincoln* announcing the end of major combat in Iraq. The Office of Communications choreographed every aspect of the event, even down to positioning the aircraft carrier so the shoreline could not be seen by the camera when the president landed and to arraying members of crew in coordinated shirt colors over Bush's right shoulder and placing a banner reading "Mission Accomplished" to perfectly capture the president and the celebratory two words in a single shot. The speech was specifically timed for the sun to cast a golden glow on Mr. Bush. One of the president's aides proclaimed, "If you looked at the TV picture, you saw there was flattering light on his left cheek and slight shadowing on his right. It looked great."[13]

Change Justifications.   The Bush administration has been skillful in adapting rationales for its policy proposals to changing circumstances. The president advocated tax cuts as a way to return money to taxpayers when the government ran a budget surplus, as a way to constrain future government growth, as an insurance policy against an economic downturn, and as a means of stimulating a stagnant economy. The facts that the surplus soon disappeared, that government had to grow substantially as a result of the war on terrorism, that an economic downturn occurred, and that most of the tax reductions would not occur for years (and thus could not provide a stimulus) were ignored.

On the issue of regime change in Iraq, the administration sought first to link Iraqi President Saddam Hussein to al Qaeda and the September 11 attacks. When those links proved tenuous, the administration proclaimed a shift in U.S. strategic defense doctrine from deterrence and containment to pre-emption of those who would use weapons of mass destruction. When critics at home and abroad complained that the U.S. was ignoring its allies in pursuit of unilateral action, the president went to New York and declared that Iraq's refusal to comply with United Nations resolutions *required* multilateral action to preserve the viability of the world organization. Similarly, the president responded to criticism that he had usurped the legislature's war powers by going to Congress and asking for a strong resolution of support for the use of force against Iraq.

After the war, as the search for weapons of mass destruction in Iraq continued without success, the president first focused on destroying the *capability* to produce such weapons rather than the weapons themselves. Then he developed yet another rationale for the war against Saddam Hussein: Iraq was to be the "linchpin" to transform the Middle East and thereby reduce the terrorist threat to the United States.

Stay Resilient.   The Bush administration has continually demonstrated resilience in its relations with the public. The summer of 2002 provides an excellent example of this pattern. By June, only 54 percent of the respondents felt Bush had strong qualities of leadership. Even worse, only 42 percent expressed confidence in his ability to deal wisely with an international crisis and only 45 percent thought he had the skills necessary to negotiate effectively with world leaders. Fifty-seven percent felt the administration favored the rich.[14] The next month, the same poll found the public evenly split on whether Bush or his aides were running the government. A plurality of 48 percent felt the U.S. was on the wrong track, 58 percent viewed business as having too much influence on Bush, and 66 percent felt the same way about business influence on the administration. Sixty-one percent of the public felt the administration's proposal for reforming corporate accounting practices showed it was more interested in protecting the interests of large corporations than those of ordinary Americans.[15]

The White House did not allow events to overtake it, however. In the week following its biggest drop in the Gallup poll since the September 11 rally began, it announced ("hurriedly" in the minds of critics) its proposals for a new Department of Homeland Security. This returned it to a proactive stance and also provided a distraction from congressional hearings that were critical of the federal bureaucracy's performance.

In August, the administration again seemed to be adrift. As it stepped up its rhetoric against Saddam Hussein and advocated a unilateral strategy for regime change, the U.S. found its allies reluctant partners. Indeed, many were openly critical of the president's policy. Even more damaging were highly visible cautionary warnings from Republican establishment figures such as James Baker, Brent Scowcroft, and Lawrence Eagleburger. Moreover, more than two-thirds of the public signaled that it was necessary to obtain resolutions authorizing going to war with Iraq from both Congress and the United Nations, authorizations the administration argued it did not require. Fifty-eight percent of the public felt the White House had not done a sufficient job of explaining to the American public why the United States might take military action to remove Saddam Hussein from power.[16] In addition, the public remained quite pessimistic about the economy.

Once again, the administration turned the tide. Putting on a full-court press, the president turned the tables on its critics by asking the UN for multilateral action and Congress for a resolution authorizing force. In short order, a majority of the American public concluded that the administration had made its case for going to war clearly.[17] As the public became convinced that there would likely be a war with Iraq and that the White House was meeting its critics at least halfway, it began moving behind the president and his approval ratings reversed some of the losses sustained over the summer.

In sum, having drifted down in the Gallup Poll as far as 65 percent in August 2002 (lower in the polls of a number of other organizations), Bush's overall approval ratings increased slightly in September. As the spotlight turned from the economy, corporate malfeasance, and failures in the intelligence community to responses to the Iraqi threat against the United States, the president's approval ratings stabilized and even increased slightly.

As the UN weapons inspectors searched for illegal weapons of mass destruction in Iraq early in 2003, the administration yet again found itself in danger of losing control of events. As international pressure built to give the inspectors more time, it appeared that opponents of the war in the UN were setting the terms of debate. In response, the administration launched a carefully coordinated series of speeches by leading figures in January and February, culminating in the presentation to the Security Council by Secretary of State Colin Powell.[18] As a result, support for invading Iraq with ground troops rose to its highest point since 2001 (see Table 2.5).

Focus on Values.   The Bush White House copied a page from Bill Clinton's (and Dick Morris's) playbook by frequently focusing on values rather than issues. For example, it has staged events around the country that focused on family-friendly issues such as fitness, homeownership, reading, and adoption—typically providing largely symbolic support. Such efforts were designed to appeal to suburban women, one of the most sought-after groups of votes, and to reach people who do not focus on politics by relating to their issues in their personal lives. Local media typically gave substantial coverage to these events.

Such events were natural outgrowths of the 2000 presidential campaign in which Bush emphasized returning dignity and integrity to the presidency, "an era of responsibility," "leave no child behind," and, of course, "compassion." The war on terrorism provided new symbols for the president to exploit, focused around the most basic of public concerns, that of safeguarding people from attack in their homes and workplaces.

Just as in the election, the White House's emphasis on values has paid off for Bush. The public has always viewed him quite positively. At the beginning of his term 65 percent of the public approved of him as a person.[19] The president has also enjoyed positive evaluations on a number of personal character dimensions, particularly as someone with a vision for the country's future and who was strong and skilled enough to achieve this vision (see Table 2.1). The public's opinion of Bush seemed consistent with the image of a straight-talking chief executive officer that both the campaign and then the White House has tried to project. Contrary to the views of his most vocal detractors, majorities of the public have felt that Bush understands complex issues and is working hard enough to be an effective president.[20]

Table 2.1 Evaluations of Bush Characteristics and Qualities

Characteristic	2/9–11/01	4/20–22/01	Saying Applies % 10/5–6/01	4/29–5/02	7/26–28/02	1/10–12/03
Has vision for country's future		74				68
Can get things done		69				
Is tough enough for the job	68	68				
Is honest and trustworthy	64	67		77	69	70
Is a strong and decisive leader	61	60	75	77	70	76
Can manage the government effectively	61		79	75	66	67
Shares your values	57	58		67	60	54
Inspires confidence	57	55	75		66	65
Cares about the needs of people like you	56	59	69	66	60	56
Understands complex issues	55	56	69	68	60	
Generally agrees with you on issues you care about	53		60	64		
Is a person you admire	49			64		
Keeps his promises		57				
Is sincere in what he says			84	76		
Provides good moral leadership				84		
Puts the country's interests ahead of his own political interests				72		
Is not a typical politician				54		

Source: Gallup Poll, "Thinking about the following characteristics and qualities, please say whether you think it applies or doesn't apply to George W. Bush."

In light of the public's negative valuations of his predecessor's character, it is worth noting that large majorities have seen the president as honest and trustworthy.

Positive evaluations of the president's personal characteristics proved to be important, because in its April 20–22, 2001 poll, Gallup found that 52 percent of Americans considered leadership skills and vision to be the most important criterion for evaluating the president's job performance—compared to 36 percent who felt that the president's stance on issues was the most important criterion. Gallup found that a plurality of all key subgroups, including Bush's natural opponents of Democrats and liberals, assigned more importance to leadership skills and vision than to agreement on issues. The importance the public accorded the president's personal characteristics may partly explain why his overall job approval rating was higher than support for his job performance in many more specific policy-related areas.

Shortly after September 11, the public was even more positive about Bush as a person, and these evaluations had not substantially changed, even after two years of his presidency. Large majorities saw him as honest and trustworthy, strong and decisive, an effective manager, inspiring confidence, caring about average people and sharing their values, and as having a vision for the country.

ACTING STRATEGICALLY

In addition to the core governing strategy of going public, the Bush White House has been attentive to other key strategic elements in its relations with Congress. Among the most important are moving rapidly to exploit opportunities, focusing on priorities, and setting the national agenda.

Moving Rapidly

Presidents must not only recognize the opportunities in their environment and devise a strategy for governing. To succeed with Congress, they must also move rapidly to exploit those opportunities. First-year proposals have a better chance of passing Congress than do those sent to the Hill later in an administration. Thus, the White House should be ready to send its priority legislation to Capitol Hill.

Despite a severely truncated transition, the Bush administration lost no time in sending priority bills to Congress. Proposals for a large cut in income taxes, education reform, and increased support for faith-based charities went to Congress in short order. Specific changes in defense policy would take longer, but the White House launched an extensive review of the nation's defense posture.

The administration was not ready with proposals for all its priority issues, however. Two very important items on the "big six" list were deferred. Social Security reform was delegated to a commission. Medicare and prescription drugs were postponed. Given the disappearance of the general revenue budget surplus, the lack of consensus on these issues, and the president's limited political capital, the delays appear to be sensible strategic choices rather than evidence of disorganization or lethargy.

Setting Priorities

New presidents are wise to resist the temptations to try to deliver on all their campaign promises immediately following their elections and to accede to the many demands that are made on a new administration. Instead, it is important to establish priorities among legislative proposals. In addition, because the Washington community pays disproportionate attention to the first major legislative initiatives, it is especially critical to choose early battles wisely.

If the president is not able to focus Congress's attention on his priority programs, they may become lost in the complex and overloaded legislative process. Congress needs time to digest what the president sends, to engage in independent analyses, and to schedule hearings and markups. Unless the president clarifies his priorities, Congress may put the proposals in a queue.

Setting priorities is also important because presidents and their staff can lobby effectively for only a few bills at a time. The president's political capital is inevitably limited, and it is sensible to focus on the issues he cares about most. Setting priorities early also can reduce intra-administration warfare over the essence of the administration.

Karl Rove, the president's wide-ranging senior adviser, maintained that Bush campaigned on six key issues: tax cuts, education standards, military upgrades and a missile defense shield, federal support for faith-based charities, partial privatization of Social Security, and Medicare reforms and prescription drug coverage for seniors.[21] If these were Bush's priorities, he did a good job of focusing on them.

First, the Bush White House made a clear choice of a large income tax cut as its highest legislative priority. This made good strategic sense for a conservative administration. The president and his advisors felt that the notable victory of enacting a major tax cut early in the administration would signal the administration's competence in governing while unifying the Republican party for the more difficult issues ahead. Equally important, by severely limiting the government's resources, cutting taxes would set the terms of debate for nearly all the policy debates that would follow and restrain the Democrats' ability to use the budget surplus for expansion of social welfare policies.

It remains an open question whether the tax cut has also undermined the administration's ability to fund its own initiatives, such as a defensive missile shield, or to respond to demands for popular programs such as a prescription drug program under Medicare. Similarly, it is unclear whether engaging in a highly partisan fight over taxes early in the administration while simultaneously seeking bipartisan support on other issues had counterproductive consequences for future coalition building.

Tax cuts were not the administration's only priorities. Education reform, an overhaul of defense policy, and greater federal support for faith-based social welfare programs were also high on the list. The White House devoted attention and energy to each of these initiatives. Each also resulted in different outcomes. Education reform came to fruition in December of 2001, defense reform was caught up in the war on terrorism, and the faith-based initiative was stripped of its core elements and became little more than an incentive to donate to charities.

In general, the George W. Bush White House rarely sends detailed legislation to Congress and takes clear stands only on a select group of issues. Thus, it has husbanded its political capital and focused it on its priority issues.

Influencing the Agenda

A major goal of every administration is dominating the political agenda. Usually this means focusing public attention on its priority issues and, if possible, keeping lower priority and potentially politically damaging issues off the agenda. The efforts of the White House to set priorities and focus on them helped to secure them a place on the national agenda. A study of the first 60 days of news coverage of the Bush and Clinton administrations found that Bush was more successful than Clinton in focusing attention on his message. Each of the five major stories about Bush was on his priority initiatives, amounting to more than a third of all stories.[22]

Setting priorities in the early weeks of a new administration is also important because during the first months in office the president has the greatest latitude in focusing on priority legislation. After the transition period, other interests have more influence on the White House agenda. Congress is quite capable of setting its own agenda and is unlikely to defer to the president for long. In addition, ongoing policies continually force decisions to the president's desk.

The Bush presidency is no exception to the challenge of controlling the national agenda. At the same time that the president was seeking support for his priority items, he had to engage in legislative battles on important issues such as campaign finance reform and a patients' bill of rights, and make a highly visible decision on stem cell research. In fact, he had to devote one of only two nationally televised addresses (scarce presidential resources) of his first seven months in office to the latter. Bush also inevitably became embroiled in the issue of Navy practice bombings in Vieques, Puerto Rico.

More damaging were his responses to the unexpected energy shortage in California and potential environmental regulations, many of which were proposed by his predecessor. His and Vice President Cheney's energy plan was widely viewed as a sop to the oil and gas industry the two served, and many people saw the administration as having a weak commitment to environmental protection.

Despite the administration's organization and discipline regarding its legislative agenda, responding to the terrorist attacks of September 11 immediately dominated the president's agenda. The emphasis on national unity in the weeks that followed the tragedy and the inevitable focus of the president's energies on national security limited the opportunities for him to push hard for his most contentious proposals.

At the same time, the terrorist attacks and the resulting war on terrorism's dominance of the public agenda had the perverse consequence of solving several intractable problems facing the president. As Congress resumed its session following its summer recess in 2001, Democrats were beginning to blame the president's tax cut for "defunding" the federal government and forcing Congress to spend the surplus provided by Social Security contributions. These funds were to have been placed in a "lock box," off limits for paying current expenses. At the same time, unemployment was climbing and news about the country's economic recession was becoming more prominent in the media. The president's initiatives on education and funding for faith-based charities were stalled, and stories were circulating that Secretary of Defense Donald Rumsfeld was being rolled in his efforts to reform the U.S. defense posture.

After September 11, the recession gave way as a news story to terrorism and preparation to wage war in Afghanistan. Later, the president could lay blame for economic problems at the feet of Osama bin Laden and his supporters. Everyone seemed to forget about the Social Security lock box, as Congress raced to provide whatever was needed to aid the victims of terrorism and to fight terrorists abroad. When consensual policy dominates the agenda, presidents do well in the polls.

When the president proposed a Department of Homeland Security on June 6, 2002, and when he made his case for regime change in Iraq later in the summer, he had no difficulty dominating the nation's agenda. Issues dealing with the security of Americans, recently shocked by terrorist attacks, easily captured the media's and the public's attention. Even a looming war with Iraq, however, could not stop people from placing the sagging economy at the forefront of their concerns.[23]

Displaying Tactical Flexibility

The Bush White House has displayed tactical flexibility when political momentum has moved against it. When public opinion regarding the administration's performance in the war on terrorism declined in the late spring of 2002 (discussed below), the White House shifted gears quickly on the Democrats' proposal for a Department of Homeland Security. Instead of opposing it, the president announced an even more extensive reorganization of government. Similarly, when the administration received low marks for its response to the corporate fraud and accounting practices scandals that came to light in 2002, the president embraced an accounting regulation measure far stronger than the one he proposed. When campaign finance reform passed, and proved to be popular, the president signed it. Similarly, when a farm bill passed in 2002 that substantially exceeded the president's budget proposal, he signed it to shore up Republican support in farm belt constituencies for the upcoming midterm elections.

SUCCESS IN MOVING THE PUBLIC

It is one thing to go public. It is something quite different to succeed in moving public opinion. How successful has George W. Bush been in his efforts to govern through a permanent campaign?

Table 2.2   Public Support for Bush Tax Cut, 2001

Poll Date	% Favor	% Oppose	% No Opinion
Feb. 9–11, 2001	56	34	10
Feb. 19–21, 2001	53	30	17
March 5–7, 2001	56	34	10
April 20–22, 2001	56	35	9

Source: Gallup Poll, "Based on what you have read or heard, do you favor or oppose the federal income tax cuts George W. Bush has proposed?"

Taxes

No policy has been more central to the George W. Bush presidency than tax cuts. They have been the answer to every economic situation. If the federal government is running a surplus, cut taxes. If the economy is stagnant, cut taxes. If the economy requires more investment, cut taxes on investments, savings, and estates.

The president made tax cuts the centerpiece of his campaign in 2000, and he wasted no time in proposing substantial tax cuts once he was inaugurated. He advocated them both frequently and forcefully. Table 2.2 shows responses to Gallup Poll questions on the president's 2001 tax cut proposal. The results show that public opinion did not change in response to the president's efforts.

In 2003, the president proposed a fundamental change in the tax structure, one that would eliminate taxes on most stock dividends and allow people to establish tax–free savings accounts. The policy did not gain traction with the public, however. The Pew Research Center for the People and the Press found that only 42 percent of the public approved of Bush's handling of taxes despite a high-profile White House campaign on behalf of its policy.[24] At the beginning of May, Pew found that only 40 percent of the public favored the president's tax cut.[25] Most respondents to a CBS/*New York Times* poll in early May said they did not think it was important to cut taxes or that doing so would stimulate the economy.[26] Similarly, the *Washington Post*-ABC News Poll found that tax cuts were of low importance to the public and that when given the choice between tax cuts and increased domestic spending, the public favored the latter by 67 percent to 29 percent.[27] Shortly before the president signed the truncated bill that eventually passed, Gallup found that more people felt the tax cuts were a bad idea than thought they were a good idea.[28]

The president originally requested a ten-year total of $726 billion in tax cuts. He repeatedly railed against the strategy of making tax cuts temporary and phasing them in over time. At the center of his proposal was the elimination of taxes on stock dividends. In the end the president signed a tax bill that cut taxes $320 billion, that was temporary and phased in, and that did not eliminate the dividend tax.[29]

Four Republican senators refused to support the full package: John McCain (Arizona), Lincoln Chafee (Rhode Island), Olympia Snowe (Maine), and George Voinovich of Ohio. The administration did not even try to pressure McCain and Chafee, knowing that it would be useless, but it did target Voinovich and Snowe. In addition, the White House did not object when the Club for Growth ran advertisements aimed at them in their home states. The administration also targeted Democrats John Breaux (Louisiana), Blanche Lincoln (Arkansas), and Ben Nelson (Nebraska).

The White House staged dozens of events around the country with administration officials and mobilized friendly interest groups to pressure senators. Sometimes these efforts seemed to equate tax cuts with patriotism. More importantly, the president took to the road, attempting to exploit his 70 percent approval ratings following the cessation of fighting in Iraq. In Ohio, the home of Republican holdout Voinovich, the president derided the Senate bill that provided $350 billion in tax cuts as a "a little bitty tax relief package" and insisted that senators who did not support him "might have some explaining to do."

In the end, the efforts had little impact and may even have backfired. Ben Nelson was the only Democrat (aside from long-time tax cut supporter Zell Miller) who supported even the $350 tax-cut bill the Senate passed. Of the four Republican opponents, only Voinovich voted for the final bill—after holding out for $32 billion of relief for the states and insisting that it be subtracted from even the scaled-down Senate bill. The White House declared victory, of course, but in reality Bush concluded that it was more important to have a tax cut than to stand on principle over its size and content.[30] The lack of success of his strategy of going public had left him no choice.

Issues

As is usually the case with presidents, Bush's overall approval exceeded approval on his handling of many specific issues. Table 2.3 presents results of five Gallup polls taken during his presidency. In the two polls in the pre-September 11, 2001, period,

Table 2.3   Issue Approval for George W. Bush

Issue	% Approve				
	4/20–22/01	7/10–11/01	3/22–24/02	7/26–28/02	1/10–12/03
Overall	62	57	79	69	58
Economy	55	54	65	52	53
Foreign Affairs	56	54	71	63	48
Defense	66		80		63
Education	62	63	63	62	57
Taxes	54	60	64		49
Budget	52		51		43
Unemployment	47		57		
Environment	46	46	53		
Abortion	43		49		39
Energy	43	45	57		
Social Security		49	47		
Health Care			52	47	41

Source: Gallup Poll.

we see that the president was rated most highly on the issues that were his highest priorities: taxes, education, and defense. It is reasonable to conclude that these issues were the most salient to the public in the early months of the Bush administration, at least partly because of the president's emphasis on them. Conversely, less than 50 percent of the public approved of his performance on Social Security, unemployment, abortion, the environment, and energy. These issues evidently were less salient in evaluations of the president.

Between September 11, 2001, and the end of March 2002, the president maintained the approval of more than 79 percent of the public, a level unprecedented in the past half century. The president's high overall approval was undoubtedly driven by the high evaluations of his performance on the issues of defense and foreign policy. However, his impressive approval levels seem to have had a halo effect, increasing his support on unrelated issues as well. The results of the March 22–24, 2002, Gallup poll show that the public's evaluation of Bush's handling of issues rose substantially not only for defense and foreign affairs, but also for the economy, unemployment, energy, and the environment. He maintained the strong support he had previously achieved on education and taxes. In that same poll, the president received 86 percent approval for his performance on preventing terrorism in the U.S. and also for fighting terrorism abroad. Seventy-two percent of the public approved of his handling of the Middle East.

Although the rally that began on September 11, 2001, was the most sustained in modern times, its decay was inevitable. Americans seemed to be growing uneasy amid terrorism warnings, a stagnate economy, and the failures of prominent institutions, including the FBI, CIA, major corporations, and the Catholic Church. The Gallup poll of June 21–23 showed only one-third of the public believed the U.S. was winning the war on terrorism. These concerns were reflected in the drop in the public's approval of the president's performance on foreign affairs, the economy, and health care (see the July 26–28, 2002, results in Table 2.3).

By January 2003, the president was doing even more poorly, falling below 50 percent approval of his handling of taxes, the budget, and foreign affairs, and reaching only 53 percent approval of his handling of the economy. Although the rally sparked by the war with Iraq bolstered his ratings on foreign affairs, even in the middle of the war he only received a 49 percent approval rating on his handling of the economy,[31] and even before the war concluded, three times as many people felt the economy was the most important problem facing the nation as felt that war or Iraq was.[32] By the fall, Bush's approval on most issues had fallen yet further in the face of the public's concerns about unemployment and the reconstruction of Iraq.

Televised Addresses

The president faced similar frustrations in increasing his public support with his nationally televised addresses. Presidents do not speak directly to the national over national television often, and when they do they frequently seek support for themselves and their policies. Table 2.4 shows the difference in presidential approval in the Gallup polls taken most closely before and after each of George W. Bush's live presidential televised address to the nation in his first 33 months in office. (In com-

Table 2.4   Changes in Approval Ratings after George W. Bush
             National Addresses

January 20, 2001	Inaugural	NA
February 27, 2001	Administration Goals	1
August 9, 2001	Stem Cell Research	2
September 11, 2001	Terrorist Attack	35
September 20, 2001	Terrorist Attack	4
October 7, 2001	War in Afghanistan (afternoon)	2
November 8, 2001	War on Terrorism*	0
January 29, 2002	State of the Union	−2
June 6, 2002	Department of Homeland Security	4
September 11, 2002	Anniversary of terrorist Attacks	4
October 7, 2002	War with Iraq**	−5
January 28, 2003	State of the Union	1
February 1, 2003	*Columbia* space shuttle disaster	−2
February 26, 2003	War with Iraq	1
March 17, 2003	War with Iraq	13
May 1, 2003	War with Iraq	−1
September 11, 2003	Reconstruction of Iraq	−7

Source: Gallup Poll

*Broadcast by only one network.
**Broadcast by only Fox, not ABC, NBC, CBS, or PBS.

paring survey results of two samples such as those employed by Gallup, differences
between the results must be about 6 percentage points before we can be reasonably
sure that the results reflect a real difference.)

The figures in the third column of the table show that a statistically significant
change in Bush's approval following a televised presidential address occurred only
twice. The first was an increase of 35 percentage points following the terrorist attack on September 11, 2001. Few would attribute the public's rallying around the
commander in chief to the president's brief comments that evening. There was another rally, this time of 13 percentage points, following the president's address on
March 17, 2003, announcing the invasion of Iraq. Again, it would be stretching to
attribute the rally to the president's short statement.

His approval went up only one percentage point in the Gallup poll following his
address to a joint session of Congress on February 27, 2001, and only two percentage
points following his August 9, 2001, address on his decision regarding federal funding
of stem cell research. In the months following September 11, when his approval was
very high, there was less potential to increase his support. Yet even when his approval declined, televised addresses still made little impact on his public support.

War with Iraq

The president's most important initiative in 2002 was preparation for war with Iraq.
In the late summer, the White House decided it should move on regime change in
Iraq and sought the public's backing. The context in which Bush sought this

support was certainly favorable. In surveys conducted over the previous 10 years, stretching back to the end of the Gulf War, majorities had generally supported U.S. military action in Iraq to remove Saddam Hussein from power. The American public has long held strongly negative perceptions of Iraq and its leader. In a December 1998 poll, Saddam Hussein received the worst rating of any public figure tested in Gallup poll history—1 percent positive and 96 percent negative.[33] In early 2002, the country of Iraq received a 6 percent favorable and 88 percent unfavorable rating, the worst of any of the 25 countries tested in that poll.[34] Since 1991, Iraq had never received even a 10 percent favorable rating.[35] Asked in February 2001 what country was America's worst enemy, Americans named Iraq significantly more often than any other country.[36]

In September 2002, Gallup reported that most Americans believed that Iraq had developed or was developing weapons of mass destruction. Many Americans felt that if left alone, Iraq would use those weapons against the United States within five years. Most Americans felt that Saddam Hussein sponsored terrorism that affected the United States. A little more than half of Americans took the additional inferential leap and concluded that Saddam Hussein was personally and directly involved in the September 11, 2001, terrorist attacks.[37]

On August 26, 2002, Vice President Cheney delivered a hard-hitting speech laying out the administration's case for invading Iraq, and then, on the anniversary of the terrorist attacks, the president delivered a nationally televised address. The next day he addressed the United Nations, demanding that it take action to disarm Iraq. Later, he asked Congress to pass a resolution authorizing him to use force against Iraq. On October 7, Bush addressed the nation again, delivering his most comprehensive presentation regarding the likely need to use force against Saddam Hussein's regime in Iraq. On February 26 and March 17, 2003, the president again made national addresses on Iraq.

It is interesting to note that Bush's October 7 speech was strictly nonpartisan, the venue for the speech was chosen for the absence of a statewide election in the midterm elections, and the subject focused on what is perhaps the most important decision a nation can take. Nevertheless, ABC, CBS, NBC, and PBS chose not to carry the president's remarks. The White House was reluctant to make a special request for airtime out of concern for fanning fears of an imminent invasion, but it would have welcomed coverage. The networks argued that the president's speech contained little that was new. In the absence of breaking news, the commander in chief was unable to obtain airtime to discuss his thinking about going to war. As a result, only about 17 million people viewed the speech.[38]

Table 2.5 shows public support for the invasion of Iraq. Public opinion did not change in response to the administration's blitzkrieg. Gallup used the phrase "sending American ground troops" in the question about invading Iraq. Some other polling organizations simply asked about "military action"—an easier threshold—and found higher levels of support. The president, of course, sought support for the use of ground troops as well as other means of projecting force. Nevertheless, surveys by the Pew Research Center and the CBS/*New York Times* Poll found little or no change in public support for invading Iraq since the summer and before the

White House's public relations effort. Indeed, Pew found that between mid-August and the end of October support for taking military action in Iraq to end Saddam Hussein's rule decreased by 9 percentage points.[39]

Furthermore, Americans expressed reservations and conditions to their support. They had a strong preference for both a congressional authorization for the use of force and securing the participation of allies.[40] They also preferred to wait for weapons inspectors to attempt to disarm Iraq before the United States took military action. At the same time, respondents said they were more concerned with the economy than with Iraq and 69 percent (including 51 percent of Republicans) complained that Bush should be paying more attention to the economy.[41]

Table 2.5 Public Support for Invasion of Iraq

Poll Date	Favor %	Oppose %	No Opinion %
February 19–21, 2001	52	42	6
November 26–27, 2001	74	20	6
2002			
June 17–19	61	31	8
August 19–21	53	41	6
September 2–4	58	36	6
September 5–8	58	36	6
September 13–16	57	39	4
September 20–22	57	38	5
October 3–6	53	40	7
October 14–17	56	37	7
October 21–22	54	40	6
November 8–10	59	35	6
November 22–24	58	37	5
December 9–10	55	39	6
December 16–17	58	35	7
December 19–22	53	38	9
2003			
January 3–5	56	39	6
January 10–12	56	38	6
January 23–25	52	43	5
January 31–February 2	58	38	4
February 7–9	63	34	3
February 17–19	59	38	3
February 24–26	59	37	4
March 3–5	59	37	4
March 14–16	64	33	3

Source: Gallup Poll, "Would you favor or oppose sending American ground troops to the Persian Gulf in an attempt to remove Saddam Hussein from power in Iraq?"

Public support for invading Iraq with ground troops stayed within a narrow range throughout the fall and winter until early February. At that point it increased five percentage points. This increase was not in response to the president, however, but to Secretary of State Colin Powell's presentation of evidence against Iraq to the United Nations. In the month following Powell's speech, support for an invasion drifted downward until the middle of March, when the president issued the final ultimatum to Saddam Hussein that marked the beginning of a rally in support of war.

Midterm Elections

In the month following the president's October 7 speech, he engaged in the most active midterm campaigning of any president in history. In the end, the Republicans gained seats in both houses of Congress, maintaining the majority in the House and regaining it in the Senate. The historic nature of these gains (exceeded only once—in 1934—during the previous century) generated considerable commentary about the president's public leadership.

Bush campaigned relentlessly, covering 15 carefully chosen states in the last five days alone, and he rallied his party. The most significant fact in the Republican success in the elections was the heavy turnout in Republican base, not Democratic abstentions. A Gallup poll taken the weekend before the election found that 64 percent of Republicans were "more enthusiastic" about voting than in the past, while only 51 percent of Democrats responded that way.[42] On the other had, the Democrats failed to rally—they had little to rally around, lacking both a message and a messenger. Voters did not necessarily support the Republicans on the issues, but the White House succeeded in turning the election into a referendum on popular president.[43]

Most people who entered the booths did not have terrorism on their minds. More were concerned about the economy and the prospect of war with Iraq. But the minority who did have terrorism on their minds was overwhelmingly Republican, and the Democrats were not able to establish positioning on enough of the other issues to counter this strong GOP advantage. The war on terrorism had shifted the public debate to national security issues that favored the Republicans and shielded the president from criticism on domestic issues that favored the Democrats.

Despite the Republican success, perspective is important. The election was very close. The *Washington Post* reported that a change of 41,000 votes in only two states out of 77 million cast nationwide would have kept the Senate in Democratic hands. As political analyst Charlie Cook put it, "This was a year of very close races that, for the most part, broke toward Republicans but in no way reflected a significant shift in the national direction."[44]

In addition, the Republicans enjoyed several advantages. Because the president had lacked coattails in 2000, there was less chance for setbacks in the midterm elections. Few Republicans held seats that lacked a substantial Republican base. In fact, since Al Gore received the most votes in 2000, we would have expected the Democrats to lose seats.

The Republicans also had gained as a result of redistricting following the 2000 census. Both the *National Journal* and *Congressional Quarterly Weekly Report* concluded that the Republican gains in the House almost exactly matched these territorial gains.[45] (The Republicans were successful, however, in boosting the security of representatives who had won narrowly in 2000.)

Democrats were also forced to play on Republican turf, trying to pick up seats in traditionally Republican areas. For example, 26 out of the country's 45 competitive House seats were in districts where Al Gore had gotten less than 50 percent of the vote in 2000.[46] The Democrats' seven strongest bids to take over Republican-held seats were in states Bush had won in 2000, and four of the six vulnerable Democratic seats were in states won by Bush while Gore had only narrowly carried the other two, Minnesota and Iowa.

The Republicans raised more money than the Democrats (although not in Georgia), and in a handful of hotly contested races, the money helped. Having more money also allowed the Republicans to concentrate their funding in battleground states and districts.[47]

The Republicans also enjoyed an advantage with candidates. The White House actively recruited quality candidates, including Senate winners Norm Coleman (Minnesota), Jim Talent (Missouri), and Saxby Chambliss (Georgia). The Democrats, on the other hand, had a weak cohort of challengers to Republican incumbents.[48] The memorial service for Minnesota Senator Paul Wellstone a few days before the election turned into a political rally that alienated some voters in a closely contested election and gave Coleman an excuse to resume his campaign.

Charlie Cook found no Republican wave except perhaps in Georgia. Instead, he concluded that the midterm elections in 2002 were mainly decided by the basics of getting out the vote.[49] Indeed, the Republicans operated a finely engineered voter-mobilization effort. In Georgia, the state with the biggest Republican successes, the party implemented a meticulous organizational plan that included computer analysis, training programs for volunteers, and a voter registration drive followed by massive mailing, telephone, and neighborhood canvasses in the closing days of the campaign. The president visited as late as November 2 to energize the Republican ranks. Aiding this grassroots mobilization were the National Rifle Association and United Seniors (an organization heavily underwritten by the drug industry).[50]

THE IMPACT OF HIGH APPROVAL ON CONGRESS

One of the perennial questions about presidential-congressional relations is the impact of the president's public approval on the support he received in Congress. Did George W. Bush's extraordinarily high approval ratings following the terrorist attacks provide him a significant political resource in his attempts to obtain congressional support for his policies? Did the patriotic response to the attacks help him to mobilize the public on behalf of his programs? Bush certainly seemed aware of the potential advantages of public support—as well as its ephemeral nature. As the president put it, "It is important to move as quickly as you can in order to spend whatever capital you have as quickly as possible."[51]

Where the public supported his policies—on fighting the war on terrorism abroad, on investigating and prosecuting terrorism at home, and in reorganizing the government to enhance domestic security—the president ultimately won most of what he sought. Even on security issues, however, the going was not always easy. He lost on the issue of privatizing airport security workers, although Congress considered the bill in the immediate aftermath of the September 11 attacks. The president also faced a protracted battle over the new Department of Homeland Security when his proposal for additional flexibility in personnel policy in the department infuriated labor unions, a core Democratic constituency.

Passing legislation was even more difficult on the divisive domestic issues that remained on Congress's agenda, including health care, environmental protection, energy, the economy, government support for faith-based social programs, corporate malfeasance, judicial nominees, and taxes. The politics of the war on terrorism did not fundamentally alter the consideration of these issues, which continued to divide the public and their representatives in Congress as they had before. The inevitable differences between the parties emerged predictably, exacerbated by the narrow majorities in each chamber and the jockeying for advantage in the midterm elections.

Bipartisanship in one arena (the war on terrorism) does not necessarily carry over in another. As the parties in Congress have become more homogeneous over time and as the number of competitive seats has shrunk, especially in the House, the differences between the parties have increased. The opposition party does not offer very fertile ground for presidents on most issues—even during wartime. Thus, the president failed to obtain many of his top-priority items in 2002, including making the 2001 tax cuts permanent and passing his fiscal stimulus program, providing government funding for a robust faith-based initiative, and obtaining drilling rights in the Artic National Wildlife Reserve. No progress was made on partially privatizing Social Security, banning cloning and certain kinds of abortion, or passing private-school tax credits, and the president experienced plenty of frustration on obtaining confirmation of his judicial appointees. He also had to sign a farm bill that was much more costly than he wanted.

In December 2001, the president concluded quiet negotiations with the Democrats led by Senator Edward Kennedy and signed a bill on education reform. The president was able to claim a victory on one of his top-priority issues, even though he had given up many of the most controversial elements of his original proposal. It is significant that to accomplish even this much, the president chose to negotiate in private rather than to go public.

In 2003, following the historic results of the 2002 midterm elections, many observers predicted that the president would be more successful in Congress. Such predictions were illusory, however. With Bush focused mostly on the war in Iraq, a small but crucial number of Republican moderates in the Senate broke ranks and dealt significant blows to several of his highest-profile policies, slicing in half the president's $726 billion tax cut proposal and defeating his plan for oil drilling in the Arctic National Wildlife Refuge in Alaska. Democrats were no easier to deal with either, forcing the president to accept a faith-based plan stripped of its essential features and to put on hold his proposals for providing a prescription drug program for seniors and for capping medical malpractice lawsuit damages. The opposition also continued to oppose effectively his nominations to appellate courts.

The modest impact of Bush's high approval ratings is not surprising. The president's public support must compete for influence with other, more stable factors that affect voting in Congress, including members' ideology, party, personal views and commitments on specific policies, and constituency interests. Although constituency interests may seem to overlap with presidential approval, they should be viewed as distinct forces. It is quite possible for constituents to approve of the president but oppose him on particular policies, and it is opinions on these policies that will ring most loudly in congressional ears. Members of Congress are unlikely to vote against the clear interests of their constituents or the firm tenets of their ideology solely in deference to a widely supported chief executive.[52]

It is interesting that at the beginning of his term, Bush's travels seemed motivated more by demonstrating his support in states where he ran well in the election than in convincing more skeptical voters of the soundness of his proposals. He did not travel to California until May 29 and visited New York even later. Instead, the White House gave priority to states that Bush had won and that were represented by Democratic senators, including Georgia, Louisiana, Arkansas, Missouri, North and South Dakota, Montana, and North Carolina.

The goal of these trips seemed to be to demonstrate preexisting public support in the constituencies of members of Congress who were potential swing votes. Whatever the president's motivations, he obtained the support of only one Senate Democrat (Zell Miller of Georgia, who announced his support of the tax cut before Bush was inaugurated) on the April 4 bellwether vote for his full tax cut.

In 2003, the president seemed to be following the same strategy as he campaigned for his tax cut proposal. His travel seemed designed to work at the margins to convince moderate senators of both parties that his tax cut proposal enjoyed public support in their states.

CONCLUSION

The George W. Bush administration has surprised many observers, who underestimated both the president's character and his political skills. The White House has made unusually focused efforts to govern strategically and gotten the most out of the context in which it is attempting to govern. However, despite its sensitivity to strategy and its discipline in implementing it, the Bush administration has faced the familiar frustrations of contemporary presidents. The public has typically been unresponsive to the president's pleas for support, and Congress has frequently failed to support his policy initiatives.

NOTES

1. Richard E. Neustadt, *Presidential Power and the Modern Presidents* (New York: Free Press, 1990), p. 4.

2. See George C. Edwards III, *At the Margins: Presidential Leadership of Congress* (New Haven, CT: Yale University Press, 1989).

3. Gallup Poll, January 15–16, 2001.

4. See Corey Cook, "The Permanence of the 'Permanent Campaign': George W. Bush's Public Presidency," *Presidential Studies Quarterly* 32 (December 2002): 753–764.

5. This discussion draws extensively on Martha Joynt Kumar, "Communications Operations in the White House of President George W. Bush: Making News on His Terms," *Presidential Studies Quarterly* 33 (June 2003): 366–393.

6. See, Jonathan Weisman, "Bush Blunts 'Fairness Question' on Taxes," *Washington Post*, May 13, 2003, p. A6.

7. Elisabeth Bumiller, "Even Critics of War Say the White House Spun It with Skill," *New York Times*, April 20, 2003, p. B14.

8. Bumiller, "Even Critics of War Say the White House Spun It with Skill."

9. Dana Milbank, "Bush by the Numbers, as Told by a Diligent Scorekeeper," *Washington Post*, September 3, 2002, p. A15.

10. Martha Joynt Kumar, "'Does This Constitute a Press Conference?' Defining and Tabulating Modern Presidential Press Conferences," *Presidential Studies Quarterly* 33 (March 2003): 221–237.

11. Dana Milbank, "No Lemons; It's All Lemonade in Bush's White House," *Washington Post*, July 22, 2001, B1.

12. Elisabeth Bumiller, "Keepers of Bush Image Lift Stagecraft to New Heights," *New York Times*, May 16, 2003, pp. A1, A8.

13. Bumiller, "Keepers of Bush Image Lift Stagecraft to New Heights,"

14. CBS News/*New York Times* poll, June 14–18, 2002.

15. CBS News/*New York Times* poll, July 13–16, 2002.

16. CNN/*USA Today*/Gallup poll, September 2–4, 2002.

17. The switch was from 37 percent agreeing the administration had made a clear case in late-August to 52 percent in mid-September. Pew Research Center poll, September 12–16, 2002.

18. Elisabeth Bumiller, "War P. R. Machine Is on Full Throttle," *New York Times*, February 9, 2003, p. 13.

19. Gallup poll, February 9–11, 2001.

20. Gallup poll, April 20–22, 2001.

21. Alexis Simendinger, "The Report Card They Asked For," *National Journal*, July 21, 2001, p. 2335.

22. The Project For Excellence in Journalism, *The First 100 Days: How Bush Versus Clinton Fared In the Press*, 2001.

23. See, for example, the Gallup polls for January 13–16, 2003; February 3–6, 2003; and March 3–5, 2003.

24. Pew Research Center for the People and the Press poll, February 12–18, 2003.

25. Pew Research Center for the People and the Press poll, April 30–May 4, 2003.

26. CBS News/*New York Times* poll, May 9–12, 2003.

27. Dana Milbank and Dan Balz, *Washington Post*, May 11, 2003 (web site).

28. Gallup poll of May 19–21, 2003. These results are based on a question asked of half the sample (N=509). Forty-six percent responded that the tax cuts were a bad idea, one percent more than thought they were a good idea.

29. It is possible, of course, that the tax cuts would be made permanent in the future. The point here is the contrast between what the president wanted and what he got.

30. Dana Milbank and Jim VandeHei, "Bush Retreat Eased Bill's Advance," *Washington Post*, May 23, 2003, p. A5.

31. Gallup poll of March 29–30, 2003.

32. Gallup poll of April 7–9, 2003.

33. Gallup poll of December 28–29, 1998.

34. Gallup poll, February 4–6, 2002.

35. Chris Chambers, Americans Most Favorable Toward Canada, Australia and Great Britain; Iran, Libya and Iraq Receive the Lowest Ratings," Gallup Poll News Release, February 16, 2001.

36. Gallup poll, February 1–4, 2001.

37. Frank Newport, "Public Wants Congressional and UN Approval before Iraq Action," Gallup Poll News Release, September 6, 2002.

38. Jim Rutenberg, "Speech Had Big Audience Despite Networks' Action," *New York Times*, October 9, 2002, p. A13.

39. See Pew Research Center survey report of October 30, 2002.

40. Editors of the Gallup Poll, "Nine Key Questions about Public Opinion on Iraq," Gallup Poll News Release, October 1, 2002; Lydia Saad, "Top Ten Findings about Public Opinion and Iraq," Gallup Poll News Release, October 8, 2002.

41. CBS/*New York Times* poll, October 3-5, 2002.

42. William Schneider, "The Bush Mandate," *National Journal*, November 9, 2002, p. 3358; Adam Nagourney and Janet Elder, "Positive Ratings for the G.O.P., If Not Its Policy," *New York Times*, November 26, 2002, pp. A1 and A 22.

43. William Schneider, "A Popularity Contest," *National Journal*, November 16, 2002, p. 3346.

44. Charlie Cook, "Off to the Races: So Much for the GOP Sweep," December 10, 2002, Washington, D.C.

45. Richard E. Cohen, "New Lines, Republican Gains," *National Journal*, November 9, 2002, p. 3285; Richard E. Cohen, "New Lines, Republican Gains," *National Journal*, November 9, 2002, p. 3285; Gregory L. Giroux, "Redistricting Helped GOP," *Congressional Quarterly Weekly Report*, November 9, 2002, pp. 2934–2935.

46. Charlie Cook, "A Landslide? That Talk is Mostly Just Hot Air," *National Journal*, November 9, 2002, p. 3346–3347.

47. Bob Benenson, "GOP Won Midterm by Winning Series of Small Battles," *Congressional Quarterly Weekly Report*, November 9, 2002, pp. 2890. See also Jim VandeHei and Dan Balz, "In GOP Win, a Lesson in Money, Muscle, Planning," *Washington Post*, November 10, 2002, pp. A1, A6, A7.

48. Gary C. Jacobson, "Terror, Terrain, and Turnout: Explaining the 2002 Midterm Election," *Political Science Quarterly* 118 (Spring 2003): 1–22.

49. Charlie Cook, "A Landslide? That Talk is Mostly Just Hot Air," *National Journal*, November 9, 2002, p. 3346–3347.

50. Peter H. Stone and Shawn Zeller, "Business and Conservative Groups Won Big," *National Journal*, November 9, 2002, p. 3355.

51. Quoted in Dana Milbank, "Bush Popularity Isn't Aiding GOP Domestic Agenda," *Washington Post*, June 16, 2002, p. A4.

52. On the question of the impact of presidential approval on presidential support in Congress, see Edwards, *At the Margins*; and George C. Edwards III, "Aligning Tests with Theory: Presidential Approval as a Source of Influence in Congress," *Congress and the Presidency* 24 (Fall 1997): 113–130.

3

The Bully Pulpit
and the
War on Terror

◆◆◆

Marc Landy

Presidential words and deeds shape the quality and character of the citizenry. The term "bully pulpit" coined by Theodore Roosevelt evokes this unique capacity of the president to influence how ordinary Americans come to make sense of the circumstances in which they find themselves.[1] The Constitution does not confer such an awesome task on the president. It declares him commander in chief, not teacher in charge. But as Sidney Milkis and I have explored in our study of presidential greatness, the outstanding rhetorical precedents set by great presidents have conspired to place this responsibility on his shoulders.[2] Such epochal utterances as Washington's Farewell Address, Jefferson's Second Inaugural, Jackson's Nullification Proclamation, Lincoln's Gettysburg Address, and FDR's response to Pearl Harbor provided crucial guidance for Americans for understanding the regime in which they lived and for coping with the great challenges they faced.

This chapter examines presidential use of the bully pulpit by focusing on President George W. Bush's rhetorical response to the crisis of 9/11 and its aftermath up through the summer of 2003. It analyzes his public utterances to see how he educated the public about the nature and meaning of 9/11, about how the government would respond in its immediate aftermath, and, after the defeat of the Taliban, why and how it would engage Iraq. It seeks to explain how Bush chose to frame the problems posed, to justify the actions that his administration was contemplating and to defend those actions against the criticisms they inspired. It concludes with a consideration of the challenges and opportunities the nation's educator in chief is likely to face as the War on Terror continues.

9/11

As of September 10, 2001, George W. Bush was a controversial figure, not greatly loved, winner of the highest office despite losing the popular vote. In the wake of 9/11, he became the indispensable person to whom a nation looked for both an explanation of the tragedy and a clear and plausible account of how the nation would respond. The events of that terrible day provided an occasion for presidential civic education unprecedented in scope and difficulty. Lincoln and FDR's wartime tasks were simple by comparison. As upsetting as the attacks on Fort Sumter and Pearl Harbor were, they fit into a readily identifiable picture of war. They were attacks on a fleet in harbor and a fort by uniformed combatants representing in one case a sovereign state and in the other a state with pretensions to sovereignty. The orders for those attacks had been given by the duly constituted governments of those states and carried out through the military chain of command. For all the horror of those events, the American public could readily comprehend what had happened, who the perpetrators were and, broadly speaking, what the nation had to do to respond. Although there were some dissenters, most Americans were prepared to say that war had been declared on them and the only plausible response was to return the favor.

The events of 9/11 provided no comparable clarity. Although the Pentagon was a military target, the far greater slaughter of thousands of civilians took place at the World Trade Center, which was not. Unlike Lincoln and FDR, Bush had to explain not only how the U.S. would respond, but who the enemy was and why the attacks had taken place. The only clear aspects of that day were the tragedy of lost lives and the mounting fear and the sense of vulnerability the suicide attacks engendered. Journalists are trained that a news story should answer the questions that are of greatest concern to the reader: when, why, what, who, and how. These same questions provided the frame for Bush's civic education project as well. Was 9/11 the act of criminals or was it an act of war? Hendirk Hertzberg, writing in *The New Yorker*, attacked the war metaphor.

> . . . a more useful metaphor than war is crime. The terrorists of September 11 are outlaws within a global polity. They may enjoy the corrupt protection of a state . . . But they do not constitute or control a state . . . Their status and numbers are such that the task of dealing with them should be viewed as a police matter, of the most urgent kind.[3]

The question of how terrorism was to be vanquished was critically related to the definition imposed on what had occurred. If it was a crime, then the rule of law clearly applied and the problem should be dealt with using the normal panoply of institutions and methods of criminal inquiry and prosecution—police forces, prosecutors, and courts. But if it was a war, then a far broader range of initiatives was possible, including Machiavelli's dictum that wars should be fought not when the problem is easy to recognize, but earlier, when it is hard to recognize, meaning proof positive of guilt is not available, but easy to cure.

Regardless of whether the 9/11 attack was an act of war or crime, the question remained, who were the perpetrators? How would we know when the war was won or the crime was solved? Were they only the people actively involved in terrorist missions or did they include all those, including sovereign states, which gave them aid and succor? Just as importantly, who were our friends? What expectations did we have of other countries who professed opposition to terror? And, what did it mean to *defeat* terrorism? These "what" questions provoked the question of "when." As Richard Neustadt states elsewhere in this volume, Americans hate long wars. If this was indeed a war, would it develop into the sort of protracted engagement implied by the epithet "another Viet Nam"? When would this nightmare be over? Would the United States have to learn to accept terrorist acts as a normal part of everyday life as the Israelis and Northern Irish had done?

The most bedeviling question of all was "why"? Each of the objects of the 9/11 attack symbolized an aspect of American life that was anathema to many around the globe, and to influential minorities at home. The very name, World Trade Center, and its location in the world capital of international finance made it the epitome of the new global economy and culture that reeked of individualism, commercialism, environmental degradation, inequality, secularism, and decadence. The Pentagon was the nerve center of a military that in the minds of many had been placed in service of worldwide oppression of the poor and the powerless.

Influential commentators saw the attacks as confirming their critiques of American institutions and foreign policy. As Susan Sontag wrote in *The New Yorker*, "Where is the acknowledgement that this was not a cowardly attack on 'civilization' or 'liberty' or humanity or the 'free world' but an attack on the world's self proclaimed super-power, undertaken as a consequence of specific American alliances and actions?"[4] Marc Cooper lamented in *L.A. Weekly* that the attacks had not led to a reconsideration of American foreign policy in the direction which the terrorists were pushing for. "There might have been some understanding that traditional U.S. support for autocratic, undemocratic regimes from Saudi Arabia to Egypt, while in no way justifying or producing the 9/11 attacks, allows them to resonate sympathetically with angry desperate millions."[5]

As the following examination of Bush's speeches shows, he unreservedly rejected such self-critical interpretations. His response to the "why" question emphasized America's virtues, not its flaws. His unqualified endorsement of the liberal-democratic principles that are fundamental to the American regime and that undergird its foreign policy was the cornerstone of his civic education campaign.

A WAR AGAINST TERROR

Bush's public education effort commenced at the prayer service held for the victims of 9/11 at the National Cathedral on September 14.[6] Although the solemnity of the occasion constrained his rhetoric, he nonetheless made two key points that would form the core of the strategy elaborated in subsequent speeches. First of all, he asserted that 9/11 was indeed the equivalent of Pearl Harbor and Fort Sumter. "War has been waged against us by stealth and deceit and murder." Although exactly who the enemy was remained to be fully determined, war had been declared against the United States. Because it was war, the objective was to win. "This conflict was begun on the timing and terms of others. It will end in a way, and at an hour, of our choosing."

Although Bush did not commit the U.S. to any particular strategy or tactic for waging war, he hinted that whatever approach was adopted would be pursued with ruthlessness and single mindedness. Winning the war would not be subordinated to other goals, however laudable, such as respecting the authority of international institutions or placating the sensibilities of friends and allies. To remind Americans that waging war required the full commitment of all Americans, Bush, who had acquired a reputation for aggressive partisanship, invoked the words of a great Democrat, Franklin Delano Roosevelt. "Today, we feel what Franklin Roosevelt called the warm courage of national unity." As if to highlight the need for bipartisanship, FDR was the only former president mentioned in the address.

On September 20, 2001, Bush addressed a joint session of the United States Congress.[7] This was his single most important statement about the crisis because it answered the key questions of who, why, and how. In explaining "who attacked our country," he declared that the perpetrators ought not to be thought of as Arabs or Muslims, because Muslims, including Arab Muslims, are peaceful and law abiding. They were traitors to Islam, people trying to "hijack" a great religion to the cause of evil. "The enemy of America is not our many Muslim friends, it is not our many Arab friends, our enemy is a radical network of terrorists."

Spiritually and philosophically these terrorists were descended not from the great Islamic prophets and sages but from the same destructive dogmas that had threatened civilization for most of the previous century. "They follow in the path of fascism and Nazism and totalitarianism." Because their aims were identical, they would suffer the same fate, "they will follow that path all the way, to where it ends: in history's unmarked grave of discarded lies."

Bush did not restrict his definition of who the enemy was to the terrorists themselves; he extended it to encompass,

> every government that supports them . . . Every nation in every region, has a decision to make. Either you are with us, or you are with the terrorists. From this day forward any nation that continues to harbor or support terrorism will be regarded by the United States as a hostile regime.

This extension of enemy status provided the crucial link between "who" and "how." Like the Romans, the U.S. would fight Philip where Philip was based. But this Philip was not a king and had no country. Therefore, the U.S. would fight Philip wherever Philip was given safe harbor and attack the countries that provided Philip with sanctuary. This war would be fought for defensive purposes but on offensive principles.

To understand this new type of war, the public would need to unlearn lessons from the past. The Viet Nam War had taught that protracted military engagements in Third World countries were "quagmires." Americans had come to expect that their wars would be fought more in the air than on the ground. Victory would come swiftly and with few if any casualties. To accustom the public to the new realities of the War on Terror, Bush warned,

> This war will not be like the war against Iraq a decade ago, with a decisive liberation of territory and a swift conclusion. It will not look like the air war above Kosovo two years ago, where no ground troops were used and not a single American was lost in combat . . . Americans should not expect one battle, but a lengthy campaign . . .

Bush's response to the "why" question gave no ground to partial apologias for the perpetrators such as those cited earlier. America had been attacked not for its vices but for its virtues, not because it undermined cultural integrity but because it promotes political freedom.

> Why do they hate us? They hate what they see in this chamber—a democratically elected government; their leaders are self-appointed. They hate our freedoms—our freedom of religion, our freedom to vote and assemble, and disagree with each other. They picked on America, because America is the leading force in the world for expanding liberty. This is not just America's fight. . . . This is the world's fight. This is civilization's fight. This is the fight of all who believe in progress and pluralism, tolerance and freedom . . . These terrorists kill not merely to end lives, but to disrupt and end a way of life . . . With every atrocity, they hope that America grows fearful, retreating from the world and forsaking our friends. They stand against us, because we stand in their way."

A RESPONSE BECOMES A DOCTRINE

The swift victory over Taliban and Al Queda forces in Afghanistan marked the end of the first, and relatively uncomplicated, phase of the War on Terror. Criticism of the invasion of Afghanistan, both in the U.S. and abroad, had been mild and muted. But as Nicholas Lemann perceptively observed, the difference between retaliating against Al Queda and declaring a war on terror was the difference between a response and a doctrine.[8] Bush's 2002 State of the Union speech was the critical occasion for expounding that doctrine and how it would apply beyond the immediate response to Al Queda.[9] Most importantly, this speech established that the war was not limited to ferreting out and capturing terrorists or to eliminating their safe harbors. It was inextricably tied to preventing either terrorists or the rogue states that supported them from threatening to use weapons of mass destruction—chemical, biological, or nuclear weapons. Bush mentioned three by name, "North Korea is a regime arming with missiles and weapons of mass destruction . . . Iran aggressively pursues these weapons and exports terror . . . The Iraqi regime has plotted to develop anthrax, and nerve gas and nuclear weapons for over a decade."

Bush claimed that "states like these, and their terrorist allies, constitute an *axis of evil* (my italics) arming to threaten the peace of the world." Like his previous effort to link terrorism to fascism and Nazism, this effort to depict the three rogue states as being part of an axis was an effort to familiarize Americans with a new enemy by conjuring up images of past one. Like most analogies, it was not entirely accurate. Unlike Japan, Italy, and Germany, this new trio had not established a formal alliance nor had it declared war on the United States. But like all good analogies, the *axis of evil* served to highlight an important truth. Like the earlier axis, these states had revealed themselves to be implacable enemies of the United States and posed a collective threat to its vital interests. Therefore they must be dealt with just as decisively as the earlier triumvirate had been.

Bush used his graduation speech to the cadets at West Point to further elaborate the differences between the War on Terror and the strategic principles that had enabled the West to prevail in the Cold War—deterrence and containment.[10]

> Deterrence—the promise of massive retaliation against nations—means nothing against shadowy terrorist networks with no nation or citizens to defend. Containment is not possible when unbalanced dictators with weapons of mass destruction can deliver those weapons on missiles or secretly provide them to terrorist allies.

But whatever the strategic differences, the moral grounds for this new war were the same as for previous ones.

> Because the war on terror will require resolve and patience, it will also require firm moral purpose. In this way our struggle is similar to the Cold War. Now, as then, our enemies are totalitarians, holding a creed of power with no place for human dignity. Now, as then, they seek to impose a joyless conformity, to control every life and all of life.

Bush also provided a more thorough refutation of the idea that the War on Terror involved a "clash of civilizations."

> The 20th century ended with a single surviving model of human progress, based on non-negotiable demands of human dignity, the rule of law, limits on the power of the state, respect for women and private property and free speech and equal justice and religious tolerance. . . . When it comes to the common rights and needs of men and women, there is no clash of civilizations. The requirements of freedom apply fully to Africa and Latin America and the entire Islamic world. The peoples of the Islamic nations want and deserve the same freedoms and opportunities as people in every nation.

At one level, this statement is disingenuous. Not all serious people agree on the single model of human progress he described, and certainly not all Muslims. But here Bush was siding with defenders of human rights of a wide variety of ideological stripes who also argue that illiberal regimes cannot hide behind the cloak of moral relativism to defend beliefs and practices that curtail human freedom. Bush acknowledged that "America cannot impose this vision" but he did not shrink from declaring it to be true.

THE NATIONAL SECURITY STRATEGY

Presidential speeches by no means constituted the exclusive form of civic education emanating from the executive branch. As required by law, the White House issued its annual edition of a document outlining the national security strategy (NSS).[11] In past years, this document had received only perfunctory attention from the press. But, because of 9/11 and because the 2002 edition contained a more expansive explanation and defense of the positions Bush had adopted and hinted at in his previous speeches, the NSS received a great deal of media scrutiny and became the subject of commentary by "talking heads" from American thinktanks and academia and their counterparts overseas.

Unlike so many government "white papers" the 2002 NSS is brief, terse and jargon free. It attempts to provide a full overview of the purposes and principles of American national security policy in a mere 31 pages. Although it set off an uproar within the foreign policy establishment, the source of that uproar, the elaboration of the doctrine of preemption, is confined to a three-page section of the document. The remainder of the text is most notable for its similarities to previous NSS incarnations, pledging its continued support for multilateral institutions and for the internationalist principles to which all previous modern presidential administrations have also been firmly attached.

In his introduction to the document the president explained how and why a new strategic doctrine was necessary.

> The gravest danger our nation faces lies at the crossroads of radicalism and technology. Our enemies have openly declared that they are seeking weapons of mass destruction . . . As a matter of common sense and self-defense America will act against such emerging threats before they are fully formed. We cannot defend America and our friends by hoping for the best. History will judge harshly those who saw this coming danger but failed to act.

In Section V, entitled "Prevent Our Enemies from Threatening Us, Our Allies and Our Friends with Weapons of Mass Destruction," the document elaborates on the danger posed at that crossroads and how to address it.

> The radicalism of our rogue state enemies makes them more likely to use weapons of mass destruction than our previous enemies led by the risk averse, status quo oriented successors of Stalin. Khrushchev and Brezhnev could be cowed by the threat of massive retaliation, Saddam and Kim, not to mention the leaders of terrorist networks like Al Queda and Hammas, cannot. Traditional concepts of deterrence will not work against a terrorist enemy whose avowed tactics are wanton destruction and the targeting of innocents. Whose so-called soldiers seek martyrdom in death and whose most potent protection is statelessness. The overlap between states that sponsor terror and those that purse WMD compels us to action.

The document acknowledges that what is most provocative about the new doctrine is not pre-emption per se, but rather its rejection of imminence as a condition for pre-emption. The rationale for a state striking first is clearest and strongest when that state is in imminent danger of attack. The document calls for a modification of this reliance on imminence based on the novel dangers that rogue states and terrorists pose. Because these adversaries rely on stealth and target innocent civilians, the idea of imminence is drained of meaning. It is impossible to predict when and where the enemy will strike.

The risks and uncertainties of such attacks are greatly compounded by the efforts that such states and terror networks are making to acquire weapons of mass destruction that "can be easily concealed, delivered covertly and used without warning." By rejecting prevailing norms of warfare—concentration on military targets, providing warning of attack, putting one's forces in uniform—the enemy has rendered the concept of imminence meaningless and therefore the United States is justified in abandoning it as a condition for preemptive attack.

Iraq

Having enunciated a set of criteria on the basis of which to justify pre-emption, Bush set about to demonstrate that Iraq met those criteria and was therefore an appropriate pre-emptive target. Although his critics did not necessarily accept his defense of non-imminent pre-emption, the subsequent debate over Iraq was dominated not by conceptual debate but by arguments over whether or not compelling evidence existed demonstrating that Iraq posed a serious threat. Bush's addressed those concerns in a speech delivered in Cincinnati on October 7, 2002.[12] Specifically, he explained why it was necessary to act against Iraq now and what the link was between Iraq and the wider war on terror. He distinguished Iraq from the other members of the "axis of evil" on the grounds that Iraq housed a greater number of different serious dangers than the others. Not only did it already possess weapons of mass destruction, but it had provided safe haven for known terrorists including members of Al Queda and had a demonstrated track record of mercilessness directed at foreign enemies and at its own citizens.

Bush was only able to argue persuasively for immediate action against Iraq because of his earlier success in inculcating the principle that the fight against terrorism was a war, not a criminal manhunt. A prospective enemy in war, unlike a criminal defendant, is not innocent until proven guilty. Therefore the key question to ask about Saddam did not involve his prior actions but rather his likely future ones. It was not essential to demonstrate that he was complicit in the events of 9/11, or even that he had extensive past intimate ties with Al Queda. Rather the key question was to what extent the events of September 11 were likely to embolden him. It was not really plausible that, given his track record and oft-stated views, he would sit idly by and let others gain the credit and the glory for attacking the West. Reluctance by the Western powers to quash him would almost certainly heighten his contempt for them and whet his appetite for revenge. In the context of war, such a calculation regarding future probabilities is sufficient grounds for offensive action.

UN Deliberations

Bush chose not to heed those within his own camp who urged him to avoid the UN and the potential for stalemate that placing the issue in the hands of the Security Council and UNSCOM entailed. He took this decision for prudential reasons. First, he hoped that indeed the UN would endorse preemptive action against Iraq, thus providing broad legitimacy for such an aggressive act. Second, poll data showed that the American public considered such a step to be a necessary precursor for preemptive action.[13] Finally, Bush's staunchest ally in the War on Terror, Prime Minister Tony Blair of the United Kingdom, viewed such an effort as necessary for maintaining the support of the British public for aggressive pre-emption.

In order to accommodate these political necessities without unduly hampering his ability to pursue his key objective, regime change in Iraq, Bush had to make the complex rhetorical case that going to the UN was a good but not a necessary thing to do. Although the United States did not desire to take unilateral action, it maintained the right to do so. Therefore, adopting a multilateral approach was a tactic in service of non-imminent pre-emption, not an end in itself.

In his Cincinnati speech he indicated why the previous approach taken by the UN was insufficient.

> The UN inspections program was met by systematic deception. The Iraqi regime bugged hotel rooms and offices of inspectors . . . forged documents, destroyed evidence and developed mobile facilities to keep a step ahead of inspectors. Eight so called presidential palaces were declared off limits to unfettered inspections. After 11 years during which we have tried containment, sanctions, inspections and selected military action, the end result is that Saddam Hussein still has chemical and biological weapons and is increasing his ability to make more. And he is moving closer to developing a nuclear weapon.

As an alternative, Bush proposed that the UN adopt a new resolution that did not depend so exclusively on inspections. Saddam would be required to enumerate all the weapons he had and destroy them under UN supervision. As a further supplement to inspections, Iraq would have to allow scientists with knowledge of the weapons program to be interviewed outside of Iraq and to be able to bring their families with them to avoid retribution against their families if they make revelations hostile to Saddam's interests.

The eloquence and cogency of Bush's case for regime change in Iraq should not be taken as evidence that his effort to mobilize international support for non-imminent pre-emption in Iraq was entirely successful. Indeed it was not. Despite the evidence that Colin Powell presented at the UN on February 5, 2003, three of the five permanent members of the UN Security Council, France, Russia and China, were not persuaded that Iraq was in "material breach" of UN Resolution 1441 which the Security Council had passed unanimously on November 8, 2002, calling on Iraq to disarm. France in particular made clear that it would veto any resolution calling for war on Iraq, at least until the inspections had been allowed to continue for many more months.

In his State of the Union speech, January 18, 2003, Bush began to prepare the nation for the possibility that the U.S. would have to fight Iraq without UN sanction.[14]

> In all these efforts (multilateral steps including working with the UN), however, America's purpose is more than to follow a process—it is to achieve a result: the end of terrible threats to the civilized world. All free nations have a stake in preventing sudden and catastrophic attacks. And we're asking them to join us, and many are doing so. Yet the course of this nation does not depend on the decisions of others. Whatever action is required, whenever action is necessary, I will defend the freedom and security of the American people.

To underscore the argument that negotiations were not ends in themselves, he invoked the most unambiguous diplomatic failure of the 1990s: The negotiations with North Korea aimed at preventing that country from obtaining nuclear weapons.

> On the Korean Peninsula, an oppressive regime rules a people living in fear and starvation. Throughout the 1990s, the United States relied on a negotiated framework to keep North Korea from gaining nuclear weapons. We now know that that regime was deceiving the world, and developing those weapons all along. And today the North Korean regime is using its nuclear program to incite fear and seek concessions . . . Our nation and the world must learn the lessons of the Korean Peninsula and not allow an even greater threat to rise up in Iraq. A brutal dictator, with a history of reckless aggression, with ties to terrorism, with great potential wealth, will not be permitted to dominate a vital region and threaten the United States.

To emphasize the impossibility of relying on inspectors to find hidden weapons of mass destruction, he reminded his audience that

> The 108 UN inspectors were not sent to conduct a *scavenger hunt for hidden materials across a country the size of California* (my italics). The job of the inspectors is to verify that Iraq's regime is disarming. It is up to Iraq to show exactly where it is hiding its banned weapons, lay those weapons out for the world to see, and destroy them as directed. Nothing like this has happened.

Instead, Saddam was exploiting the presence of the inspectors to deceive the international community.

> From intelligence sources we know, for instance, that thousands of Iraqi security personnel are at work hiding documents and materials from the UN inspectors, sanitizing inspection sites and monitoring the inspectors themselves. Iraqi officials accompany the inspectors in order to intimidate witnesses.

Bush did not close the door on working with the UN He announced that on February 5 he would send Secretary of State Powell to New York to make the American case that Saddam had failed to comply with the Resolution. But Bush made it quite clear that if the UN did not respond positively to Powell's brief, the U.S.

would be forced to pursue a pre-emptive strike on Iraq without UN approval. "We will consult. But let there be no misunderstanding: If Saddam Hussein does not fully disarm, for the safety of our people and for the peace of the world, we will lead a coalition to disarm him."

Thus was born the concept of the "coalition of the willing" that would dominate U.S. rhetoric throughout the ensuing phase in which it became clear that the U.S. and Britain could not obtain a majority of Security Council votes, and that even if they had been able to do so, France was committed to vetoing any resolution endorsing the use of force.

Neither the actual decision to go to war and flout the Security Council nor the end of hostilities that Bush announced aboard the Aircraft Carrier USS Abraham Lincoln brought any new important civic teachings. The bitter debate at the UN had so solidified opinion pro and con that little more remained to be said. As for the war itself, the pictures of statues of Saddam tumbling down and of mass gravesites proved more eloquent and evocative than mere words.

THE RHETORICAL FUTURE

It is in the nature of education to be incomplete, and this is especially true regarding matters of war and peace. Bush's civic teachings up to the present can only be a partial guide to his future lesson plans, because those teachings must be adapted to the course of events, over which he has only partial control. Perhaps the most important contingency of all regards the actual lessons that various parties have drawn from the Iraqi conflict. If indeed rogue state candidates like Iran and Syria conclude that the fate of Iraq demonstrates that harboring terrorists has become more dangerous than purging them, then the War on Terror and the accompanying presidential rhetoric will simmer down. The War might even devolve into a worldwide police action in which the counter-terrorism forces of former rogue states cooperate with the U.S. and other nations to root out terror. But it is also possible that some state or states will conclude that it is imperative to acquire weapons of mass destruction before the U.S.-led dragnet fully closes, or that harboring terrorists is still a worthwhile gamble, or both. Then the president faces the unenviable task of mobilizing public opinion for yet another pitched battle.

Most likely, hostile nations, even if they are ultimately willing to cooperate with the U.S. and its allies, will test American resolve. Therefore Bush will have to make a case for going to war again, even if in the end it is not necessary to do so. As we have seen, in his West Point speech he showed the public why the War on Terror is dissimilar to the Cold War. The 2002 National Security Strategy reiterated that message. But, post-Iraq, as the U.S. seeks to influence the behavior of less committed "rogues," a crucial aspect of Cold War strategy, deterrence, will play a critical role. Precisely because the U.S. does not want to fight wars around the globe, it must make a credible case to any hostile nation in particular that the U.S. will attack if that nation continues to abet terrorism. Such an ostentatious willingness to fight is the essence of deterrence.

Bush's ability to impart this lesson is made more difficult by the unsettling course which events in Iraq have taken. The war was surprisingly easy, but the peace has proven aggravating and deadly. The American public has been troubled both by the steady stream of American deaths and the sullen ingratitude shown by many different segments of the Iraqi populace. This disappointment has been fanned by the media, both national and foreign, which set absurdly high expectations for what would happen in Iraq after the military victory was won, as if this were the first war which ever ended with widespread looting or that a people deprived of political freedom for more than a generation would immediately behave like model citizens.

Also, from an educational standpoint, Bin Laden, Sheik Omar, and Saddam Hussein were too evil. They were sent by central casting to play the part of "rogue state dictator" or "Dr. Terror." Of those currently auditioning for those roles, only Kim Sung Il shows any real aptitude for it. Other leaders and other terror networks project a more nuanced public image. How is Bush to teach the public to think about countries like Saudi Arabia and Pakistan which profess to be supporting the war on terror, and make some gestures in that direction, but also harbor terrorists? What is he to make of Hammas and Hezbollah, which in addition to training and outfitting suicide bombers also run food kitchens for the poor?

For deterrence to work, Bush must accustom Americans to longer battles against more subtle enemies. And he must teach that in all probability the hardest battles will be fought after the shooting stops. For, as deterrence theory teaches, only if potential enemies are truly convinced of American resolve to fight and to "nation build" will they take the painful and difficult and steps necessary to prevent American attack—evict terrorists and eliminate weapons of mass destruction. Thus, whatever the contingencies, the key to long-term success is a high level of American public resolve. Such resolve, in the face of suffering and reversals, requires deep conviction of the essential rightness of the American cause. That is why Bush's unapologetic response to the question of "why they hate us" and his vigorous assertion of the virtues of the American constitutional order have proven and will continue to prove critical to long-term success.

As Bush has argued, the terrorists and their allies hate the essential character of the regime itself—its commitment to unalienable rights and to the constitutionally delimited institutions and formalities that secure those rights. Americans are fighting to preserve a way of life in which liberty and equality flourish. The better Americans understand that essential truth, the more they will sacrifice to keep it alive and the less they will be deterred by discovering that the enemies of liberty are not all "monsters." Bush can and must continue to encourage Americans to understand that the freedoms and privileges they enjoy are fragile and that they are engaged in a long-term struggle to protect those precious possessions, not in a Quixotic campaign to rid the world of evil.

American resolve also depends upon sound and sober public expectations of what the War on Terror can reasonably hope to accomplish. This in turn requires greater realism about how nation-states relate to one another and therefore what any foreign policy can hope to accomplish. The difficulties Bush will encounter in instilling the necessary level of intellectual and emotional sobriety can be partially gleaned from criticisms made of current and past policy.

Some critics have harped on America's willingness to aid Saddam in his war against Iran during the 1980s, only to turn against him during the 1990s when he attacked Kuwait, as evidence of the hypocrisy of U.S. policy.[15] Such criticism is mistaken because it misapplies the principle of hypocrisy. Hypocrisy occurs when one says one thing and does another, not when one shifts course in line with one's interests. When the U.S. is accused of hypocrisy what is really meant is that the U.S. is not acting on the basis of friendship. It has failed to take the needs of other countries to heart as a true friend would. It does not really *care* about countries like Iran and Kuwait. At some level this charge is true. But, properly understood, it is not a criticism. Countries are not friends. Only individuals can be friends. Therefore, it is not a violation of friendship for nations to shift alliances when interests and circumstances change. Perhaps the greatest educational challenge Bush will face in the future is to disabuse the public of the sort of hopes and longings that such misplaced invocations of "hypocrisy" and "friendship" represent.

As France's behavior during the UN debate in 2003 displayed, evocations of the past—images of American soldiers liberating Paris in 1944, being embraced by grateful mademoiselles and giving food to hungry children—could not compete with the French government's calculation of its national interest in determining its course of action in the present. From an educational standpoint, France and Germany's willingness to ignore past American friendship is of immense value. It should make it far easier for the president to teach Americans emotional sobriety. It provides an object lesson about what Americans should *not* expect from Iraq. For, if they believe that liberation and reconstruction will place Iraqis in America's emotional debt, a chit to be cashed in whenever America chooses, they are sadly mistaken. To allow Americans to hope that such lasting emotional bonds will develop is to court dangerous disillusion in the future.

The most incessant drumbeat of criticism since the end of the war regarded the failure to find conclusive evidence that Iraq possessed weapons of mass destruction (WMDs). Critics argued that Bush and Blair had made the dangers posed by such weapons the central rationale for prosecuting the war. Sen. Robert Byrd accused the White House of justifying the war on the basis of intelligence that was "bent, stretched or massaged to make Iraq look like an imminent threat."[16] Making use of leaks and other statements provided by competing intelligence agencies, critics like Seymour Hersh argued that a "cabal" at the Pentagon had systematically interpreted ambiguous evidence to "prove" that Iraq had WMDs.[17] These assertions vary from trivial to unproven. Hersh and like-minded critics disparage the Pentagon for its inattention to ambiguity. But they fail to acknowledge the tenuousness of their own information, which comes from resentful bureaucratic rivals of the Pentagon and which they cannot independently verify.

The furor over the alleged exaggeration of WMD reached its highest pitch when the White House admitted that a statement Bush made in his 2003 State of the Union speech had been based on insufficient evidence. Bush had said, "the British government has learned that Saddam Hussein recently sought significant quantities of uranium from Africa."[18] Critics distorted this apology into being an admission of an outright fabrication. They spoke as if Bush had claimed that the Iraq had actually purchased uranium when all he said was that the British learned that Iraq "had sought" to make such a purchase. Nor did the White House admit that the claim was false, but only that it now considered the existing evidence insufficient for inclusion in such an important speech.[19]

More serious than the shrill tone and exaggerations of these criticisms is the mistaken view of international relations on which they are premised. The ability to garner accurate intelligence, particularly with regard to an authoritarian regime, is extremely limited. One relies on the reports of defectors and other equally hard to verify sources. But however inadequate the information, there is no choice but to make inferences from it. Therefore, the right question to ask is not whether the case against Iraq regarding its WMD program was proven before the war but rather what was the most appropriate inference to make. As Bush said, the Iraqis had repeatedly interfered with the UN weapons inspection effort. Solid evidence did exist of systematic efforts to bug inspectors' rooms and prevent them from conducting thorough and expeditious inspections.

As John Yoo persuasively argues,

> What is important from the perspective of international law is not whether Iraq had WMD in the end. What matters is whether, at the time of the invasion, it appeared reasonably necessary to defend against Iraq's threat to U.S. national and international security . . . Rather than prove its harmlessness, Iraq instead did everything it could to suggest that it possessed WMD and would be willing to use them. Hence the games played with UN arms inspectors and the rumors that Iraq would use chemical weapons if coalition forces neared Baghdad. . . . As recently as November 2002, the Security Council decided that Iraq "has been and remains in material breach of its obligations" to eliminate its WMD program, and reaffirmed its original 1991 authorization to use force against Iraq.

Given the lack of serious demurral prior to the war, the fuss about the WMD issue being made post-war is hard to take seriously. And indeed the American public has not done so. According to the polls, many Americans readily, perhaps too readily, concede that the Bush administration overestimated the threat posed by Iraqi weapons of mass destruction. But, by a wide margin, they also believe that Iraq did possess such weapons when the war broke out and they continue to demonstrate overwhelming approval for Bush's Iraq policy. According to a Pew Center poll, as of August 5, 2003, 63% of the public agreed that the U.S. made the right decision to go to war with Iraq and only 30% disagreed.[20] According to a July 25, 2003 CNN/USA *Today* poll, 60% approved of Bush's handling of the situation in Iraq while only 38% disapproved.[21] As of July 25, 2003, 62% of those surveyed in a *Newsweek* poll believed that American national security was stronger as a result of Bush's Iraq policy while only 28% thought it was weaker. *Newsweek* found that although 41% believed that the Bush administration had misinterpreted intelligence data relating to the threat of Iraqi WMDs, 70% thought that Iraq actually had banned chemical or biological weapons right before the Iraq War started.[22]

The good sense of the American people revealed in the poll data shows that sustaining American resolve even in the face of an avalanche of vitriolic and purportedly high-minded criticism is possible. But as this chapter has stressed, future enemies of the U.S. are unlikely to appear as unambiguously evil as Saddam and Osama, and the case for war is unlikely to be as overwhelming. As Bush and his successors look for guidance in how to talk to the American people about maintaining their resolve in the face of frustration and disappointment, they will discover that the rhetorical legacy bequeathed by former presidents is a highly problematic one. Modern American presidents have abetted and nourished the very longings for permanent peace and global brotherhood that Bush should be at pains to discourage. From Wilson's paean to a "war to end war" to FDR's promise of the UN as a permanent solution to international strife, to LBJ's commitment to winning over the "hearts and minds" of the Vietnamese people and Bush Senior's quest for a "new world order," presidents have fed false hopes and impossible dreams.

American military superiority is so great that perhaps George W. Bush can likewise get away with feeding a false sentimentalism. But the risks of doing so are very great. The War on Terror will be long and victory will be incomplete. Indeed international terror is best viewed as a chronic problem to be coped with more or less forever rather than a problem to be disposed of. Living with it does not mean appeasing it. But its successful prosecution requires a realistic understanding of the inherently rivalrous nature of international affairs, and the unquenchable resentment that the weak feel towards the mighty. If Bush can help Americans to come to grips with these realities he will succeed where even his most illustrious predecessors have failed.

NOTES

1. As William Muir notes, there is no direct evidence that TR ever used the term. It is attributed to him because in a eulogy to Roosevelt, publisher George Putnam recalled that TR had used that expression. See William K. Muir, Jr., *The Bully Pulpit: The Presidential Leadership of Ronald Reagan* (San Francisco: Institute for Contemporary Studies 1992), 44, n.227.

2. For a more extensive discussion of presidential rhetoric and civic education see Marc Landy and Sidney Milkis, *Presidential Greatness* (Lawrence, KS: University of Kansas Press, 2000).

3. Hendrik Hertzberg, "Tuesday and After," *The New Yorker*, September 24, 2001, reprinted in Micah L. Sifry and Christopher Cerf, eds, *The Iraq War Reader: History Documents and Opinion* (New York: Touchstone, 2003), 220–221.

4. Susan Sontag, "Reflections on September 11," *The New Yorker*, September 24, 2001, reprinted in *The Iraq War Reader: History Documents and Opinion*, 215.

5. Marc Cooper, "A Year Later, What the Right and Left Haven't Learned," *L.A. Weekly*, September 13–19, reprinted in *The Iraq War Reader*, 225.

6. http://www.whitehouse.gov/news/releases/2001/09/20010914-2.html

7. http://www.whitehouse.gov/news/releases/2001/09/20010920-8.html

8. Nicholas Lemann, "The War on What? The White House and the Debate About Whom To Fight Next," *The New Yorker*, September 9, 2002, reprinted in *The Iraq War Reader*, p. 283.

9. www.whitehouse.gov/news/releases/2002/01/20020129-11.htm

10. www.whitehouse.gov/news/releases/2002/06/20020601-3.html

11. www.whitehouse.gov/nsc/nss.html

12. www.whitehouse.gov/news/releases/2002/10/20021007-8.html

13. "Times Poll: Americans Wary of War But Willing to Let Bush Wage It," Ronald Brownstein, *Los Angeles Times*, February 4, 2003.

14. www.whitehouse.gov/news/releases/2003/01/20030128-19.html

15. See for example Joost R. Hiltermann, "The Men who Helped the Man Who Gassed His Own People," *The Iraq War Reader*, 41–44. Hiltermann is the former director of the Iraqi Documents Project at Human Rights Watch and the former executive director of Human Rights Watch's Arms Division.

16. John Yoo, "Why Iraq's Weapons Don't Matter," *Legal Times*, August 4, 2003.

17. Seymour Hersh, "Selective Intelligence," *The New Yorker*, May 12, 2003, 44–52.

18. BBC News World Edition, "White House warned over Iraq claim." July 9, 2003.

19. Fred Barnes, "The Phony Scandal," *The Weekly Standard*, July 28, 2003, 23.

20. Pew Research Center for the People & the Press survey conducted by Princeton Survey Research Associates. July 14–Aug. 5, 2003. N=2,528 adults nationwide. MoE ± 2.

21. CNN/USA *Today*/Gallup Poll. July 25–27, 2003. N=1,006 adults nationwide.

22. *Newsweek* Poll conducted by Princeton Survey Research Associates. July 24–25, 2003. N=1,002 adults nationwide. MoE ± 3.

News Organizations as a Presidential Resource in Governing:

Media Opportunities and White House Organization

◆◆◆

Martha Joynt Kumar

When a president comes into office, he needs to have a communications operation in place ready to handle the queries of reporters and to take advantage of the enormous number of opportunities for a chief executive to speak to his various audiences, including those outside of the United States. It is not a matter of choice for a president and his team. Looking at some facts and figures relating to the presence of reporters in the White House and recent patterns of public presidential remarks, one can understand a president's need for an effective communications operation to manage his relations with the news organizations that carry his words to the public. This chapter explores the number of opportunities a president has to communicate with the public. Although not equally successful in using these opportunities, all four presidents elected to two terms since World War II had a state-of-the-art communications operation. President George W. Bush came into office appreciating the central role of presidential communications and created an organization to match his perceived needs.

News organizations represent a source of pressure on a president and also serve as an important resource as he seeks to govern. In the 1990s and now in the new century, a president can expect to answer the queries of reporters two or three times a week and to make public addresses and remarks, including a weekly radio address, on an average of more than once a day, six days a week. Such appearances are regularly broadcast nationally on cable television. Gone are the days when presidential remarks were delivered to a select audience and only that audience. Now a president's responses to reporters' questions and his remarks to groups are broadcast live on more than one cable television channel. For a president in the new century, there are no off-the-record remarks, and speeches to a limited audience. Even if a President tries to make remarks off the record, they seep into the public record. The presidency today is on the record and broadcast live to audiences around the world.

REPORTERS AT THE WHITE HOUSE: QUESTIONING THE PRESIDENT

When President Bush came into office, there was in place at the White House a communications operation with nearly 100 reporters at their station ready for the new president to make news. Then and now, television reporters are prepared to broadcast from the North driveway from an area known as "Pebble Beach" where 13 news organizations, five of whom are assigned two positions each, can go live with their regular and breaking news reports. The Press Room is in operation with radio and wire reporters housed in ten and two booths, respectively, set aside for use for their frequent reports, five booths for individual television network correspondents as well as space for their crews, and assigned space for those working for daily news papers and news magazines, including the photographers. Although on a typical day not all of the spaces are occupied, there are others around who sometimes fill those places. On a normal day when there is an event to cover, there are 10 to 15 photographers around the Press Room as well as 20 camera people working as television crews. Thus, the president faces an operation in place poised to cover the chief executive over which he and his staff have no directional authority. The approximately 100 people included among those regularly working at the White House for news organizations expect a president to make news and for the White House staff to provide them on a regular basis with the information they need in order to file their reports and go on the air.

Because news organizations view chronicling the presidency in terms of covering the president himself, their reporters focus their attention on getting the president on the record on a daily basis. In particular, they seek his public responses to their queries in preference to getting his views as spoken by his surrogates. Although reporters do not get to query him every day, they expect to see and hear from him daily and to question him in at least a brief session two or three times a week. The expectations of White House reporters are based on their recent experiences. President Clinton and his immediate predecessors left behind for President Bush a record of meeting fairly frequently with reporters to answer their queries. Although the longer press conferences reporters prefer are not as frequent as the shorter question and answer sessions, in recent years news organizations have had significant opportunities to directly query a president. When a new president comes into office, news organizations anticipate the pattern of frequent access will continue.

With the expansion of cable news networks from a lone network, CNN (established in 1981), to the addition of MSNBC (1996) and Fox (1996), the expectations of regular queries from reporters grew during the Clinton years. Not only did reporters expect the president to meet with them on a fairly regular basis in a press conference setting, they anticipated he would take their queries at sessions before and following official presidential sessions with members of Congress, the Cabinet, and visiting foreign and international leaders. The sessions regularly take place prior to or following sessions where the president is conducting official business with a visiting individual or group whose presence the chief executive and his staff want to highlight. Such meetings differ from news conferences in terms of the length of the session, the questions asked, and the participants. When a president calls in reporters before or after an Oval Office meeting with a visiting official from a foreign country, such as President Bush did in January 2003, with President Kwasniewski of Poland, a "pool" represents the interest of all reporters.[1] Since there is not sufficient room to bring in all reporters covering the White House, news organizations in a sense "pool" their resources and have a small group represent them in such sessions. The two wire services, Associated Press and Reuters, are allowed in as a regular part of every pool. Radio and print reporters (newspapers and news magazines) have one person representing each group on a rotating basis, as do magazine photographers. In April 2003, there were 27 newspapers and newspaper chains in the rotating "in town" pool, 5 television networks, 9 radio organizations, and 3 magazine photographers.[2] These sessions typically take between three and five minutes with perhaps four reporters getting in a question, as was the case in this session. Reporters covering the White House can expect the president to hold sessions with a pool two or three times a week. When he does not do so, the Press Secretary will receive complaints in the two daily information sessions he holds with reporters.

When Karen Hughes was setting up the communications operation for the Bush White House, she could have gotten a good idea of their staff needs by looking at the number of question and answer sessions the new president could expect to have during his term in the White House. If one looks at 261 business days a year for a White House where almost all question and answer sessions occur during weekdays and using as a guide the Clinton numbers of eight years of 1,042 short question and answer sessions with reporters as well as his 193 press conferences, one can see that a president can expect to face a group of reporters for a public session an average of every other day. Table 4.1 demonstrates the frequent sessions President Clinton had with reporters during his tenure, especially during his first two years.

At the beginning of his term, some reporters could expect to see President Clinton almost every day in one or another venue. In addition to the sessions he held with the pool and the press conferences he had, President Clinton also gave interviews to reporters representing the print and the electronic media. The question and answer sessions, and to a lesser extent the interviews with individual journalists and groups of reporters, take place at the White House, but also in locations around the country and in settings abroad. In short, when President Bush came into office the reporters covering him anticipated he would respond to their queries wherever he conducted official business and do so on an almost daily basis. The president and

Table 4.1   President Clinton's Public Interchanges with Reporters[a]

	1993	1994	1995	1996	1997	1998	1999	2000–2001	1993–2001
Public Question and Answer Sessions Other Than Press Conferences—By Location	242	142	107	125	122	88	99	117	1,042
White House, including Camp David, Air Force One, Blair House	202	92	84	88	90	58	62	82	758
In Washington, D.C.	5	2	1	6	1	1	3	4	23
Outside of D.C., inside the U.S.	26	28	12	19	17	7	9	18	136
Outside of the U.S.	9	20	10	12	14	22	25	13	125
Press Conferences	38	45	28	22	21	13	18	8	193
Interviews with News Organizations[b]	52	79	34	24	16	32	36	95	368
Total Interchanges with Reporters	332	266	169	171	159	133	153	220	1,603

[a] *The Public Papers of the Presidents of the United States* has as two document categories, "Exchanges with Reporters" and "Remarks and Exchanges," both of which refer to sessions where either the whole event is one where the president takes questions from reporters or remarks where he takes questions, usually following his speech. These sessions differ from presidential press conferences in their shorter length, their restricted access, and sometimes their restriction to a particular subject or subjects. Press conferences include those sessions included in the "news conferences" category in the *Public Papers*. The figures are calculated by calendar year rather than by elapsed time in office.

[b] The number of interviews found in the *Weekly Compilation of Presidential Documents* and the *Public Papers of the Presidents* does not reflect the total number of interviews conducted. Only a portion of the transcripts of interviews with news organizations were released by the Clinton or the Bush administrations. Even in the Clinton administration, there are transcripts that have not been made public. Both administrations accepted the traditional observance where media control the release time of their interviews and how much is released. Additionally, there are interviews, especially radio ones in the Clinton administration, where no permanent written record was made of the president's remarks. On November 6th and 7th, 2000, for example, President Clinton conducted 21 and 27 "get out the vote" radio interviews from his home in Chappaqua, New York. No transcripts were made. These figures come from an internal record kept by staff in the Clinton White House. "William Jefferson Clinton, Presidential Radio Interviews. As of January 15, 2001." A staff member who was present for the interviews said these were "individual interviews one after another after another after another. We started at about 2:00 P.M. on Monday the 6th and went until about 7:30 P.M. that night," she said. "And then on the 7th we went from about 6:30 A.M. to 8:00 A.M. and 9:30 A.M. until 2:00 A.M." Background information. I have included additional television interviews found on a list kept internally by White House staff: "President William Jefferson Clinton: Presidential Television Interviews 1993–2001."

Table 4.2   President George W. Bush's Public Interchanges with Reporters[a]

	2001	2002	2003	Totals
Public Question and Answer Sessions Other Than				
Press Conferences—By Location	144	96	49	289
White House, including Camp David, Air Force One,				
Blair House	91	48	25	164
In Washington, D.C.	5	5	2	12
Outside of D.C., inside the U.S.	37	33	17	87
Outside of the U.S.	11	10	5	26
Press Conferences	19	20	22	61
Interviews with News Organizations[b]	49	34	24	107
Total Interchanges with Reporters	212	150	95	467

[a] Through October 10, 2003, except for the interview figures which go through October 28.

[b] The interview numbers are ones provided to me by the White House. The numbers found in the *Weekly Compilation of Presidential Documents* and the *Public Papers of the Presidents of the United States* reflect only a portion of the interviews conducted. Only a few of the transcripts of interviews with news organizations have been released by the Bush Administration—2 in 2001 and 18 in 2002. Even in the Clinton administration, there are transcripts that have not been made public, especially ones with print media. Both administrations accepted the traditional observance where media control the release time of their interviews and how much is released.

his staff needed to set up their own communications operation outside as well as inside of the White House.

Like his predecessors, President Bush has met with reporters in settings favorable and comfortable to him and did so often, particularly in his first year. Table 4.2 provides a view of his sessions with reporters where he responded to their queries. In his third year, the number of such sessions fell off dramatically. Although in his first year he met with reporters for a short question and answer session or a press conference an average of a little more than three business days out of five, from October 2002 to the end of April 2003 such sessions fell to an average of approximately once every four days. With the buildup for and conduct of the war in Iraq, the president chose to routinely be less visible than those in his administration who were publicly explaining policy on an almost daily basis, such as Secretary of Defense Donald Rumsfeld speaking from the Pentagon, General Tommy Franks and his spokesmen in Qatar, and Press Secretary Ari Fleischer at the White House.

President Bush followed the practice of President Clinton of meeting more frequently with reporters in question and answer sessions in his first year than he did in his second one. In Clinton's case in his second year he held a little more than half the White House question and answer sessions with reporters he entertained his first year in office. In part there is a natural curiosity in the early months where each side gets to know one another in a greater number of sessions than later will be the case. With President Bush as well, the place where the sessions dropped off was at the most important venue for question and answer sessions: at the White House.

In comparison with his two immediate predecessors, President Bush has held relatively few press conferences (Table 4.3). At 994 days into his four-year term,

Table 4.3   Solo and Joint Presidential Press Conferences, 1953–October 10, 2003

President	Total	Solo	Joint	Joint Sessions/ Total Conferences (%)	Joint with Foreign Leaders	Joint with U.S. officials
Eisenhower	193	192	1	0.05	0	1
Kennedy	65	65	0	0	0	0
Johnson	135	118	17	12.7	0	17
Nixon	39	39	0	0	0	0
Ford	40	39	1	2.5	1	0
Carter	59	59	0	0	0	0
Reagan	46	46	0	0	0	0
G. Bush	142	83	59	41.5	47	12
Clinton	193	62	131	67.9	129	2
G. W. Bush	61	9	52	85.2	51	1

Source: Adapted from Martha Joynt Kumar, "Is This a Press Conference?" Defining and Tabulating Presidential Press Conferences, *Presidential Studies Quarterly*, 34 (March 2003): 221–237. See the article for a treatment of the press conference patterns of recent presidents.

President Bush has held somewhere near half the number of press conferences held by President George H. W. Bush and President Bill Clinton. President George W. Bush has had 61 while Presidents Clinton and Bush had 102 and 105 press conferences, respectively, at the same point in their presidencies. With only 21 and 19 press conferences, respectively, Presidents Nixon and Reagan had substantially fewer than President George W. Bush. In their cases, though, the two presidents had many more evening East Room press conferences than is true of the current president. President Nixon had nine evening East Room sessions at the 994 day mark while Reagan had ten in the same time period. President Bush has had two of the high-stakes evening East Room sessions. Those sessions that could last anywhere up to an hour in the Nixon and Reagan years were replaced by a much lower risk session that now has become the standard: the joint press conference.

Both Presidents George H. W. Bush and Bill Clinton maintained about the same frequency of press conferences in their second year as their first. With President Bush, however, his sessions varied greatly from those held by his two immediate predecessors. In both years, President Bush has held few solo press conferences. Of President Bush's 61 press conferences, only 9 have been solo ones. The difference between the two types of press conferences is more than just the number of participants. In joint press conferences in his two and a half years in office, President Bush has received approximately one-quarter of the questions he gets in a solo press conference.[3] The sessions are so short that reporters cannot deeply press the president on any one issue.

With only three or four questions to respond to, the difference between the joint press conference and a question and answer session in the Oval Office is sometimes marginal. In a January 31st session at the White House with Prime Minister

Tony Blair, President Bush called on three reporters while Blair took a like number. The whole session took 13 minutes, including their opening statements.[4]

A look at the practices of his predecessors at the same point in their presidencies (Table 4.4) demonstrates the degree to which President Bush is eschewing traditional press conferences, and, at the same time, is picking up on the joint press conference practice observed by Presidents George H. W. Bush and Bill Clinton.

Although the president in recent years has made himself available to the large number of reporters stationed at the White House and in the Washington community, he has done so in ways that fit in with his own style. In order to set up the sessions with reporters in ways that meet his needs and, to a lesser extent those of news organizations, presidents have needed to have communications operations capable of making appropriate determinations and arrangements.

NEWS ORGANIZATIONS AS A PRESIDENTIAL RESOURCE

A president needs an effective communications operation for both defensive and offensive reasons. He seeks to define himself and his programs and to keep to a minimum threat level the efforts of others to portray him in terms not of his choosing and that of his staff. A president's staff members often believe themselves to be in

Table 4.4   Solo and Joint Presidential Press Conferences,
994 Days into a Presidency

President	Total	Solo	Joint	Joint Sessions/ Total Conferences (%)
Eisenhower—1st term	75	74	1	1.3
Eisenhower—2nd term	73	73	0	0
Kennedy	63	63	0	0
Johnson	69	64	5	7.3
Nixon—1st term	21	21	0	0
Nixon—2nd term*	9	9	0	0
Ford*	40	39	1	2.5
Carter	52	52	0	0
Reagan—1st term	19	19	0	0
Reagan—2nd term	14	14	0	0
G. H. W. Bush	105	66	39	37.1
Clinton—1st term	102	34	68	66.7
Clinton—2nd term	48	13	35	72.9
G. W. Bush	61	9	52	85.2

Source: Adapted from Martha Joynt Kumar, "Is This a Press Conference?" Defining and Tabulating Presidential Press Conferences, *Presidential Studies Quarterly* 34 (March 2003): 221–237. See the article for a treatment of the press conference patterns of recent presidents.

*Presidents Nixon and Ford did not serve out the full 994 days in these terms.

an environment where the stakes are high and at the same time it is difficult for the chief executive and his team to present their views and proposals in a way the public can see, hear, and understand. In talking about the difference between peace and wartime in terms of their communications effort, White House Communications Director Dan Bartlett spoke of getting through to the public and the importance of doing so, especially in war setting. "The microphone is even bigger, our ability to puncture through the clutter of what's out there is even more powerful, and the international component of it, that we're not just speaking to our citizenry; we're speaking to the world even more so than just being the President of the United States, leader of the free world. During times of war it's even that much more."[5] The clutter people in a White House see comes from many quarters, including alternate messages filtering into the Washington community from members of Congress, interest groups, the opposing political party, and disaffected members of the bureaucracy. They want to define themselves and, while they are at it, they often aim to portray the president in their own terms, not his.

Presidents view the problems they deal with as sometimes as difficult to explain, as they are important to understand. President Bush talked to his staff after the terrorists' attacks on September 11th about the importance of communicating to the public on a subject whose elements are not always obvious. Dan Bartlett described the difficulties and needs the president outlined to his communications team. The president said to Karen Hughes, Ari Fleischer, and Bartlett that "his role as educating the American people about the nature of this conflict is very important. It's important they hear it from him." Bartlett indicated the president thought explaining the war on terrorism involved different elements than the types of war people were familiar with. "It's going to be different. It's going to be fought in the shadows. Things like that he was very keen on." They would need to think through carefully what they say in a time of war as "there are real consequences for what we do," the president told them. "This is not a political campaign. This is not about passing this or that. When you're communicating, when you can do so, it has real impact. That's how the President communicated to Karen, myself and Ari [Fleisher]."[6]

With the presence of network cameras ready to broadcast live from the White House whenever news organizations decide to do so, a president and his staff have a rich resource to use to get to the public whose understanding and support the chief executive needs in order to govern. Rather than have to depend on a daily basis on newspapers and magazines to relay what information they want to provide, those working in a White House today can make use of all of those news organizations whose representatives are stationed in and around the Press Room from early morning to late at night. Routinely, Press Office staff come into their offices beginning with an early morning team that needs to be there prior to the morning television news programs that begin at 7:00 A.M. and remain until the last reporter leaves, sometimes near midnight when there is a late presidential event.

Since the Eisenhower Administration when television was taken seriously by the staff as a presidential resource, presidents and their staffs have created ways to use the presence of the networks as well as all of the other news organizations to broadcast the president's goals, his programs, and his brand of leadership. It is a rare

Table 4.5   President Clinton's Addresses and Appearances Available
for Use by News Organizations

	1993	1994	1995	1996	1997	1998	1999	2000–2001	1993–2001
Addresses to the Nation	7	5	3	2	2	5	3	3	30
Oval Office	4	4	2	0	0	1	2	1	15
Other White House	0	0	0	1	0	2	0	1	4
Congress [a]	3	1	1	1	2	2	1	1	11
Weekly Radio Addresses	46	51	51	52	50	52	52	56	410
Addresses and Remarks[b]	410	475	426	531	438	545	567	645	4,037
Total Appearances	463	531	480	585	490	602	622	704	4,477

[a] This section includes State of the Union messages as well as Inaugural addresses and other addresses found in the Document Category, "Addresses to the Nation" found in the *Public Papers of the President of the United States, William J. Clinton.*

[b] In many instances in the events listed in Addresses and Remarks, there are sessions before or after the event when the president had an exchange with reporters where he took a small number of questions from reporters, usually a pool of reporters coming into the meeting at a specified time for a brief session. Counted here are the Addresses and Remarks where the president did have an exchange with reporters as well as one where he did not talk with reporters afterwards.

day at the White House when the president is not publicly visible in one or more events featuring some aspect of his presidency. All public events are available for media coverage under one or another set of rules.

President Clinton's appearances, shown in Table 4.5, demonstrate the frequent schedule of public presidential events. In addition, one can see that as the cable networks increased their presence at the White House in 1996, the president's public appearances increased. His increase in public speeches contrasts with the marked decrease in the number of press conferences and short question and answer sessions he had with reporters. As coverage by television of presidential events increased, the sessions where the president had to take reporters' questions decreased. He and his staff want him to appear in settings where his vulnerability is minimal. No matter whether it is a Democrat or a Republican in the White House, presidents and their staffs prefer to present him in settings where there is less chance of his being met with surprises.

Based on the public appearances of President Clinton, President Bush could anticipate an active public schedule with many opportunities to make statements in person as well as to address his various audiences. His appearances are shown in Table 4.6. In looking at his eight years in office, President Clinton had a public event on the average of almost twice a weekday, including one on Saturdays, when his weekly radio address was broadcast. President Bush maintained close to the same averages in his first two years in office.

Table 4.6   President George W. Bush's Addresses and Appearances Available for Use by News Organizations, through October 10, 2003

	2001	2002	2003	Total
Addresses to the Nation	7	4	5	16
Oval Office	1	0	1	2
Other White House	1	1	2	4
Joint Session of Congress, including State of the Union and Inaugural	3	1	1	5
Other	2	2	1	5
Weekly Radio Addresses	48	51	40	139
Addresses and Remarks	453	484	239	1,176
Total Appearances Available for Media Use	508	539	284	1,331

The schedule for President Bush for the week of February 3 to 7, 2003, gives one an idea of what events are on the public presidential calendar.[7] On Monday the 3rd, the president toured the Vaccine Research Center of the National Institutes of Health and spoke there on his BioShield Initiative, which he had mentioned in his State of the Union address. Tuesday he was to meet with the King of Bahrain and the following day the president of Poland. Because of the accident of the space shuttle Columbia, the meeting with the King of Bahrain was put off to a later date in order for the president to travel to Houston for a memorial service for the astronauts. Usually when a president has a session with a foreign or international leader, a pool of reporters will be brought into the Oval Office to query the president. On Thursday the president began his day at the National Prayer Breakfast and later spoke on energy independence at the National Building Museum. Although there were no scheduled public events on Friday, often ones are added as the week progresses.

Some of the broadcast organizations, including C-Span, will carry the president's appearances live while others will use some clips from the sessions. All news organizations with a White House presence report to the public on these events in some way. Thus, although the events can be seen in one light as ones where the president is appealing to a particular audience, in reality he and his staff are targeting his appearances to a far larger public audience. The audience is at home and at work throughout the United States.

Today presidents are visible on an average of between two and three times a day conducting the business of government in public settings. He speaks from a variety of White House venues and travels around the country and abroad as well. In all of those locations, reporters follow him and are ready to go live when events warrant. Table 4.6 demonstrates the myriad opportunities President Bush has taken to appear publicly to explain his goals and programs as well as his actions. News organizations are the delivery system that allows him to get directly to the public. Although not all of these sessions were covered by news organizations, many were. Especially after September 11th, the cable news networks daily provide coverage of presidential events, including broadcasting his whole speeches and presentations.

In addition to presidential events, cable networks are regularly broadcasting briefings by the president's surrogates, most often his press secretary who has a daily televised briefing when the president is in town, and some of his Cabinet secretaries, particularly Secretary of Defense Donald Rumsfeld and State Department spokesperson Richard Boucher. On a regional basis, departmental secretaries regularly speak for the administration's programs and goals.

The presence at the White House of cable news networks has made possible the broadcast of daily presidential appearances. In addition to the expansion of the number of news organizations, covering presidential events is much easier than it once was because of developments in broadcast technology. The lead time for organizing White House events for broadcast coverage has dramatically fallen and the flexibility of a president and his staff to choose locations other than the Oval Office for presidential addresses has dramatically increased. Both are due in large measure to technological changes among news organizations and to improvements to the infrastructure of the White House. An historic structure with a limited capacity to handle heavy demands on its electrical system, the main building and the West Wing as well were limited in their ability to handle the loads used by electronic media. Well into President Clinton's second term, in order for television networks to cover a presidential event in the East Room or in any other public room other than the Briefing Room and the Oval Office, the television crews had to lay cable from a location near the West Wing door, down the driveway and under the North Portico, up and over the terrace on the East Side of the White House, and then through a metal slot in one of the French doors on the east side of the East Room. The process of laying cable required an event begin its set up a couple of hours beforehand. In that environment, a president had little flexibility in the locations he could use to go live quickly with a presidential address. It is not surprising that President Clinton used the Oval Office to give almost all of his presidential addresses to the nation that came from the White House. With developments in technology allowing for a president to go live elsewhere in the White House complex without prior setup, President Bush has used the Oval Office for only two addresses to the nation.

COMMUNICATIONS ORGANIZATIONS DESIGNED TO MEET PRESIDENTIAL NEEDS

President Bush and his staff view communications as having a place in a White House unlike that of organizations in the private or even elsewhere in the public sector. "I hear people describe the purposes of the White House as to maximize the value of the president's time, voice," commented Clay Johnson, who served as a senior adviser in the Bush White House and who spent considerable time in the private sector in earlier years.[8] "And I guarantee you no other company defines their headquarters' role as maximizing the value of their chairman's time and voice." What the president says matters and where and how he says it make a difference to the perceptions the public has of him. In response to a question whether a president can influence public opinion, Karl Rove commented: "Look, if you don't believe a president can affect public opinion then it really doesn't matter what the president says, does it? Or how he says it."[9] He continued: "I find it hard to believe that you can't [influence public opinion]." Rove as well as other senior aides in most recent administrations have operated on the notion they can and should seek to move public opinion in the president's direction and that his communications organization is a prime way of doing so.

At the heart of the communications operation of President Bush is a management precept that the president "makes news on his terms," an observation made by Jim Wilkinson, the Director for Planning in the Office of Communications.[10] Making news on the president's terms requires an organization focused on planning and getting ahead of events. Good communications requires organization supporting the president's own communications abilities. "Communicating is communicating," said Mary Matalin in response to a question about the differences between communications in campaigning and governing.[11] "It has to be clear, it has to be repetitive, it has to be coherent, it can't be internally or intellectually inconsistent." In addition, you have to have a "receptive zone," she said. "You've got to make people want to hear what you're saying. It has to have relevance. So you have different tactics for different places." Hitting all of those zones requires a well-tuned organization. As a result, the president and senior advisers set in place a staff operation with the following core organizational elements.

Strategy Level: People and Instruments

Creating an effective communications operation in the Bush White House involved creating an organizational structure with three levels of staff and a set of institutions that includes preexisting White House units as well as new offices and titles associated with those at the strategic level. In the combined area of communications offices, there are three levels of operations: Strategy, Operations, Implementation. It is a system with delineations of people and tasks accompanied by a well recognized and accepted chain of command starting off with those who develop the plans and then the staff who translate the plans into events and appearances and, finally, the people who carry them out.

The organizational structure the President and his senior advisers developed to translate strategies into operations contains a group of four basic White House units with additional resources for those at the strategic level. The existing communications units found in the last three administrations are tied together through those at the strategic level. Karen Hughes, Counselor to the President and now an outside adviser in regular contact with those at the White House, had the communications portfolio coordinating planning with Senior Adviser to the President, Karl Rove. The offices with the operations and implementation responsibilities are the Office of Communications, the Press Office, the Office of Media Affairs, and the Speech-writing unit. All four units handle tasks associated with publicity operations no matter who is president. What varies from one administration to another are the supervisory arrangements for the units. The Office of Strategic Initiatives and the other offices in the grouping of political outreach units headed by Rove, is a resource for the communications operation. Like the Hughes operation, Rove's office coordinates preexisting units dealing with political and interest group relations, including the Office of Political Affairs, the Office of Intergovernmental Affairs, and the Office of Public Liaison. Between them, Hughes and Rove covered White House relations with nongovernmental groups and institutions. Both of the chief strategists are involved in the process of identifying goals and having them adopted.

Having the communications and political operations represented together is important beyond the fact Hughes and Rove are the most trusted long-term political and communications advisers the president has in the White House. During a year, the president operates in more than one environment, one mode. There are rhythms to a year and during some parts and with some issues a president is going to be working in a political environment. At others, it will be more of a nonpartisan one. "He also understands in different environments, you've got to be in the environment you are," said Matalin in October, 2003.[12] "This is a political environment. Then discuss it in ways that people can understand." Thus, in discussing Homeland Security in the weeks prior to the November congressional elections, the president spoke in very political terms. On the other hand, when the State of the Union address is on the decks for discussion, bipartisanship is the presidential mode. To represent the president in all his environments, both advisers are important for the strategies discussed and the options chosen.

Goal Setting: Campaign Agenda and the State of the Union Message.   At the midpoint in the president's term, there have been two basic instruments used for administration goal setting: the campaign agenda and the State of the Union message. The campaign platform was comprised of goals he discussed on a regular basis and, once in the White House, he devoted an individual week to exploring what he planned to do on each one of them. Building up military defense, education, tax cuts, faith-based initiatives, were all items discussed in his campaign, which formed his agenda as he came into office. Each week had a set of events highlighting the issue under discussion. Prior to coming into the White House, Karl Rove developed a 180-day plan to carry forward their campaign agenda. Well into the first year, the president and his staff drew from their campaign agenda for their initiatives though alterations were made based on governing needs.

Following September 11, the major statement of the president's governing goals is found in his State of the Union address. Dan Bartlett, who heads the Office of Communications and served as deputy to Karen Hughes, described the way in which they use the State of the Union message to operationalize the stated goals. "What we have done with this from a messaging standpoint, we basically take State of the Union which outlines the President [George W. Bush]'s national goals for the year—winning the war on terrorism, protecting the homeland, defeating the recession—and knowing over the course of the next years we're going to want to keep coming back to those three core themes."[13] They have what they call "pillar events and messages" that you come back to each month. "You're always going to want to talk about the war in a given month. You're always going to have the President talking about protecting the homeland in a given month and you're going to want him talking about the concern of those who have lost their jobs and such as we recover from a recession." All of those are items that can be planned several months out.

When she was Counselor to the President, Karen Hughes was responsible for communications planning three to four months out. At the beginning of the administration, there were meetings on Wednesday and Friday where the staff thought through their events for a three to four month period. Working with the general goals they had, the group worked through strategies for following up and defining them. Coordination is what they did in these meetings with perhaps two dozen people from the basic offices reaching outside of the White House either to governmental or non-governmental units. Those at the strategic level then and now make certain the days are full of White House statements reflecting what they want to say rather than what others want them to say. That requires a great deal of organization with representation of the various White House offices providing information and resources. Now those sessions deal more with carrying out plans rather than developing them. "We have message meetings twice a week but they really have become—they're really more implementation meetings to get all the groups together and make sure everybody is on the same page and everyone is going forward together," Hughes commented.[14] At the end of her tenure, Hughes no longer went to that meeting on a regular basis as "it's become more of looking at the week ahead and making sure that everything's in place and everybody's on the same page."

Carrying Strategy into Messages and Appearances

President Bush established an organization that retained the four basic elements of the publicity structure found in most administrations since that of Richard Nixon. Those offices are the Press Office, the Office of Communications, the Office of Media Affairs, and the Speechwriting unit. The numbers of people on staff in the four offices is fairly similar in the Bush and Clinton White Houses. The Bush people had a total of 43 people in 2001 while the Clinton people had 39 in 1998. The difference lies in the emphasis of each. The Bush White House favors the long-range planning operations and puts their resources there while the Clinton White House had more people assigned to the Press Office.

Press Office: Daily Operations. As it has traditionally done, the Press Office is focused on the daily operation. The Press Secretary plays little role in the overall communications strategies because of the daily emphasis of his office and the volume of work he deals with each day. Ari Fleischer explained his focus. "The Press Office is much more operational, much more implementation," he said.[15] The Press Office is the place where daily press relations are handled and where plans developed elsewhere for daily coverage are carried out. In modern White Houses, including the Bush one, the scope of Press Office activity is limited to the day in front of them. Next week, next month, and next year belong to the communications operation and to others working on general strategic planning.

As she carried out his work, Flesicher speaks with Hughes but is not micromanaged by her. "Karen's really the big picture. Karen kind of changes the fundamental direction of something that's moving, or puts speed into it when something is moving. Once it's moving, Karen's not the type who said, 'Here are the words you have to use.' If I have questions or doubts to what's sensitive, I always reached out to Karen, and still will, because she really is good. So she can help me think it through and sort out generally as to how far do you want to go, on what don't I go."[16]

In the Bush White House, the Press Office is a pared down unit with 10 people in 2001 and 12 in 2002. In the Clinton years under Press Secretary Mike McCurry, it had 24 people. The major difference in the two operations is that in the Clinton White House the operation that today is the Office of Media Affairs was under the Press Office and today it is responsible to the Assistant to the President for Communications. With the addition of email as a way to distribute press releases and other information that once was printed out and put in Press Room bins, there is less printing work that needs to be done by junior staff in the Press Office. The main tasks of providing reporters with information in briefings and in walk-in responses remain as do the preparations necessary for the morning and afternoon briefings provided by the Press Secretary. Although the Press Office is involved in advance work on trips, most everything done out of the office relates to the daily information coming from the White House.

Office of Communication: Events Management and Integration with Other Institutions.

Communications is responsible for creating the focus for the day, organizing the planning up to four months out, and coordinating with White House and administration personnel. Dan Bartlett, who heads the office, also handles an assessment of how their work was received. Although the Office of Communications is the unit where internally events are planned and executed, it is also the place where they find out how they are doing and develop strategies in response to what they are discovering. Jim Wilkinson, the deputy for planning in the office in 2002, was often involved in taking their message to the Hill. "Literally, tactically, Jim Wilkinson [Deputy Communications Director for Planning] goes to the Hill and pulls together meetings with the press secretaries, and depending on the issues, that communications person goes up with that substance person," said Matalin.[17] "He had me go up there on energy, to bring the substance person, and I did the energy hoorah thing, and he does the across-the-board issue." Wilkinson set up the meetings with [House Majority Whip] Tom DeLay's office. "We sat around and brainstormed, came up with concepts that were purely communications devices. Like we had a nationwide energy town hall meeting held on the same night Cheney keynoted one. . . . All across the country at the same time, with the same message, we were holding town halls."

Office of Media Affairs: The "Echo."

This office deals with the regional and local press. Specialty press, such as Hispanic, Polish, and African-American news organizations, are taken care of through this office as well as radio. In addition, the web site is managed through this office.

In this administration, the office is particularly geared towards the follow up for presidential events. When he goes on the road following a major speech, for example, the Office of Media Affairs handles the local press. The Media Affairs operation is broken down into regional portfolios with those handling them responsible for getting information to news organizations within the assigned areas, but also for finding out how the president's initiatives played in those locations. One of the responsibilites of the director is to set up calls with White House officials and representatives of news organizations, especially when there is an important speech and event taking place. In addition, working with the Cabinet is an important aspect of developing a resonance to presidential goals and themes. For a summer housing initiative, Media Affairs called on the HUD Secretary to meet with reporters as well as some other people in departments. "With the housing rollout, we had—we kind of guided and directed HUD's activities," said Nicolle Devenish, who headed the office in 2002.[18] "We asked Secretary Martinez to do something with the Hispanic press. There was an Under Secretary that did something with the African-American press. I think we set up some conference calls with reporters from all around the country. And it's a little bit—I won't say low tech, but a lot of it is just getting our reporters to get on a conference call."

Speechwriting: The Words.   President Bush came into the White House with a preexisting set of expectations on the part of those used to dealing with presidents. News organizations, government officials at every level, and interest groups counting themselves as important to the president's policy interests, all had expectations of hearing from the president in response to their interests. In their individual ways, each sector preferred to hear publicly from the president in his own words, rather than those of surrogates, whether they were Cabinet secretaries or the Press Secretary.

When they came into office, the Bush communications team had to immediately prepare for presidential appearances in the forms of speeches and remarks and then sessions where the president responded to reporters' questions. All of the earlier mentioned sessions, whether they involved responses to reporters' queries or simply creating remarks and developing the location and timing for doing so, the communications operation, especially the speechwriting unit, has an enormous load of work where mistakes must be kept to a minimum in order for the president's publicity to be effectively presented. As the White House has grappled with the enormous speech burden, the unit has gone from 10 to 12 staff members from 2001 to 2002.

Coalition Information Centers and Global Communications: Communicating Abroad.   The Bush White House added units to focus their communications operations on a world-wide market. They did so with the Coalition Information Centers created after the September 11th attacks and aimed at responding to the publicity attacks against the U.S. in Afghanistan and in Muslim countries where we were under attack. Tucker Eskew, who headed the Office of Media Affairs at the time of the September attacks, moved to London to coordinate publicity with Alastair Campbell, spokesperson for Prime Minister Tony Blair. The idea was to have an offensive and defensive operation where the American government and our allies could act within the same news cycle as our opponents, most especially the Taliban. Eskew explained the impetus for the office: "We were being inflicted with disinformation, misinformation, outright lies largely by a Taliban public information officer based in Islamabad in the days following the beginning of the bombing in Afghanistan," he said.[19] Prime Minister Tony Blair's government told the White House they were getting beat on the news cycle. "I think we acknowledged that we needed to re-spond more aggressively, more rapidly to defend ourselves in that global news cycle and to do it more quickly so that we weren't letting the ten hours lapse from Islam-abad's morning to D.C.'s morning."

Once discussions began then "Alastair [Campbell] and Karen cooked up this idea of Coalition Information Centers designed to more effectively, rapidly respond and coordinate information resources across agencies within the United States Government and between governments in the coalition. . . . So there's a briefing process at the White House. There is certainly one at Number 10 as well." Where the problem came in the briefing process was Islamabad. Campbell and Hughes de-cided there needed to be a briefer in Islamabad to counter the ones held by the Tal-iban. "We had to do it because the press were getting briefed by this Taliban infor-mation officer. . . . The campaign became so successful that we didn't just rout the Taliban from most of Afghanistan; we routed that guy out of Islamabad. There was somewhat less need to respond to all of that but still a concentration of interna-tional media and regional media that was often very conspiracy minded and in some ways anti-America. So throughout November and December particularly we briefed, briefed frequently, and regularly, daily in fact, and we knocked down some stories." Once the daily firefighting operation was no longer needed, then those in-volved in the operation here and in Great Britain began to think "proactively and thematically, strategically if you will, about ways to get our message across. Our mes-sage was this is not a war against Islam." That led to their initiative on behalf of women of Afghanistan that included Laura Bush and Cherie Blair.

A more formal and broader effort to combat an unfavorable U.S. image resulted in the creation of the Office of Global Communications, a unit established in the White House Office in July 2002, and then through an executive order in January 2003. Eskew, who now heads that office, in June explained its origins as they were planning its launch. "It is going to be strategic and thematic. It is going to be proac-tive. It's going to coordinate among agencies to try to take the president's construct, his framework for communications, and integrate it in to what we're already doing and it's also to provide support for and elevate good ideas, good programs so that they can become part of the president's schedule or part of the president's agenda, part of his legislative and governmental agenda. If there's something good that's communications related that we found out in our process of interacting with and as-sessing government communications programs and it deserves to be on the presi-dent's schedule or agenda, we'll help elevate it to that level."[20] The office is part of the White House Office, which indicates the office's importance to the president. One of the things Jim Wilkinson said he had learned while working in the Office of Communications "is the importance of it being here at the White House, that real estate matters, and having that [Global Communications] here at the White House is critical, because it sends a signal to the rest of the bureaucracy this is important to the President personally."[21]

"WINNING THE PICTURE": THE IMPLEMENTATION LEVEL

Once those at the strategic level decide what the themes are they want to communicate, then the operations people decide how the event will be structured and the implementers work at setting up the event and the pictures to carry out what the planners want to get across. Perhaps the best of those who carry goals into results in the television area is Scott Sforza. He is a professional with a television and White House background and uses both experiences to translate messages into words and pictures. He develops the backdrops behind the president when he speaks in a variety of locations around the country, such as when he spoke in Kansas City with the words "Protecting the Homeland" along with the image of a firefighter appearing on a wallpaper like background.[22] At the White House itself, the setting serves as the backdrop though message banners might be used when he speaks in Room 450 of the Eisenhower Executive Office Building. "I sort of use the rule of thumb," he said, "if the sound were turned down on the television when you are just passing by, you should be able to look at the TV and tell what the President's message is; if you are passing by a storefront and see a TV in the window, or if you are at a newspaper stand and you are walking by, you should be able to get the President's messages in snapshot in most cases."[23]

When President Bush addressed the nation on October 7, 2001 to announce our campaign of military strikes against Al Qaeda and Taliban targets in Afghanistan, he chose a site no president had spoken from. In speaking in the Treaty Room in the White House where President McKinley signed the treaty ending the Spanish-American War, the president and his staff selected a location where the picture itself communicated a basic message. Delivered at 1:00 in the afternoon, viewers could see the traffic passing in the distance on Constitution Avenue. "The President wanted to really address the nation in a different way than he had before," said Scott Sforza who serves as Deputy Communications Director for Production.[24] "He enjoyed the history of the room and what it was all associated with." He continued by discussing the moving traffic in the background. "We wanted that [visible traffic]; we'll send a message to the world that, we're still in business here."

The White House of President George W. Bush is more effectively organized to express the interests and carry out the wishes of the president than is true of most recent similar operations. It is a system they brought with them rather than one developed through a process of accretion and experience. They came in with a full-fledged organization in place. When the president and his staff entered the White House, they knew what they wanted to accomplish and the organizational scheme they would put in place to carry out their goals. With a well thought out transition, they had their organization structured and their goals established prior to coming in. Like the bulk of the White House organization, the communications operation reflects the priorities and interests of the president and his staff.

Organization is important as the element aiding in optimizing the use of the president's voice in those settings designed to achieve the administration's personal, political, and policy goals. News organizations are the vehicle through which presidents and their communications staff communicate to the public. Although the president and his White House staff regard the news media as a presidential resource, they also are very aware of his and their need to respond to the queries posed by reporters. A president and his staff may not provide the answers journalists want or at the time they want information, but those serving in a White House are aware they cannot ignore the queries of those housed less than 100 feet from the president's office.

NOTES

1. The White House, Office of the Press Secretary, "Remarks by President Bush and President Kwasniewski of Poland," the Oval Office, January 1, 2003.

2. There are four types of pools: In-House Pool, In-Town Travel Pool, Travel Pool, and Expanded Pool. The first refers to events taking place in the White House complex, the second to the pool traveling to events taking place within the Washington, D.C., area, the third to the pool traveling with the President when he goes out of town, and the fourth on occasions, such as Air Force One arrivals, where additional organizations are brought in to cover the occasion. The information on what constitutes a pool is taken from *"Where the Rubber Meets the Road: The White House Press Office, Lower Press Office Manual*, last updated January 20, 2001" a manual used by Press Office staff in the Clinton White House. The news organizations in the April 2003 pool rotation included the following. The Print Pool includes: *Austin American Statesman, Baltimore Sun, Boston Globe, Chicago Tribune, Christian Science Monitor, Columbus Dispatch, Copley News, Cox News, Dallas Morning News, Gannett News, Hearst Newspapers, Houston Chronicle, Knight Ridder, Los Angeles Times, McClatchy, Newhouse, Newsday, New York Daily News, New York Post, New York Times, Pittsburgh Post,* Scripps Howard, United Press International, *USA Today, Wall Street Journal, Washington Post,* and *Washington Times*. The Radio Pool includes nine radio organizations: ABC, American Urban Radio Network, Associated Press, Bloomberg, CBS, National Public Radio, Standard Radio News, Talk Radio, and Voice of America. The Television Pool includes the five networks: ABC, CBS, CNN, Fox, and NBC. The Magazine Photo Pool includes *Newsweek, Time,* and *US News and World Report*. This information is taken from a listing sent out to email recipients of Press Office information, "April 2003 Pool Rotation," sent on March 24, 2003. Associated Press and Reuters are in each pool.

3. Tabulated by the author from the transcripts as found in the *Weekly Compilation of Presidential Documents*.

4. The White House, Office of the Press Secretary, "Remarks by the President and British Prime Minister Blair," Cross Hall, January 31, 2003.

5. Interview with Dan Bartlett, Martha Joynt Kumar, Washington, D.C., May 22, 2002.

6. Interview with Dan Bartlett.

7. The White House, Office of the Press Secretary, "The Week Ahead, Monday, February 3 / Friday February 7, 2003," January 31, 2003.

8. Interview with Clay Johnson III, Martha Joynt Kumar, telephone, August 9, 2002.

9. Interview with Karl Rove, Martha Joynt Kumar, Washington, D.C., May 8, 2002.

10. Interview with James Wilkinson, Martha Joynt Kumar, Washington, D.C., July 3, 2002.

11. Interview with Mary Matalin, Martha Joynt Kumar, Washington, D.C., October 3, 2002.

12. Interview with Mary Matalin.

13. Interview with Dan Bartlett.

14. Interview with Karen Hughes.

15. Interview with Ari Fleischer, Martha Joynt Kumar, July 11, 2002.

16. Interview with Ari Fleischer.

17. Interview with Mary Matalin.

18. Interview with Nicolle Devenish, Martha Joynt Kumar, Washington, D.C., July, 2002.

19. Interview with Tucker Eskew, Martha Joynt Kumar, Washington, D.C., June 13, 2002.

20. Interview with Tucker Eskew.

21. Interview with James Wilkinson, Martha Joynt Kumar, Washington, D.C., July 3, 2002.

22. Dana Milbank, "In Missouri, Bush Promotes Homeland Security Agency," June 12, 2002.

23. Interview with Scott Sforza, Martha Joynt Kumar, Washington, D.C., June 27, 2002.

24. Interview with Scott Sforza.

CHAPTER 5

Leading and Competing:

The President and the Polarized Congress

◆◆◆

Barbara Sinclair
University of California, Los Angeles

The U.S.'s weak parties and the resulting lack of party cohesion in Congress have conventionally been seen as the great barrier to effective presidential legislative leadership. Members elected to Congress by their own efforts and so responsive to the parochial concerns of their districts owe little to the national party and the president, the argument goes. Consequently the president cannot count on the support of his fellow party members in the Congress.

In the last two decades the supposedly fragmented and weak congressional parties have been transformed. In both chambers, partisan polarization has increased enormously; the parties are more internally ideologically homogeneous and more ideologically distant from each other than at any time in the last half century. If the lack of cohesion was a problem for the president, is this high cohesion a blessing? What is the impact of partisan polarization on presidential legislative leadership and success?

To answer these questions, I use a data set consists of bill-level data for 11 congresses from 1961 through 1998 as well as some data on the 107th Congress (2001–2002). The analysis proceeds as follows. In the first section I briefly examine the development of partisan polarization in Congress and the impact that the greater polarization has had on the rate of agreement between the president and key congressional actors. Next, I consider how a stronger congressional majority leadership of his party can aid the president and also the ways in which a more cohesive and organized opposition party can compete with him in agenda setting, framing debate and shaping legislation. Presidential strategies to counter a more aggressive and cohesive opposition party are examined in section three; the emphasis is on veto threats and "going public." In the fourth section, I assess presidential legislative success; analysis of the quantitative data discussed earlier allows me to determine the impact of partisan polarization and of other key variables on the rate and character of presidential success on all major legislation and on his own agenda.

POLARIZATION OF THE CONGRESSIONAL PARTIES AND ITS IMPACT ON POLICY AGREEMENT BETWEEN THE PRESIDENT AND CONGRESS

Although American political parties' lack of cohesion has sometimes been exaggerated, the middle years of the 20th century were a period of low intra-party ideological agreement, especially within the majority Democratic party. The late 1960s and early 1970s saw cohesion reach a nadir, with numerous congressional Democrats, mostly conservatives from the southern states, voting more often with opposition Republicans than with their party colleagues.[1]

Party voting data tell the story of how the congressional parties have changed. In the 1960s and 1970s (1961–1980), Republican and Democratic majorities on average opposed each other on 40 percent of the recorded votes in the House and 42 percent in the Senate. By the 1990s (1991–2000), 58 percent of the roll call votes in the House and 57 percent in the Senate were party votes.[2] Furthermore, on party votes, members were increasingly likely to vote with their party colleagues and against their partisan opponents. As Figure 5.1 shows, the difference between how Democrats and Republicans voted on party votes was considerably greater at the end of the 20th century than at any time in the previous half century. The Poole and Rosenthal DW-nominate scores, which can be interpreted as locating members of Congress on a left-right dimension, show that increasingly there is almost no overlap between the parties, that the most conservative Democrat is to the left of almost all Republicans and conversely the most liberal Republican is to the right of almost all Democrats.[3]

This partisan polarization can be traced to an alteration in the constituency bases of the parties. The change in southern politics that the Civil Rights movement and the Voting Rights Act set off resulted in the conservative southern Democrats so common in the 1960s and before being replaced either by even more conservative Republicans or by more mainstream Democrats. As African-Americans became able to vote and as more conservative whites increasingly voted Republican, the supportive electoral coalitions of southern Democrats began to look similar to those of their northern party colleagues. As a result, the legislative preferences of northern and southern congressional Democrats became less disparate.[4]

The increasing proportion of House Republicans elected from the South made the Republican party more conservative but accounted for far from all of the change in the party's ideological cast. A resurgence of conservatism at the activist and primary voter level resulted in fewer moderates being nominated; increasingly the Republicans who won nominations and election, especially to the House, were hard-edged, ideological conservatives. Perhaps in response to the polarization of the

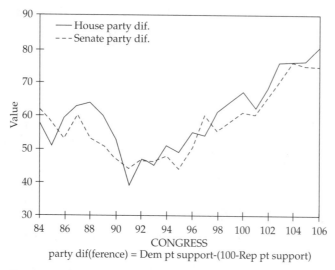

party dif(ference) = Dem pt support-(100-Rep pt support)

Figure 5.1   Congressional Party Polarization, 1955–2000

parties' elected officials and party activists, party identifiers also became more polarized on policy issues.[5] Thus constituency sentiment at both the activist and voter level underlies congressional partisan polarization, especially in the House with its smaller and more homogeneous districts.

What has been the impact of such polarization on presidential legislative leadership? Has the increased cohesion of his party in Congress made the president's task easier?

The Madisonian division-of-powers system the U.S. Constitution established provides the president with sharply limited powers in the legislative process and with relatively meager resources for inducing members of Congress to vote contrary to their own legislative preferences.[6] Consequently the president's legislative success should be, in large part, a function of the extent of agreement between what the president wants and what various key congressional actors want. To what extent and under what conditions does the president agree or disagree on specific legislation with congressional actors in the legislative process?

To answer that question, I gathered bill-level data for 11 congresses from 1961 through 1998. I examine major legislation as identified by *Congressional Quarterly* and augment that with legislation on which key votes occurred, again as identified by *Congressional Quarterly*. This yields a list of between 42 and 59 measures per Congress.[7] *Congressional Quarterly* is a specialized publication aimed at the Capitol Hill community (members of Congress, their staffs and lobbyists); CQ's list of major legislation is a list of what knowledgeable contemporary observers considered the major—but not just landmark—legislation of the day and can reasonably be interpreted as the active congressional agenda. I chose the congresses so as to provide variation on a number of crucial variables, especially partisan control of the branches (divided versus unified) and level of partisan polarization in Congress.[8]

The sequential and bicameral legislative process means that there are multiple stages at which agreement is important and multiple sets of members whose legislative preferences can make a difference.[9] Using *Congressional Quarterly* accounts, I coded presidential support/agreement or opposition/disagreement (or an intermediate, mixed position) for every major measure at each stage of the process. In the vast majority of the cases, CQ explicitly discussed the president's views and the coding was straightforward. Presidential opposition does not necessarily—and, in fact, infrequently—means that he opposes any bill on the issue; it simply means he opposes the bill in the form it emerged from that stage—the House committee, for example.

Table 5.1 shows the rate of agreement between the president and the House and Senate reporting committees, the chamber floors and the Congress's final bill (that is, the bill that emerged from House-Senate reconciliation procedures). There is more agreement than disagreement at all stages, but disagreement is hardly rare. The distribution on bills as they emerged from successful House-Senate reconciliation is similar to that at earlier stages, except that the rate of agreement is higher and the rate of disagreement lower than at any of the earlier stages. This suggests that at least some bills are altered towards the end of the congressional process in ways that make them more acceptable to the president and provides a hint of possible presidential influence.

Even when U.S. parties are at their weakest, members of a party tend to share policy preferences. One would thus expect that, when the president and the majority of the members of the House and of the Senate are of the same party, agreement should be more frequent and disagreement less frequent than when they are of different parties.[10] As hypothesized, agreement is much more frequent and disagreement much less so when control is unified than when it is divided (see Table 5.2). When the president's party commands a congressional majority, the president supports most of the legislation reported by the committees and passed by the chambers and he opposes very little of it. In contrast, when the other party controls Congress, both committees and the floor are quite likely to approve legislation in a form the president opposes and considerably less likely to approve legislation in a form he unequivocally supports. Shared partisanship does provide the basis for considerable agreement across the branches, while conflicting preferences are more likely when the branches are controlled by different parties.

Table 5.1   Presidential Support for and Opposition to Bills at Various Stages of the Legislative Process

President's position on	House committee	House floor	Senate committee	Senate floor	Final bill
Support	50	48	53	57	59
Mixed	17	17	18	19	22
Oppose	33	34	29	25	19

Table 5.2   The Relationship of Presidential Support for and Opposition to Bills and Divided versus Unified Control

Bill	Control	Support	Opposition
House committee	Unified	84	5
	Divided	28	52
House floor	Unified	77	6
	Divided	31	52
Senate committee	Unified	79	9
	Divided	28	49
Senate floor	Unified	82	5
	Divided	33	43
Final bill*	Unified	83	4
	Divided	40	31

*97th Congress is excluded because control was mixed.

The configuration under divided control is not, however, a mirror image of that under unified control; when control is divided, a president does not do as badly as his counterpart does well under unified control. Additionally, when control is divided, the bill that emerges from House-Senate conference (or other reconciliation procedures) tends to be considerably better from the president's perspective than the bill at any of the earlier stages; at that point and in contrast to all of the earlier stages, the president is actually more likely to support than oppose the bill. Since the same members approved the final bill as the bill that earlier passed their chamber, different preferences cannot explain this shift. Rather presidential influence is suggested. Later sections explore this suggestion further.[11]

What has been the effect of increasing partisan polarization on the relationship between presidential-congressional agreement and partisan control? Table 5.3 divides the congresses into three periods—the 91st and before (1970 and before), a period of relatively low polarization; the 94th through 97th (1975–1982), an intermediate period; and the 100th and later (1987 and later), a period of higher and increasing polarization.[12]

From the first to the second period, agreement between the president and Congress decreased under both unified and divided control, but the decrease was much steeper under divided control. Increasing polarization, the reforms, or both seem to have made the Congress less accommodating—not only but especially to presidents of the other party. From the second to the third period, agreement under unified control goes up to exceed, often significantly, agreement during the initial period; agreement under divided control continues to decrease, with the result that the effect of partisan control becomes massive. What is most notable is that presidents lost considerably more under conditions of divided control than they gained under conditions of unified control. Considering the frequency of divided control in recent decades, that is of major consequence for presidential success.

Table 5.3   The Relationship of Presidential Support for Bills and Divided versus Unified Control in Three Periods of Increasing Partisan Polarization

		House			Senate		
Bill	Control	91st and Before	94th, 95th and 97th	100th and after	91st and Before	94th, 95th and 97th	100th and after
Committee	Unified	82	76	94	85	67	89
	Divided	57	30	19	44	28	23
Floor	Unified	74	66	94	88	76	83
	Divided	61	38	19	42	33	31

CONGRESSIONAL PARTIES AS ALLIES AND ADVERSARIES

As the congressional parties became more cohesive, they became potentially more valuable as allies for the president but also more formidable as opponents. In the House of Representatives, greater ideological homogeneity made possible the development of a stronger and more activist party leadership.[13] By the mid-1980s, majority party members had granted their party leadership significant new powers and resources and had come to expect the leadership to use them aggressively. A president whose party controlled the House could expect the majority party leadership to use those powers and resources on his behalf. To be sure, congressional party leaders are elected by and thus agents of their own members and furthering their members' policy and reelection goals is their first priority. Yet, increasingly in a time of high partisan polarization, that means passing the president's program. Members of Congress are likely to have similar policy goals to those of a president of their party—not infrequently his program includes policy proposals that originated with them; furthermore, members are aware that the president's success or failure will shape the party's reputation and so affect their own electoral fates.

A president whose party controls the House can expect the majority party leadership to work with (and, if necessary, lean on) the committees to report out his program in a form acceptable to him and in a timely fashion; to deploy the extensive whip system to rally the votes needed to pass the legislation; to bring the bills to the floor at the most favorable time and under a special rule that gives them the best possible chance for success; and, if necessary, to use the powers of the presiding officer to advantage the legislation.[14]

The special rules under which bills are brought to the House floor, because they, unlike much of the aid the leadership provides, are public, offer a particularly good illustration of the help the majority party leadership can and does give a president of its party. The rule sets the conditions governing the consideration of the specific bill. Rules that restrict the amendments which may be offered reduce uncertainty and protect the legislation from alteration; thus they are prized. During the 103rd Congress (1993–94), the Democratic House leadership brought 67 percent of President Clinton's program to the floor under restrictive rules compared with 54 percent of other major measures that were so protected.[15] The Republican House leadership provided even more protection for George W. Bush's program in the 107th Congress (2001–02); 85 percent of his agenda items were considered under restrictive rules, considerably higher than the 68 percent of other major measures so considered.[16]

In the Senate, the increased ideological homogeneity of the parties has meant that senators are more likely to act as party teams than they were in the past. However, Senate rules constrain the assistance that the majority party leadership is able to give to a president of its party. The Senate is not a majority-rule chamber; to force a vote over the objections of any senator requires an extraordinary majority of 60 votes; and amendments to most bills need not be germane.

The Majority Leader works with the president if he is of the same party; he uses his significant informal influence to persuade committees to report legislation the president wants in the form he wants it and in a timely fashion; through persuasion and bargaining, he tries to construct a winning coalition for the president's program; he uses his considerable influence over the floor agenda to bring the president's priorities to the floor and at a favorable time—if, that is, no filibuster is threatened. However, unless he commands 60 votes, he cannot even assure the president's priorities floor consideration. Political polarization and narrow margins in the chamber often make the necessary 60 votes hard to get.

In fact, as the parties polarized, the minorities making use of Senate rules concerning extended debate and nongermane amendments have increasingly become partisan ones. The organization and numbers the minority party commands means that its use of those Senate prerogatives presents the majority and the president with a much greater problem than when individuals and small groups were the primary users. The minority party can extract concessions on legislation that a majority supports. During the 103rd, for example, minority Republicans forced concessions on motor voter (voter registration) and national service legislation among other Clinton priority bills.

The difference in the majority party leadership's powers and resources in the two chambers does seem to affect the fate of the president's program. In the 103rd, Democrats had substantial majorities in both House and Senate; yet 92 percent of legislation on Clinton's agenda passed the House and only 84 percent passed the Senate. Of the items that failed enactment, 63 percent ran into a problem in the Senate but not in the House.

The more cohesive, more aggressively led congressional parties are much more formidable opponents when control of the Congress and the presidency resides in different hands. An opposition-party controlled House is an especially great problem for a president. The powers and resources that aid him when his party controls the chamber will be used against him when the opposition does. The opposition majority party leadership is unlikely to block consideration of a newly elected president's top priority initiatives; most congressional leaders believe that the American people expect Congress to give a new president a chance. However, a bill written by an opposition party majority in the committee and brought to the floor under a rule designed by an opposition party leadership may well emerge from the House in a form far from the president's preferences. The first George Bush repeatedly faced this problem—on clean air legislation and on the Americans With Disabilities bill, for example.[17] When Democrats lost control of Congress in the 1994 elections, President Clinton was confronted with a highly aggressive House leadership that regularly passed bills in a form he strongly opposed, sometimes not even allowing Democrats a vote on a Democratic party alternative. In the 104th Congress, Clinton opposed 70 percent of major bills in the form in which the House passed them.

Because Senate rules do not allow a narrow but cohesive majority to work its will as House rules do, an opposition party controlled Senate is a lesser problem for the president. The president's supporters, even if in the minority, can usually stop legislation he opposes from getting out of that chamber. But, by the same token, the opposition majority party leadership can block passage of legislation the president wants. Thus, after Senator Jim Jeffords' switch from Republican to independent in late May 2001 gave Democrats control of the Senate, a number of Bush initiatives—the faith-based initiative and reauthorization of the 1996 welfare reform law, for example—bogged down in the Senate. Neither party was willing to make the compromises necessary to get the 60 votes needed for passage. Others passed the Senate but in a form the President opposed. With Democrats making up a majority of the Senate delegation to any conference—and with Majority Leader Tom Daschle assuring that only Democrats who supported the party position were chosen conferees—most such legislation never emerged from a House-Senate conference. Energy legislation and the patient's bill of rights were among the major bills that suffered this fate.

The contemporary congressional parties now challenge an opposition party president in the public as well as in the legislative arena. Both parties in both chambers regularly generate agendas of their own and attempt to participate in national political discourse so as to shape debate on issues and burnish their party image.

By the 1980s, divided control of Congress and the presidency increasingly appeared to be the norm and the parties had moved much further apart ideologically. As the seemingly permanent House majority party but seldom the presidential party, Democrats became more and more restive with presidential supremacy in agenda setting.[18] New Speaker Jim Wright in 1987 at the beginning of the 100th Congress proposed an agenda consisting of issues such as clean water legislation, a highway bill and aid to the homeless that were broadly supported within the Democratic party. He relentlessly kept the spotlight on those items and used leadership resources aggressively to facilitate their passage. By the end of the Congress, all the items had become law and the Democratic Congress had gained considerable favorable publicity. Thereafter Democrats expected their leaders to developed agendas to guide legislative action and to enhance the credit their party could claim from legislative productivity. During the course of the 1980s and the 1990s, congressional leaders and the congressional parties became more vocal and visible competitors to the president as agenda setters. In 1994, minority House Republicans developed the

"Contract with America," an agenda of specific policy proposals, and made it the centerpiece of a nationalized congressional campaign. In the 104th Congress (1995–1996), Newt Gingrich, the primary architect of the Contract and the new Speaker of the House, for a time eclipsed the president as the nation's premier agenda setter.[19]

Members also came to expect their leaders to play a prominent role in national political discourse. During the long period of divided control, Democrats came to understand that the president's great access to the media advantaged him enormously in political and policy struggles, and that they as individuals could never compete with the president in the realm of public opinion. The skill with which Ronald Reagan used the president's media access to further his policy and political agenda and denigrate Democrats made congressional Democrats realize they needed spokesmen to counter the president. Democrats came to expect the Speaker to use his access to the media to promote the membership's policy agenda and to protect and enhance the party's image.

To promote their agendas and in their attempt to shape debate, the congressional parties have developed sophisticated media operations.[20] A number of party entities—especially the Caucus/Conferences and the policy committees—have greatly enhanced their ability to take part in the enterprise of communicating the party message. These party organs engage in extensive press contacts—sending out press releases, talking to reporters, holding press conferences. They also produce a great deal of information—everything from "the message of the day" to fat issue briefs—for dissemination to their membership. This constitutes a service to members but is also an attempt to nudge them into "singing from the same hymn book." The "message of the day" is often prominently displayed and the arguments most favorable to the party's position are emphasized, often in the form of "talking points"; the hope is that members will used these messages in their contacts with their local media.

Various party organs facilitate member media-contact activities that leaders hope will enhance members' reelection prospects and aid in the promotion of the party message. The Senate Democratic Technology and Communications Committee has television studios, extensive video editing capabilities, and facilities for satellite hookups with local television stations that senators can use; the staff helps senators organize media events by doing everything from contacting reporters and selling them the story to reserving the room (Sellers 1999).[21] The Senate Republican leadership provides similar services for its members through the Republican Conference.

House Democrats have a Message Group consisting of party leaders and particularly media savvy members who meet daily to agree upon a message of the day; a larger group of members is charged with disseminating the message, especially through the one-minute speeches that begin the House's legislative day. The House Republican "Theme Team" performs a function similar to the larger Democratic group; made up of 50 members, it is responsible for "communicating the majority party's legislative issues, plans and ideas . . . during speeches given on the House floor"[22] The one-minute speeches sometimes take on the character of set-piece battles with waves of well-trained troops from the two parties waging a sometimes bitter rhetorical fight.

All these efforts by no means enable the congressional parties to compete with the president on an even basis; the president still has the biggest megaphone around. Yet, when the congressional party is advocating the popular side of an issue that the media find attractive, the president can be forced to yield or pay a significant political price. In the late 1980s, for example, congressional Democrats advocated a bill forcing companies to provide their workers with notification before closing a plant. President Reagan opposed the bill. Among the many efforts to promote the cause, Democrats and their labor union allies staged a series of media events around the issue; because they would make good copy, sympathetic victims of sudden plant closures were prominently featured. The purpose of the campaign was to pressure President Reagan to not veto the bill and it succeeded. In 1996 congressional Republicans confronted President Clinton with a similarly unpalatable choice on welfare reform and he too eventually gave in.

When the president's party controls both chambers of Congress, the opposition party has more difficulty getting heard. Yet even then the president must contend with an organized opposition media operation. In early 2003, House Democrats' economic stimulus proposal receive considerable press coverage, in part at least because they scooped the president.

Furthermore, Senate rules sometimes make it possible for the minority party to focus media attention on an issue the majority and the president would rather avoid and sometimes even pass legislation they oppose. In the 1990s, exploiting Senate prerogatives to attempt to seize agenda control from the majority party became a key minority party strategy. The lack of a germaneness requirement for amendments to most bills severely weakens the majority party's ability to control the floor agenda. The minority may be able to offer its agenda as amendments to other bills and, if the effort is accompanied by an adept public relations campaign, may be able to force it through the chamber. In 1996 Senate Democrats used this strategy to enact a minimum wage increase and, in later years, forced highly visible floor debate on tobacco regulation, campaign finance reform, gun control and managed care reform. Until 2001, Senate Democrats had an ally in the White House who used his bully pulpit to amplify their message. However, the strategy can work even when the president is opposed. Campaign finance reform was forced onto the floor and passed the Senate in 2001 before Democrats took control of the chamber.

PRESIDENTIAL STRATEGIES IN AN ERA OF PARTISAN POLARIZATION

Presidents have altered their legislative strategies to counter the more aggressive congressional opposition. They more frequently "go public" and they use veto threats in their bargaining with Congress a great deal more.

"Going public" consists of "a class of activities that presidents engage in as they promote themselves and their policies before the American public," with the aim of "enhance[ing their] chances of success in Washington."[23] Sometimes the strategy is conceptualized as going over the head of Congress directly to the American people in order to stimulate the public to pressure the Congress into supporting the president's initiatives. That, however, is a highly ambitious goal that presidents can seldom hope to achieve.[24] More frequently the president hopes to increase the saliency of an issue that benefits him and frame the debate on the issue in such a way as to advantage his stance and so enhance his bargaining position and his power of persuasion. Given the political inattentiveness of the American public and the jealousy with which the TV networks guard their time, the vehicle presidents choose for going public is seldom the big prime-time speech and the audience they target is seldom the entire American public. Less grand speeches and other appearances targeted at carefully selected audiences are less costly in presidential resources.

Presidents frequently choose to travel outside Washington for such appearances. "Beyond the beltway," a presidential visit is assured of ample local news coverage; local media are more likely to provide favorable coverage than the national media; the ideal audiences are often located outside the capital. In his first 100 days in office, President George W. Bush traveled to 26 states on 24 different days; he thus surpassed his nearest competitor Bill Clinton who took domestic trips on 22 of his first 100 days, visiting 15 states, and far surpassed his father who visited 15 states on 15 days.[25] Carter and Reagan lag far behind, in the single digits.

A number of Bush's appearances were devoted to promoting his tax cut plan and took place in states he had won handily but were represented by Democratic senators. Edwards shows that Bush did not succeed in moving national public opinion on his tax cut; nor did he persuade the Democratic senators.[26] Clearly, going public does not assure success. Yet Bush may have succeeded in solidifying the support of those already predisposed to support him, his fellow Republicans—in the electorate and in the Congress. His efforts may have prevented a stronger opposition from developing. Certainly no president can yield the public forum to his opponents.

The Bush administration's "going public" strategy at least with respect to domestic issues appears to be increasingly tilted towards cultivating and activating the Republican base and away from converting the uncommitted middle. How else to explain sending Treasury Secretary John Snow to Ohio, home of Republican senator George Voinovich, to promote Bush's 2003 tax cut proposal? Voinovich, who is up for reelection in 2004, had expressed serious doubt about the wisdom of the proposal. It seems likely that Bush was attempting to activate the Republican base to put pressure on Voinovich.

In this period of high partisan polarization and frequent divided control, veto bargaining has become an important presidential strategy for influencing legislation. When control is divided a president threatens to veto legislation unless it is changed to conform more closely to his preferences. The opposition party knows it cannot muster the two-thirds vote needed to override a presidential veto and so often does make at least some alterations. Table 5.4 shows the increase in veto threats of major measures in selected congresses between 1961 and 1998. When the president's party controls both houses of Congress, presidents seldom issue veto threats. However, the frequency under conditions of divided control has gone up enormously; since the late 1980s, veto threats are the rule, not the exception, on major measures, varying from almost half in Reagan's last congress to over two-thirds in 1997–98, the last for which data are available.

Table 5.4   The Increasing Frequency of Veto Threats
(% of "vetoable" measures subject to)

Congress	Dates	Veto Threats
87	1961–62	0
89	1965–66	0
91	1969–70	15
94	1975–76	40
95	1977–78	18
97	1981–82	25
100	1987–88	48
101	1989–90	55
103	1993–94	4
104	1995–96	60
105	1997–98	78

Bold are divided-control congresses.

Do veto threats work? Do they, in fact, move legislation towards the president's position? The evidence indicates that the strategy is effective.[27] Table 5.1 showed the president to be more successful at the end of the legislative process than at earlier stages, suggesting presidential influence. Especially when the Congress is in opposition party hands, the president tends to win more and lose less on final disposition of legislation than on either chamber floor initially (see Table 5.2). He is more likely to support legislation at the end of the process than in the form it emerges from committees controlled by the other party. Can these shifts be linked to veto threats?

The variable indexing presidential support for or opposition to legislation at a number of stages in the process makes tests of the effects of veto threats possible. One can gauge whether a bill changed **in terms of presidential support** between when, for example, it was reported from the House committee and its final form. If the president opposed the House committee bill but supported the final bill, that would be considered a change in the bill in the president's direction. If the president supported the House committee bill and supported the final bill, that would be considered no change. If the president had a mixed response to the House committee bill and opposed the final bill, that would be a change away from the president's position. Only bills that were enacted are analyzed.

Table 5.5 shows that the likelihood of change from any preliminary stage (committee or floor in either chamber) to final form is much higher for legislation under a veto threat than for other legislation. The direction of movement in legislation tends to be disproportionately towards (rather than away from) the president's position whether or not the president has issued a veto threat, but the movement is always more towards the president's position when a veto threat has been issued than when it has not.

Presidents do seem to be able to use veto threats strategically to move legislation towards their preferred position and, in a period of high partisan polarization,

Table 5.5 **The Impact of Veto Threats: Change in Bills from Earlier Stages to Final Bill—Presidential Support Variables (enacted bills only)**

Initial Stage		House committee	House floor	Senate committee	Senate floor
% that changed	No veto threat	24	23	23	19
	Veto threat	59	47	52	38
% that changed pro Pres. position	No veto threat	69	81	64	63
	Veto threat	84	89	84	78

presidents who face opposition party control in one or both chambers need to use every tool available to them.

PARTISAN POLARIZATION AND PRESIDENTIAL SUCCESS

What then is the effect of high partisan polarization on presidential success in the legislative arena? Does it aid presidents when their party controls Congress? The only instance of totally unified control in the period of high polarization (1987 and after) for which data are available is the 103rd Congress (1993–94), Clinton's first, and one should take care in generalizing too much from one case. Nevertheless, that case suggests that the benefits are mixed. Clinton fared better in the committees of both chambers and on the House floor than presidents who enjoyed unified control in less partisan eras (see Table 5.2). This did not, however, translate into greater success on the final disposition of legislation, whether one examines all major measures or the president's agenda only. Particularly on the latter, the Senate where a simple majority is not enough was most often the stumbling block.

Presidents confronting a Congress in which one or both chambers are opposition-party controlled fare considerably worse in the period of high polarization than similarly situated presidents did when polarization was less. In the pre-100th Congress period, such presidents scored clear wins on final disposition on 33 percent of their agenda and scored a win of any sort on 54 percent (categories 1 and 2 on the 5-point scale); in the later period, presidents scored clear wins on only 18 percent and scored a win of any sort on 33 percent.[28] If all enacted major measures are considered, the results are similar. Presidents clearly won on final disposition on 30 percent of major measures enacted in the earlier period and 17 percent in the latter period; they won on balance on 26 percent of enacted measures in the earlier period and only 18 percent in the latter.

GEORGE W. BUSH, THE WAR ON TERRORISM AND THE FUTURE OF POLARIZED POLITICS

Can we expect any significant decrease in partisan polarization in the near future? Does the post-9/11 environment with its seemingly perpetual war on terrorism force a lessening of overt partisanship in Congress and an increase in support for the president? The evidence to date strongly suggests the answer is "not much."

Congressional partisanship as measured by roll call voting did decrease sharply in the immediate post-9/11 period but it rebounded quickly, as Table 5.6 demonstrates. The events of 9/11 instantly changed the agenda and depressed partisanship, especially on issues directly related to terrorism.[29] However, on issues beyond terrorism, the effect on the level of partisanship was relatively short-lived. By 2002, domestic issues—and some terrorism-related ones as well—again split members of Congress along partisan lines. Overall, the 107th Congress was about as partisan as its immediate predecessors.[30]

Members' voting behavior on domestic issues, which make up the lion's share of the congressional voting agenda, even in the post-9/11 era, was not permanently altered because the views of their constituents on such issues were not altered. Public opinion polls and members' myriad contacts with their constituents showed that Democratic voters and Republican voters continued to differ substantially in their domestic policy preferences. Members who desire reelection will generally reflect their constituents' views in their votes. Furthermore, when partisan divisions with their roots in domestic issues bled over into terrorism-related issues, such as on the airline security bill in the House and the matter of civil service protections for Homeland Security Department workers, terrorism-related issues divided members along party lines. And, when the question of war with Iraq began to divide Republicans and Democrats activists and then voters, that too was reflected in members voting behavior.

Bush's legislative success in the 107th reflected these cross-cutting forces. He won, at least on balance, on 67 percent of his agenda items that were directly related to 9/11 as compared with 57 percent of those not directly 9/11 related. Most of Bush's

Table 5.6   Partisanship over the Course of the 107th Congress

Period	Party Votes (%)	
	House	Senate
Senate Republican	67	71
Senate Democratic	56	52
Immediate Post-9/11	42	33
2002 pre-election	57	44
Post-election	79	43
TOTAL	56	51

Votes on suspensions excluded for the House.

losses on non-9/11 related bills occurred when bills he wanted did not become law, primarily because they were stopped in the Democratic-controlled Senate.

In the context of continued partisan polarization, Bush's gamble in going all out in campaigning for congressional Republicans in the 2002 elections makes sense. Without unified control of Congress, his chances of legislative success, at least on his domestic priorities, were dim. Even with a Republican-controlled Congress, Bush still has to worry about the Senate in which the Republican margin is very thin and his co-partisans certainly do not command the 60 votes so often necessary to pass legislation.

NOTES

1. Barbara Sinclair, *Congressional Realignment* (Austin, TX: University of Texas Press, 1982).

2. Data are from *Congressional Quarterly Almanacs*, various dates.

3. Keith Poole's web site address is http://voteview.uh.edu. See also Keith T. Poole and Howard Rosenthal, *Congress: A Political-Economic History of Roll Call Voting* (New York: Oxford University Press, 1997).

4. David Rohde, *Parties and Leaders in the Postreform House* (Chicago: University of Chicago Press, 1991); Jeffery Stonecash, Mark Mariani, and Mark Brewer, *Diverging Parties: Social Change, Realignment, and Party Polarization* (Boulder, CO: Westview Press, 2002); Stanley Berard, *Southern Democrats in the House of Representatives* (Norman: University of Oklahoma Press, 2001).

5. Gary C. Jacobson, "Party Polarization in National Politics: The Electoral Connection," in Jon Bond and Richard Fleisher, eds. *Polarized Politics: Congress and the President in a Partisan Era* (Washington, DC: CQ Press, 2000).

6. These may be a function of constituents' views or of the member's own views and, mostly likely, of both.

7. The total number of cases is 585 and for most analyses all cases are used. For the analysis of enactment specifically I excluded these key vote measures on which controversy was confined to the amendment on which the key vote occurred and the underlying legislation was not controversial (and thus enactment of the legislation itself is not of interest), unless the amendment carried either the president's or the majority party leadership's agenda. With these exclusions N=561.

8. The Congresses are: 87th (1961–62); 89th (1965–66); 91st (1969–70); 94th (1975–76); 97th (1981–82); 100th (1987–88); 101st (1989–90); 103rd (1993–94); 104th (1995–96); 105th (1997–98).

9. See B. Sinclair, *Unorthodox Lawmaking* (Washington, DC: CQ Press, 2000).

10. George Edwards, Andrew Barrett, and Jeffrey Peake, "The Legislative Impact of Divided Government." *American Journal of Political Science* Vol. 41 (April 1997), 545–563; J. Bond and R. Fleisher, *The President in the Legislative Arena* (Chicago: University of Chicago Press, 1990).

11. For that reason, the remainder of this section only considers bills earlier than the final bill.

12. The breaks also coincide with the pre-reform period; the period of adjustment to the reforms; and the period of growing party leadership strength, especially in the House. See Rohde, *Parties and Leaders*; Barbara Sinclair, *Legislators, Leaders and Lawmaking* (Baltimore: Johns Hopkins University Press, 1995).

13. Ibid.

14. See Barbara Sinclair, "Trying to Govern Positively in a Negative Era: Clinton and the 103rd Congress." In *The Clinton Presidency: First Appraisals*, pp. 88–125. Edited by Colin Campbell and Bert A. Rockman. Chatham House Publishers, 1996 and "Context, Strategy and Chance: George W. Bush and the 107th Congress," in Colin Campbell and Bert Rockman, ed., *The George W. Bush Presidency: An Early Appraisal*, (Chatham, NJ: Chatham House Publishers, forthcoming 2003).

15. Modified closed and closed rules are here considered restrictive. See Sinclair, *Unorthodox Lawmaking*, pp. 20–28.

16. 107th data, other than that in Table 6 is preliminary.

17. Barbara Sinclair, "Governing Unheroically (and Sometimes Unappetizingly): Bush and the 101st Congress," in *The Bush Presidency*, pp. 155–184, edited by Collin Campbell and Bert Rockman (Chatham, NJ: Chatham House Publishers, 1991).

18. Sinclair, *Legislators, Leaders and Lawmaking*.

19. E. Drew, *Showdown: The Struggle Between the Gingrich Congress and the Clinton White House* (New York: Simon and Schuster, 1996); D. Koopman, *Hostile Takeover: The House Republican Party 1980–1995* (Lanham, MD: Rowman and Littlefield 1996); D. McSweeney and J. Owens, ed., *The Republican Takeover on Capitol Hill* (London: MacMillan, 1998).

20. Patrick Sellers, "Winning Media Coverage in the U. S. Congress," in Bruce Oppenheimer, ed, *Senate Exceptionalism* (Columbus: Ohio State University, 2002) ; Daniel Lipinski, "Communicating the Party Record: How Congressional Leaders Transmit their Messages to the Public," paper delivered at the 1999 meetings of the American Political Science Association, Atlanta, GA, Sept. 2–5.

21. Sellers, ibid.

22. House Republican Conference web site.

23. Samuel Kernell, *Going Public*, 3rd ed. (Washington: CQ Press,1997) p. ix.

24. George Edwards, "Riding High at the Polls: George W. Bush and Public Opinion," paper prepared for delivery at the conference on "The Presidency, Congress and the War on Terrorism: Scholarly Perspectives," University of Florida, Gainesville, FL, February 7, 2003, Table 8.

25. Data are from a table in the *Los Angeles Times*, April 29, 2001. The data are attributed to the White House.

26. Edwards, "Riding High at the Polls," Table 8.

27. See also Charles Cameron, *Veto Bargaining* (New York: Cambridge University Press, 2000).

28. *Congressional Quarterly*'s account is used to assess the success of the president on each major measure on the chamber floor and on final disposition along a five point scale ranging from clear win to clear loss.

29. Barbara Sinclair, "Patriotism, Partisanship and Institutional Protection: The Congressional Response to 9/11," paper prepared for delivery at the conference on "The Presidency, Congress and the War on Terrorism: Scholarly Perspectives," University of Florida, Gainesville, FL, February 7, 2003. My heartfelt thanks to Keith Poole, that most generous of political scientists, for giving me access to the roll call data early.

30. Ibid. p. 8.

CHAPTER 6

Bush and Congress:

Old Problems and New Challenges

◆◆◆

Stephen J. Wayne
Georgetown University

The legislative component of the modern presidency may be the least satisfying and most frustrating part of a new president's job. Established by precedence, reinforced by statute, and hyped by promises made in an elongated election campaign, the legislative challenges a new president faces are Herculean. The mating of campaign promises, leadership imagery, and a diverse set of policy goals gives birth to legislative expectations that are usually unrealistic and unattainable in a constitutional system that divides powers among separate institutions, a governmental system that decentralizes power within those institutions, and an electoral system that reinforces individual autonomy and constituency-oriented decision making in Congress.

The problem is particularly acute for Washington outsiders such as George W. Bush who have not experienced Congress first hand and operate as if it were a replica of the state legislature with which they dealt as governor. Moreover, campaigning against Washington's politics-as-usual environment frequently produces an attitude in which professional legislators and their career staffs are perceived as the problem to be torched or circumvented, not dealt with as equals. Finally, there is the difficult transition from campaigning to governing and all that goes with it: organizing the new team, prioritizing the agenda, forging a governing coalition, and mobilizing public support (Jones, 1998, p. 54). It was not designed to be easy nor has it been for most contemporary presidents.

Moreover, George W. Bush came into the presidency in a weaker position than have most newly elected presidents. Not only could he not claim a public mandate for his policy agenda, he couldn't even point to a popular victory. Even his Electoral College margin was razor thin and controversial. Democrats picked up seats in both houses of Congress.

The new president's governing coalition had to be formed from an electoral minority, amid more than the usual discontent from the opposition party. Thus, the bar was low, Bush's only advantage. He began his legislative presidency with little political capital. He had to earn it.

INITIAL CHALLENGES

Bush had three initial tasks upon taking office. He had to heal the political divide, which was magnified by the Florida vote controversy, reward his political supporters by sticking to his campaign agenda, and, finally, establish himself as president.

Healing the Political Environment

To circumvent the legislative hurdles that stood in the way of achieving his political goals, the president initiated a charm offensive while the White House clothed him in appropriate presidential garb. Democrats were befriended in a highly personal manner; they were invited to the White House; the president attended their caucuses; he even gave some of them his endearing nicknames. What more could they want?

Congressional Democrats called for the president to jettison his campaign agenda in the light of the election outcome. Bush refused. Worried about the ideological right—he remember how they turned against his father—desiring to establish his credibility early, pursuing a policy agenda in which he had come to believe, the president reaffirmed his campaign priorities and promises.

To demonstrate a presidential dimension and overcome the negative stereotypes from the campaign, especially Bush's alleged verbal inadequacies and cognitive challenges, the White House staged presidential appearances around the country, scripted policy-oriented talks which he dutifully rehearsed prior to the event, kept Vice President Cheney in the shadows, and after every major decision, leaked to the media that Bush had "really" made it. Moreover, the Bush administration took advantage of Clinton's messy departure—the furniture, pardons, executive orders and monument proclamations, White House vandalism—by reinforcing the president's nice guy image. Bush stayed above the fray, the good cop, while the White House played the "gutter" politics of the bad cop.

SETTING THE POLICY AGENDA

Bush began with his campaign agenda. Most of it had a legislative dimension. Tax relief, educational reform, military strengthening and restructuring, a faith-based initiative, and a new energy strategy were his principal priorities. The problem was that, with the exception of education, his priorities were not the public's.

Pre 9/11: An Uneventful Beginning

Most of Bush's agenda had a legislative dimension. With the exception of improving education, however, the president's principal priorities differed from those of the

Table 6.1   Top National Priorities, January 2001

Priorities	All %	Rep. %	Dem. %	Indep. %
Keeping the economy strong	81	78	84	81
Improving educational system	78	76	81	76
Reducing crime	76	69	82	72
Securing Social Security	74	67	80	74
Adding Medicare drug benefits	73	60	80	72
Securing Medicare	71	64	79	69
Regulating HMOs	66	54	77	60
Reducing middle class taxes	66	63	65	67
Dealing with problems of the poor	63	48	75	62
Protecting the environment	63	45	74	68
Providing insurance to uninsured	61	46	74	60

Question: "I'd like to ask you some questions about priorities for President-elect Bush and Congress this year. As I read from a list, tell me if you think the item that I read should be a priority. Should it be a top priority, important but lower priority, not too important, or should it not be done?" This table indicates the percentage of respondents who considered the item to be a top priority.

Source: Pew Research Center for the People and the Press, January 11, 2001.

public during and following the 2000 election. Table 6.1 lists the top priorities for the country and partisan support for them at the beginning of 2001; Table 6.2 notes the president's priorities.

According to the Pew survey of January 11, 2001, strengthening the military did not even make the list of the 10 most pressing issues. It was listed as a top priority by less than half of the population (Republicans 63%, Democrats 45%, and Independents 41%) while a component of that objective, developing a missile defense, was mentioned as a top priority by only 41 percent (Republicans 49%, Democrats 36%, and Independents 37%).

Table 6.2   Bush's Top Legislative Priorities

Policy	Date of White House Initiative
Educational Reform	January 23, 2001
Faith-Based Initiative	January 30, 2001
Tax Reform	February 8, 2001
Defense	February 27, 2001
Immigration	February 28, 2001
International Trade	May 10, 2001
Energy	June 28, 2001
Medicare	July 12, 2001

Source: White House Archives, www.whitehouse.gov

Table 6.3   Presidential Job and Issue Approval, January 2001–July 2001

Job/Issue Approval	Pres.*	Cong.	Econ.	Foreign	Edu.	Defense	Taxes	Energy	Envir.
Feb.	57	53	53	46	—	—	—	—	—
Mar.	58	55	55	52	65	—	56	—	—
April	62	55	55	56	62	66	54	43	46
May	56	49	51	55	—	59	—	41	—
June	55	51							
July	57	49	54	54	63	—	60	45	46

Source: Gallup Polls

*In months with multiple polls, I cite the one in which issue approval was also measured.

Despite his pursuit of a partisan agenda, the president succeeded in gaining public approval for his presidency in general and for his economic and foreign policy performance in particular as well as for his specific initiatives on education, taxes, and national defense. Only in the areas of energy and the environment did his approval ratings drop below 50 percent. Table 6.3 lists presidential and congressional job approval and presidential issue approval for the first six months of the Bush presidency.

In short, the president controlled the agenda and received plaudits for his job performance even though his actual policy achievements were "few and far between."

Responding to the Terrorist Attack

The president did even better in agenda control following 9/11. The administration's legislative response to the terrorist attack was a series of measures designed to enhance national security at home and aboard. With Bush enjoying broad, bipartisan popular backing, Congress deferred to his leadership. The president's national and homeland security agenda became theirs for the remainder of 2001. These include:

- A Resolution authorizing the president to use force if necessary to bring the terrorists and those who harbor them to justice;
- A supplemental spending bill ($40 billion) to help recovery from the attacks, enhance national security, and provide monies in anticipation of a military response;
- Airline bailout ($15 billion);
- Anti-terrorism legislation (USA Patriot Act) that provided expanded surveillance and enforcement powers for the federal government;
- Aviation security.

As the second session of Congress approached, the president paid lip service to his domestic policy goals, but his attention remained focused on national and homeland security and on the corporate scandals that began with Enron's failure. Table 6.4 indicates the public priorities at the beginning of the second session of the 107th Congress. With the exception of the administration's anti-terrorism and national security initiatives and its campaign to prevent the ten-year tax cut from being reversed, its priorities again differed from those of the public.

Despite these differences, the economic downturn, and the failure to address health concerns and other issues, the president's popularity remained high. It was not until July 2002 that public approval of the president's economic performance dropped under 60 percent (see Table 6.5) despite the commonly held perception that the economy was only fair or poor.

Bush's high approval ratings following 9/11 continued to elevate most of his issue approval ratings, more so at the beginning of the year and after the 2002 midterm elections.

ONGOING CHALLENGES

Every new president must establish his administration's presence on Capitol Hill, develop a strategy for dealing with Congress, and then operationalize that strategy in pursuit of his key priorities.

Fashioning a Legislative Presence

As previously noted, Bush assumed his presidency with little congressional experience and even less political capital. The legislative lessons he learned from his Texas days as governor were that personal relations matter, ideological convictions can overcome partisan loyalties, and vetoes can prevent an oppositional majority from imposing its judgment. Bush adopted the first two of these lessons in his dealings with the 107th Congress.

Table 6.4   Top National Priorities, 2002

Defending the country from future terrorist attacks	83%*
Strengthening the economy	71
Improving the job situation	67
Improving the education system	66
Waging a military campaign to destroy terrorist groups around the world	64
Making Social Security financially sound	62
Making Medicare financially sound	55
Adding a prescription drug benefit to Medicare	54
Strengthening the military	52
Dealing with the moral breakdown in the country	45

Source: Pew Research Center for the People and the Press, January 17, 2002

*Percentages indicate the proportion of the population that considered the item a top priority.

Table 6.5   Presidential Job and Issue Approval, August 2001–January 2003

Job Approval	Pres.*	Cong.	Economy	Foreign Affairs
Aug.	57	48.5	—	—
Sept.	51+/ 88	42	47#	—
Oct.	87	84	72	81
Nov.	87	73	71	—
Dec.	86	72	—	—
Jan.	84	62	64	83
Feb.	82	62	66	79
Mar.	80	63	65	75
Apr.	76	57	60	70
May	76	57	61	70
June	76	52	63	66
July	73	54	55	67
Aug.	67	46	—	—
Sept.	66	52	—	—
Oct.	67	50	49	58
Nov.	68	47	55	59
Dec.	63	50	49	59
Jan.	84	62	64	83

Bold—After 9/11.

Source: Gallup Poll

*In months with multiple polls, I cite the one in which issue approval was measured. Issue polls conducted twice during the same month were averaged. Gallup conducted one specific issue poll, March 22–24, 2002. The president received better than 50 percent approval in all areas except Medicare (44%), Abortion (49%), Campaign finance reform (48%), Social Security (47%), and Government support for faith-based organizations (46%).

Poll conducted by Pew Research Center for the People and the Press, September 6, 2001.

To counter his limited knowledge of the intricacies of Congress, the president hired an experienced White House and K-street lobbyist, Nick Calio, and then allowed him to choose the liaison heads for each of the executive departments. The objective was to make sure that all the administration's top lobbyists were singing out of the same hymn book that the White House composed and would rewrite over the course of the session.

Calio ran a top-down operation, as did most other White House shops. Assisting him were deputies Jack Howard, David Hobbs (House) and Ziad Ojakli (Senate), former top staffers to Trent Lott, Dick Armey, and the late Paul Coverdall. The rest of the liaison staff had considerable Hill experience as well (Ota, 2002, p. 3251).

The Bush team maintained a visible presence on Capitol Hill. They walked the halls, working out of the vice president's Senate office and the House Whip's office as well as a conference room controlled by the Ways and Means committee. Two Senate liaisons were positioned outside the Senate chamber to corral those entering and leaving (Ota, 2002, p. 3251).

The president was a reasonably active legislative lobbyist on his own behalf. In addition to hosting the weekly breakfasts with congressional leaders, he regularly invited members of Congress to the White House for private discussions, usually without congressional aides present. He would phone wavering members of Congress when requested to do so by his liaison staff. Here's how Press Secretary Ari Fleischer described the president's efforts on behalf of fast-track:

> On Friday afternoon and into the wee hours of Saturday morning, the President worked the phones for trade promotion authority. He spoke to six members of Congress. The last member he spoke to was at 2:20 a.m. The last phone call he made was at 3:40 a.m. He talked to Nick Calio more than a dozen times. . . .
> . . . He and Nick just kept in real close touch. There are times when he'd talk to Nick and Nick would literally hand his phone to a member and the President would talk to that member into the wee hours (Fleischer, 2002).

Designing an Inside Strategy

From the outset, the new administration tried to control the legislative agenda, use the bully pulpit to define the issue debate, and push the budget for FY 02, tax relief, and educational reform in that order. "Our strategy is to always stay on the offensive and keep moving," stated Calio. "We started off driving the debate on key issues. And we are going to continue to drive it, with the president leading the way" (Ota, 2002, p. 3253).

As he had promised during the campaign, the president toned down the partisan rhetoric that characterized the Clinton-Gingrich era while he pursued a conservative and partisan Republican agenda. The administration provided Congress with blue prints of its key initiatives and then relied on the Republican House leadership to draft the legislation. This strategy had the advantage of placating the conservative ideologues who controlled the House leadership and the Republican committee chairs. GOP unity in the House, buttressed by the administration's initial focus on the budget and the tax cut, enabled White House lobbyists to concentrate their efforts on the more moderate, slower moving, less unified Senate.

Their plan in the Senate was to identify the Republican core and then reach out to enough Democrats to enact the legislation: Zell Miller and Ben Nelson on taxes, John Breaux and Joe Lieberman on education. With a House bill that could be expected to conform to its proposal, the White House had room to compromise if it had to do so. Compromise, while certainly not a dirty word in the Bush lexicon, was perceived as a last resort, not an early option, and one to be used only when necessary.

Playing Offense

The administration concentrated its major policy initiatives prior to 9/11 on taxes, education, and defense; it focused on anti-terrorism legislation and appropriations following 9/11, and finally, on national security and homeland security in the period leading up to and following the midterm elections.

Taxes.   On tax relief, an article of faith for most Republicans, including the president, the White House held firm until the opposition of Republican Senate moderates, Lincoln Chafee, Arlen Specter, and James Jeffords threatened to break open the tax package that the House had enacted (Taylor, 2001, p. 908). Jeffords' defection from the Republican Party added another dimension to the administration's problem, Democratic control of the Senate. After a public campaign directed toward moderate Democrats failed to gain enough adherents for the president's proposal and fearful that a Democratic Senate would be even less inclined to write a bill that the administration favored, the White House accepted the $1.3 trillion tax cut which the Senate enacted as the best it could get and then moved quickly to pressure House conferees to adopt it as well rather than hold out for a figure closer to their bill.

The president's advisers wanted to avoid a lengthy conference battle. They reasoned that a quick victory on this key priority, their first major legislative accomplishment, would provide the president with political capital and give the economy with a much needed boost.

Education.   On education, however, a softer and more traditionally Democratic issue, the administration bought into a bipartisan bill drafted by the House Committee on Education and the Workforce in early May 2001. The tradeoff for Democratic support in the committee was the elimination of the administration's proposals for annual testing and private vouchers. But once the bipartisan bill passed the House, the administration dug in its heels and resisted further changes. What followed was a battle royal in the Senate in which personalities and policy differences combined to stall the legislation.

It was not until Senate committees reverted to Democratic control that the principals had the incentive and were in position to work out a deal. The new chair of the Senate Health, Education, Labor, and Pensions Committee, Ted Kennedy, wanted more money for education. He initially requested $14.4 billion; the White House countered with $2.6 billion. As the negotiations proceeded, Kennedy lowered his request $4.8 billion and the White House upped its to $4.0 billion. These figures set the parameters for the final financial part of the deal (Lizza, 2001).

Substantive policy differences remained, however. These included how much flexibility states and school districts would have in spending the money, testing provisions and the amount of time schools would have to meet higher standards, supplementary funds for special needs children, targeted programs for the poorest schools, and use of school facilities by groups which discriminate on the basis of gender and sexual orientation, such as the Boy and Girl Scouts. It took six months for Senate conferees to enact legislation on which conference representatives could agree. In the end the conferees modified or jettisoned the most controversial points of contention and compromised on the others (McQueen, 2001).

Military.   In the area of defense, the administration had proposed a program that included an anti-missile defense shield, more money for salaries and benefits for uniformed personnel, but maintained controls on overall spending. In the developmental stage was an internal DOD debate over new strategies and weapons systems for the 21st century. The battle over these issues heated up in the summer of 2001 when rumors of the changes that the secretary wished to impose echoed through the corridors of the Pentagon and Congress and on the public air waves.

Representatives of the military branches objected to the new force structures and the technologies that went with them at the expense of existing programs and weapons systems. Democrats raised questions about the cost, feasibility, and desirability of the anti-missile shield. The dispute became heated; the White House stayed out of the fray; the news media had a field day.

The events of 9/11 essentially ended the new versus old debate among the administration and the uniformed military and their allies. With national security now the top concern, with partisanship silenced, with Congress supporting the president, the administration had little difficulty in getting its way on most of the 9/11 military issues.

Although the faith-based initiative, energy policy, and health proposals were mired in the labyrinth of committees, competing interests, and the personalities that championed them, the administration had succeeded in achieving its three principal objectives for its first year in office—a successful one from the president's perspective.

Playing Defense

On its key ideological initiatives, the FY 02 budget, family planning, and congressional attempts to limit presidential authority, the administration hung tough. Veto threats, although used sparingly, were reserved for "conviction" issues. During the first session, the administration voiced strong objection and threatened to veto the Foreign Relations Authorization Act, Fiscal Years 2002 and 2003 (HR 1646) after a compromise in the House International Relations Committee removed the restriction on foreign aid for international groups that engaged in abortion counseling. Strong objection was also made to the Agriculture, Conservation, and Rural Enhancement Act of 2001 (S 1731), legislation that authorized aid in amounts that exceeded the $5.5 billion that the president requested in his budget. In raising objections to the legislation, the OMB stated in its statement of administration policy that if the bill was not changed, the president's senior advisers would recommend that he veto it.

Two House resolutions and one Senate resolution also provoked administration opposition: H.J. Res. 55 opposed the extension of the Jackson-Vanik waiver authority for Vietnam; H.J. Res. 50 disapproved extending normal trade relations with China; and S.J. Res. 28 relaxed budget enforcement mechanisms in view of the recession and terrorist attack. None of these resolutions, however, received the support of the other chamber.

During the second session, the administration objected to the House's version of the National Defense Authorization Act (HR 4546), which would have restricted the president's ability to reallocate funds originally requested for the Army's Crusader artillery piece, and the Senate's defense authorization bill, which reduced spending for the anti-missile defense shield. In both cases the objection came in the form of a veiled veto threat that if the objectionable provisions were not removed, the president's senior advisers would recommend a veto. Similarly, the administration threatened to veto the Lieberman bill to create a Department of Homeland Security (S 2514) because the legislation did not grant the secretary of the new department as much flexibility as the president desired over budget and personnel matters, flexibility desired by and for other secretaries as well.

Early on, Bush threatened to veto any appropriation or supplementary spending bill that exceeded his budget request (Allen, 2001, p. A04; Parks, 2002, p. 1009). Although reality politics forced him to back off this threat, the OMB continued to pressure Congress to stay within the parameters of the president's budget (Parks, 2001, p. 903). In December 2001, the White House threatened to veto a Democratic attempt to add $15 billion to a defense spending bill to finance the war on terrorism (Parks, 2001, p. 2893). Similarly, Bush said that he would veto an omnibus appropriations bill to finance most of the domestic agencies for the remainder of the 2003 fiscal year if it exceeded his $385.9 billion target (Fram 2003; Morgan, 2003, p. A06) as well as a defense department appropriation (HR 3338), approved by the Senate Finance Committee, that exceeded his request. Veiled veto threats were made on a supplemental appropriation bill (S 2551) that compelled release of nonemergency funds, an appropriation (H 2506) that permitted foreign aid for groups that engaged in abortion counseling, a bill that restricted government outsourcing, and an emergency spending bill which would have prevented the administration from canceling the army's Crusader without the approval of Congress. No vetoes were actually exercised, however.

Even though the president opposed federalizing all air security personnel, increasing crop subsidies for farmers, some of the reforms in the McCain-Feingold campaign finance reform bill, he did not threaten to veto any of these bills, but did say that he would not sign a patient's Bill of Rights that included the litigation provision Senate Democrats desired (Carney, 2001).

CONDUCTING THE OUTSIDE CAMPAIGN

Since the Reagan administration, it has become customary for presidents to reinforce their administration's inside lobbying with an external public relations campaign. That campaign serves three purposes: to indicate to Congress the importance the president attaches to each of his initiatives, to demonstrate the general level of public support, and to mobilize interest groups to which members of Congress look for political support and policy guidance.

Going Public Pre 9/11

The president's principal legislative efforts in the public arena were directed at building and maintaining popular support in order to pressure Congress to enact the administration's key initiatives on education, taxes, and the military. (See Table 6.6.)

Table 6.6 Policy-Oriented Presidential Public Relations Activity, Pre 9/11

	Formal Actions	Presidential Statements and Press Releases	Photo Ops	Radio Addresses	Remarks Before Groups	Nominations	Total
Taxes	1	8	5	5	15	0	34 (13%)
Education	4	10	10	9	24	16	73 (29)
Defense	9	16	2	0	12	22	61 (24)
Environment	4	11	2	0	0	1	18 (7)
Energy	7	8	1	2	5	12	35 (14)
Health Care	0	5	0	0	2	0	7 (3)
Social Security	2	3	0	4	2	0	11 (4)
Medicare	0	3	0	0	1	0	4 (2)
Immigration	0	4	0	0	1	0	5 (2)
International Trade	1	3	1	0	0	0	5 (2)
Total	28 (11%)	71 (28)	21(8)	20 (8)	62 (25)	51 (20)	253 (100)

Source: Compiled and categorized by author from White House Archives.

Education.   Educational reform generated the most presidential activity. Bush met with 24 groups, appeared in 10 photo-ops, mostly with school children, and beginning with the nomination of Secretary Roderick Paige, used the appointment of educators to trumpet his reform proposal.

The classroom venue was a particular favorite of the public relations group in the White House. Prior to the enactment of his educational plan, the president visited 8 schools, and had 31 events in a total of 16 states and the District of Columbia. In fact, he was in a Florida second grade classroom when the terrorist attack on 9/11 occurred.

The "PR" campaign on the educational initiative, titled "Leave No Child Behind," was also designed to reinforce the president's compassionate image in contrast to the harder ideological edge which his tax cuts and defense build up suggested. Moreover, the educational campaign in which the White House placed the president with students, parents, and teachers helped to illustrate his down-to-earth quality, the human dimension.

Much of the education-oriented, "PR" activity occurred in the months of March and April 2001 and was timed to speed enactment of the legislation in the House. The Jeffords' defection undercut this effort in the Senate, providing incentives for Democrats to raise concerns about the bill, thereby stalling its progress. As attention turned to the sagging economy and to the events of 9/11, the educational initiative faded from the public spotlight and the president's schedule.

Defense.   The public campaign for the administration's defense initiatives was initially designed to raise the nation's consciousness about the need for a strong defense in the absence of a direct threat to U.S. national security. Elevating Bush's image as president with the ceremonial accoutrements of the Commander-in-Chief's role was a second goal of the offensive while educating the public and building support for a new military strategy for the twenty-first century, an anti-missile shield, and other new weapons systems that took advantage of America's advanced technology, was a third.

From the outset, Bush used his "bully pulpit" to call for these reforms and for increased federal funding for defense. He met with active duty and veteran groups, and issued memoranda to his Secretary of Defense.

Taxes.   In comparison to the media-oriented campaigns for the administration's educational and defense initiatives, the president's tax plan did not generate as much White House-directed publicity. Tax relief was not at the top of the public's agenda. Moreover, the magnitude of the cuts, the payoff for those in the highest income bracket, and the complexity of the legislation discouraged the White House from organizing as many public events, although the president did meet with 15 groups and staged 5 photo ops in 15 states, most of which were carried by Bush in 2000 and were represented by at least one moderate Democratic senator. Internal Republican unity in the House of Representatives combined with the Congressional Budget Office's prediction of a large budgetary surplus over the next decade ($5.6 trillion) reduced the need for an outside campaign to build public support for the tax plan.

Nonetheless, the interest groups were out in force on this issue and the administration dealt with them on a continuing basis. A Tax Relief Coalition consisting of the United States Chamber of Commerce, the National Association of Manufacturers, the National Association of Wholesalers and Distributors, and the National Federation of Independent Businesses banded together in support of the legislation. The coalition's cohesion hinged on the **absence** of special tax breaks for business. Were Congress to reopen the package, then each group would have had to pursue its own special interests. The administration lobbied hard to keep the tax relief measure intact. Opposing the president's plan was a coalition of liberal groups, labor unions, the NAACP, and the Sierra Club while a coalition of chemical, forestry, and paper industries along with the investment community lobbied for the inclusion of specific benefits for themselves (Nitschke, 2001, p. 470).

Although the administration was successful in maintaining its balancing act, getting the bill through the House and onto the Senate floor, the defection of several moderate Republicans, as noted earlier, forced the president to compromise. Periodic attention was focused on other issues such as on energy during and after the California blackouts. However, the administration in general soft-pedaled the public dimension of the energy issue to avoid further alienating the environmental community, already angered by the holds placed on Clinton's last-minute environmental orders and proclamations. After the failure of Enron, the refusal of the White House to provide the General Accounting Office with the identities of the people with whom Vice President Cheney consulted, and the senate opposition to drilling in Alaska's Arctic National Wildlife Refuge, the administration continued to steer clear of the energy issue. Social Security, Medicare, and immigration policy were downplayed as well. (See Table 6.7.)

Going Public After 9/11

The terrorist attack of 9/11 naturally turned the White House "PR" operation toward national and homeland security. The president was presented as a unifying figure, a crisis manager, and a Commander-in-Chief around whom the country could grieve, heal, coalesce, and rally. Approximately two-thirds of the president's public activities were devoted to these types of events for the remainder of his first two years.

Unlike the pre 9/11 efforts that placed Bush physically before supportive groups, the post 9/11 activities were funneled primarily through the press office. Public statements, press conferences, formal memoranda, presidential directives and findings, and actions were announced almost daily to show a concerned president hard at work. There were, of course, public appearances, but the principal image was a president in the White House with his advisers developing national policy, forming an international coalition, overseeing the war in Afghanistan, and staying on top of anti-terrorism matters. Tom Ridge, presidential adviser and later secretary of the new department, became the prime spokesperson. It was Ridge, not the president, who met with various groups of enforcement officials, first-responders, other emergency personnel, and concerned citizens. (See Table 6.7.)

Table 6.7   Policy-Oriented Presidential Public Relations Activity, Post 9/11–2002

	Formal Actions	Presidential Statements and Press Releases	Photo Ops	Radio Addresses	Remarks Before Groups	Nominations	Total
Education	3	7	8	0	8	1	27 (6%)
Defense	19	20	0	0	9	2	50 (12)
Environment	14	8	0	0	2	0	24 (6)
Energy	4	7	0	1	3	0	15 (4)
Health Care	0	4	3	2	0	2	11 (3)
Corporate Responsibility	2	15	0	0	0	0	17 (4)
National Security	29	100	28	5	3	0	165 (39)
Homeland Security	10	38	0	1	16	4	69 (16)
Economics and Budget	11	21	1	3	6	1	43 (10)
Medicare	0	3	0	0	0	0	3 (1)
Total	92 (22%)	223 (53)	40 (9)	12(3)	47 (11)	10 (2)	424 (100)

Source: Categorized and compiled by author from White House Archives.

With Bush enjoying strong bipartisan support for most of this period, high public approval ratings, and little opposition in Congress to his national security policy initiatives, there was little need to direct presidential public activities toward legislative outcomes. As the midterm elections approached, however, the president moved into his campaign mode and stressed national and homeland security. This emphasis had the additional benefit of diverting attention from economic and social issues less advantageous to Republican Party candidates. Bush combined daily public events with private fund-raiser evenings.

The strategy worked well. Republican victory in the midterm elections provided the impetus to enact the president's proposals for a Department of Homeland Security and an insurance indemnification program.

ASSESSING THE RESULTS

Credit-taking is a major political component of the legislative presidency. Presidents evaluate and are evaluated on the basis of their successes on the Hill. This evaluation constitutes a political balance sheet, used for the purpose of building and maintaining political capital, political approval, and a legislative reputation.

The Administration's Congressional Scorecard

Generally, the House and the Senate, when they were controlled by the Republicans, were supportive of presidential efforts as evidenced by the statements of administration policy. The Democratic takeover, following Jeffords' defection, threatened to undermine that support. Majority leader Daschle began to emphasize his party's agenda of minimum wage, health care, and prescription drugs while other Democrats raised serious questions about the president's new defense policy and spending, particularly the anti-missile defense shield. Partisan politics, however, were interrupted and muted by 9/11.

Congress supported most of the 9/11-related anti-terrorism and national security legislation. The issues that incurred the most partisan division were the creation of the Department of Homeland Security and the legislation to indemnify insurance companies against further terrorist attacks. Democratic opposition to the president's request to give the new department secretary additional flexibility on budget and personnel matters, however, faded after the midterm elections in which the Republicans won back control of the Senate. Both measures were enacted in the lame-duck session of the 107th Congress.

Although the Democratic-controlled Senate did enact legislative measures on energy, HMOs, and bankruptcy in forms which the administration strongly opposed, the principal hurdle Senate Democrats put in the way of the president's program was delay. The administration only objected to three Senate bills and two resolutions in the first session of the 107th Congress and four bills in the second. Objection was also made to two House-initiated bills and two House resolutions in the first session and two House resolutions in the second. In short, the administra-

Table 6.8   Administration Positions on Authorizing Legislation, 107th Congress

Position	Session I		Session III		
	H	S	H	S	Total
Strongly Support	11	3	20	1	35
Support	27	7	11	0	45
No Objection	2	0	1	0	3
No Position	0	0	1	1	2
Oppose	1	1	2	3	7
Strongly Oppose	3	3	2	1	9
Total	44	14	37	6	101

Source: Statements of Administration Policy, Office of Management and Budget

Table 6.9   Administration Positions on Appropriation Bills, 107th Congress

Position	Session I		Session II		
	H	S	H	S	Total
Strongly Support	2	0	1	1	4
Support	4	1	6	0	11
No Objection	2	0	0	0	2
No Position*	6	6	0	0	12
Oppose	0	0	0	1	1
Strongly Oppose	0	0	0	2	2
Total	14	7	7	4	32

Source: Statements of Administration Policy, Office of Management and Budget

*Includes legislation in which the administration takes no overall position but indicates its willingness to work with Congress on parts of the legislation in which it has concerns.

tion was quite supportive of the authorizing legislation reported out of committee to the floor. Tables 6.8 and 6.9 summarize the administration's response to this legislation in its official statements of policy.

THE PRESIDENT'S LEGISLATIVE RECORD

How well did Bush do with his legislative agenda? Was he a successful legislative president during his first two years in office? Did he amass political capital for the next two years?

A Dominant Public Image

There are a number of criteria that can be used to assess Bush's legislative presidency. On a personal level, he succeeded in toning down much of the strident, partisan rhetoric of the 1990s by befriending Democrats. He was Mr. Congeniality, using his "good guy" imagery that the White House so artfully reinforced. The negative adjectives used to describe his predecessors, (Reagan—"out of it," forgetful, unencumbered by detail; Bush I—wimpy, lacking vision, unable to communicate; Clinton—slick, manipulative, untrustworthy, inconsistent, overly partisan) did not seem to fit George W. Bush.

Moreover, as president, Bush succeeded in overcoming the negative stereotype by which the media and Democratic opposition portrayed him during the 2000 campaign, that he was cognitively challenged and communicatively impaired, a light weight in a heavy-weight job. Even before 9/11 and certainly after it, Bush had successfully established his leadership credentials, presented his own distinctive image as a skillful politician, an effective communicator, and a decent human being, at least in the eyes of the American people. There was no question who was president and who was vice president, another key objective of White House gurus Karen Hughes and Karl Rove.

Crisis Manager as Legislative Leader

A second criterion for evaluation turns on the president's legislative proposals and his achievements. Of the 9/11-generated legislation, the president got most of what he wanted although he had to accept the federalizing of the air security personnel and wait until the lame-duck session to get the new Department of Homeland Security with the personnel and budgetary flexibility that he desired and the insurance indemnification legislation. He also got Congress to repeal workplace ergonomic rules, which had been established in the Clinton administration, give him the money he requested to pay the debt which the United States owed the United Nations, extend the moratorium on Internet taxation, and implement the NAFTA protocol which allows Mexican trucks to use U.S. highways.

In the second session, the president received "fast-track" authority, an increase of $46 billion in the defense budget, a bill to establish federal standards for corporate accounting, legislation to stockpile vaccines and other medicines against biological and chemical terrorism, and finally, a resolution authorizing the use of force to disarm Iraq's weapons of mass destruction. Not bad.

A Mixed Domestic Record: The Triumph of Politics Over Ideology

Here the record is mixed. Legislation was enacted on the president's principal initiatives, tax relief, education reform, and military revitalization, but modifications were also made to Bush's tax and education proposals. The events of 9/11, and the bipartisan unity it produced, propelled the defense authorization and appropriation bills along the lines that the administration desired. Additionally, the White House succeeded, for the most part, in holding the line on domestic spending, the agricultural bill being the principal exception.

A number of administration priorities were not enacted, however. The House and Senate could not agree on a patient's Bill of Rights, a prescription drug plan for seniors, bankruptcy legislation, an energy bill, employee pension protections, broadband deregulation, faith-based community service, and a bill to outlaw human cloning. Moreover, Congress only enacted two appropriation bills for FY 2003, did not extend unemployment benefits beyond the end of the year, did not rewrite the export control law, and did not reauthorize the 1996 welfare legislation. In fairness to the administration, however, the 2002 election strategy and presidential campaign for a Republican Congress sublimated public and private lobbying efforts for many of these bills.

Finally, the administration was saddled with legislation it did not want but could not veto for political reasons: the Bipartisan Campaign Finance Reform Bill (McCain-Feingold), the $780 billion dollar farm bill, and an electoral reform bill that authorized $440 million for improved registration and vote tabulation procedures. Moreover, Congress created an independent commission to investigate the pre 9/11 intelligence and security failures, a commission that the administration had initially opposed. The judicial confirmation process also delayed and stymied appointments, particularly at the appellate level. For the first two years, the Senate confirmed 77 percent of Bush's judicial nominees.

A Quantitative Grade

A third type of evaluative criteria that is often employed by political scientists to assess presidential effectiveness in Congress are legislative support scores, the percentage of time members voted in agreement with the president. The problem with such scores is that they do not differentiate votes on the basis of presidential priorities. Whether the data set include just key votes, non-unanimous votes, multiple votes on a single issue, or all votes, the roll calls are counted equally as a measure of support.

Bush does well in such a quantitative evaluation. Table 6.10 lists the scores as calculated by the *Congressional Quarterly*. Only Eisenhower and Johnson scored higher than Bush in their first years and only Johnson in his second year. Bush benefited from strong Republican unity across issues; he also received considerable Democratic support in the Senate, approximately twice as much as he received from Democrats in the House. But since the House operates on the basis of majority rule, and the Republican majority remained unified, Democratic opposition in the House was, for the most part, immaterial.

Finally, the president's overall popularity may be an indicator of his legislative achievements and/or a contributor to those achievements (see Table 6.5). The problem with using overall popularity, however, is the spike that 9/11 produced and sustained throughout most of 2002. However, one of the reasons that the spike may have sustained itself as long as it did was the skillful projection of anti-terrorism and national security themes that obfuscated other issues. Even when asked about

Table 6.10   Presidential Support in Congress:
The First Two Years

Eisenhower	1953	89.0%
	1954	82.8
Kennedy	1961	81.0
	1962	85.4
Johnson	1964	88.0*
	1965	93.0
	1966	79.0
Nixon	**1969**	**74.0**
	1970	**77.0**
Ford	**1974**	**58.2***
	1975	**61.0**
	1976	**53.8**
Carter	1977	75.4
	1978	78.3
Reagan	**1981**	**82.4**
	1982	**72.4**
Bush	**1989**	**62.6**
	1990	**46.8**
Clinton	1993	86.4
	1994	86.4
G.W. Bush	**2001**	**87.0**
	2002	**87.8**

Source: Congressional Quarterly, "Presidential Support,"
December 14, 2002, p. 3275.

*Succession; abbreviated term; **Bold** indicates divided government.

whether they approved the president's performance on economic affairs, at a time when a majority assessed the economy as fair or poor, respondents seemed to take Bush's post 9/11 performance into account in their assessments. In short, the events of 9/11 introduced an exogenous element that seemed to affect positively almost everything the president did. For this reason, the next two years may produce a more accurate test of Bush's legislative skills and domestic legislative leadership.

CONCLUSION

The legislative process is always a challenge for a new president. That challenge is conditioned by the partisan political environment, persistent institutional rivalries, and the public and congressional expectations set by the campaign. Some of these factors are relatively stable, changing slowing over time. Others are more variable, shifting with the political winds that help bring a new president to office. Both represent the challenges which a president must overcome.

The Conventional Wisdom Affirmed

President Bush succeeded in getting his items on to the congressional agenda. Unified government contributed to his initial legislative success; divided government threatened it until 9/11 expanded presidential influence as members of Congress and the general public rallied round the flag. Bush used, and some would say, extended the crisis for his political benefit. That benefit subsequently worked to his legislative advantage in the lame-duck session of the 107th Congress. The result was a pretty good legislative record.

All of this confirms the conventional wisdom about the president and legislative agendas, that early agendas emanate from the campaign (Conley), that presidents are successful in imposing them on Congress (Edwards and Barrett, 2000), that achievement in a form closest to the president's proposals is more likely to occur in a unified government, in part because contemporary Congresses have become more partisan (Sinclair, 2000), that presidents regularly go public to mobilize external support and direct it to Congress (Kernell, 1997), but must also play an inside game by stroking members, granting favors, providing information, and sometimes also political benefits or threats of sanctions (Andres and Griffin, 2002), and that during a crisis, Congress tends to rally round the president (Mueller, 1973).

The Challenges Ahead

The challenges for the legislative presidency remain. Had it not been for 9/11, Bush would have faced them earlier in his term. These challenges stem from partisan parity and polarity in Congress, reflected in the composition and behavior of its members; the increasing policy differences between the parties, reinforced by ideology; and the strengthening of the congressional leadership, particularly in the House.

This congressional environment creates both difficulties and opportunities for the legislative presidency, both of which are magnified by divided or unified government.

The difficulties, which are considerable when the institutional separation is reinforced by partisanship, have created incentives for presidents, increasingly over the course of their presidencies, to short-circuit or quicken Congress' decision-making by couching policy initiatives within the context of crises to pressure Congress to forego its deliberative processes and follow the president's lead. Moreover, when presidents anticipate opposition or delay, they also are tempted to circumvent Congress entirely by exercising their unilateral executive powers. Either presidential action undercuts the give and take of the legislative process and contributes to an even more hostile political environment for the president down the road.

On the other hand, unified government creates incentives for presidents to work through Congress and through its strengthened party leadership. The president becomes a prime minister with a partisan majority as long as Senate rules and procedures do not impose an unattainable supermajority vote. So long as the ideological purity of the congressional majority does not make politically unreasonable policy demands on the president, so long as personal leadership issues on the Hill do not interfere with presidential direction and credit-taking, so long as congressional constituency influence does not undercut the administration's national policy objectives, unified government contributes to a potentially strong legislative presidency.

Still, much depends on the ability of presidents and their advisers to send clear signals to the Hill, to anticipate accurately the attitudes and behavior of members of Congress, to touch all the necessary bases as they pursue their inside and outside campaigns, all the while showing proper deference to Congress's legitimate, policy-making role.

REFERENCES

Allen, Mike. "Bush May Veto Excess Spending, Official Says," *Washington Post*, March 4, 2001, A04.

Allred, Victoria. "Versatility with the Veto," *Congressional Quarterly*, January 20, 2001: 175–177.

Andres, Gary and Patrick J. Griffin, "Successful Influence: Managing Legislative Affairs in the Twenty-first Century," in James A. Thurber, ed. *Rivals for Power*, 2nd ed. Lanham, MD: Rowman and Littlefield, 2002: 141–162.

Barshay, Jill. "A Year of Power Struggles and Common Purpose," *Congressional Quarterly*, December 22, 2001: 3018–3021.

_____. "The Duel of Bush and Daschle: Men of Genteel Steel," *Congressional Quarterly*, January 26, 2002: 216–219.

Birnbaum, Jeffrey. "Bush's Bulldog Collars Congress," *Fortune*, August 20, 2001. www.fortune.com/fortune/print/0,15935,367334,00

Carney, James. *Time*, online edition. www.time.com/time/nation/article/0,8599,166000,00

Conley, Patricia Heidotting. *Presidential Mandates*. Chicago: University of Chicago Press, 2001.

Edwards, George C. III. *At The Margins*. New Haven, CT: Yale University Press, 1989.

Edwards, George C. III. and Andrew Barrett, "Presidential Agenda Setting in Congress," in Jon R. Bond and Richard Fleisher, *Polarized Politics*, Washington, DC: *Congressional Quarterly*, 2000, 109–133.

Fleischer, Ari, "Excerpts from Press Briefing," July 29, 2002.

Fram, Alan. "Farm Aid Dispute Hinders $396 B Deal," Associated Press, February 11, 2003.

Goldstein, Amy and Dana Milbank. "Hill GOP, Bush Split on Tax Cuts, Medicare," *Washington Post*, February 14, 2003, A01.

Groeling, Tim and Samuel Kernell, "Congress, the President, and Party Competition via Network News," in Bond and Fleisher, *Polarized Politics*, 73–95.

Jones, Charles O. *Passages to the Presidency*. Washington, DC: Brookings Institution, 1998.

Kernell, Samuel. *Going Public*. 3rd ed., Washington DC: *Congressional Quarterly*, 1997.

Lizza, Ryan. "White House Watch: Double Play," *New Republic*, May 14, 2001. www.tnr.com/051401/lizza051401.

McQueen, Anjetta. "States, Schools Looking Ahead to How Overhaul Will Work," *Congressional Quarterly*, December 15, 2001: 2972–2974.

Morgan, Dan. "Veto Threat Aimed at Spending Bill," *Washington Post*, February 6, 2003, A06.

Mueller, John. *War, Presidents, and Public Opinion*. New York: John Wiley, 1973.

Nather, David. "Compromises on ESEA Bills May Imperil Republican Strategy," *Congressional Quarterly*, May 5, 2001: 1009–1011.

_____. "Education Bill Nears Final Hurdle With 'Deal Breakers' Swept Aside," *Congressional Quarterly*, June 16, 2001: 1431–1433.

_____. "Education Bill Passes in House with Strong Bipartisan Support," *Congressional Quarterly*, May 26, 2001: 1256–1257.

_____. "Education Bill Picks Up Pace As Conferees Reach Accord on Several Thorny Issues," *Congressional Quarterly*, November 3, 2001: 2609.

Nitschke, Lori. "Coalitions Make a Comeback," *Congressional Quarterly*, March 3, 2001: 4760–4764.

Ota, Alan K. "Calio's Assertive Style Moves Legislation, But Hill Republicans Have Paid a Price," *Congressional Quarterly*, December 14, 2002: 3251–3254.

Parks, Daniel J. "Bush's Pre-Emptive Spending Challenge Sets Up Showdown with Appropriators," *Congressional Quarterly*, April 20, 2002: 1019–1021.

_____. "Bush Starts to Deal on Budget, Only Hardening Resolve of Some," *Congressional Quarterly*, April 28, 2001: 903–908.

_____. "Latest Supplemental Request Hits a Freer-Spending Hill," *Congressional Quarterly*, March 30, 2002: 866–867.

_____. "Veto Threat May Bounce Office Supplemental's Momentum," *Congressional Quarterly*, June 8, 2002: 1513–1515.

_____. "White House Shows Some Muscle in Supplemental Spending Clash," *Congressional Quarterly*, December 8, 2001: 2893–2895.

Sinclair, Barbara, "Hostile Partners: the President, Congress and Lawmaking in the Partisan 1990s," In Bond and Fleisher, *Polarized Politics*, 134–153.

Taylor, Andrew. "After First Hundred Days, Bush Emerges as Pragmatic Warrior," *Congressional Quarterly*, April 28, 2001: 907–908.

CHAPTER

7

Challenging (and Acting for) the President:

Congressional Leadership in an Era of Partisan Polarization[1]

◆◆◆

John E. Owens
The University of Westminster

Presidents need votes from Congress "all the time and all kinds of votes. . . . You need votes to enable you to build up a record, to win reelection, to win—who knows? a place in history. Indeed, come to think of it, you need votes in Congress to enable the government to function at all. . . . The only kind of votes that you as president do not need, impeachment apart, are votes to sustain you in office."[2]

Over the last 25 or so years, the task of garnering congressional votes—especially votes from the opposition party—has become much more difficult. As the ideological and policy preferences of the respective parties' activists and electoral coalitions increasingly diverged and became more homogeneous, Congress has acquired the most ideologically homogenized and most polarized parties since the early twentieth century.[3] In the process, House and Senate majorities have become much closer, split-party government has become the prevalent pattern of partisan control, and Congress' political center of gravity has shifted to the right.

POLARIZED POLITICS

Figure 7.1 shows histograms indicating the extent of the changes: whereas in the 91st Congress (1969–70), both parties in the House (and Senate) were arrayed towards the liberal/moderate end of a liberal-conservative dimension and displayed

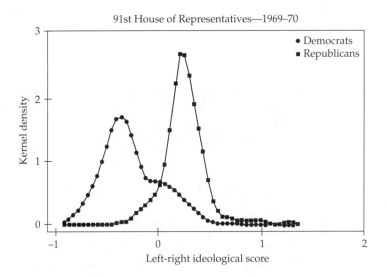

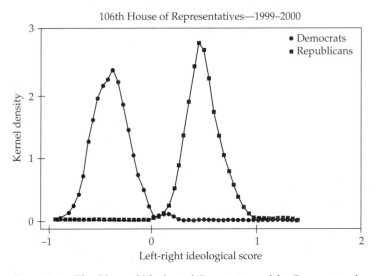

Figure 7.1 The Changed Ideological Composition of the Congressional Parties, 1969–2000.

Source: The horizontal axes show first dimension DW-NOMINATE ideological scores available from Keith Poole's website at http://voteview.uh.edu. The left-hand scales indicate frequencies of members for each score.

I am grateful to Sarah Binder for this figure.

substantial overlapping between Democratic centrists and conservatives, by the 106th Congress (1999–2000) the ideological center of gravity had shifted significantly to the right, and the two parties occupied almost no common ground as congressional Democrats clustered towards the liberal end, Republicans occupied the conservative pole, and barely a handful of members populated a political no man's land that formed in the center.[4] Table 7.1 shows the effects of increased partisan competitiveness and polarization on majority parties' pluralities and prevalent split-party government.

The most visible symptoms of these developments are the almost continuous partisan spats within the Congress and between the Congress and the president—culminating in congressional attempts to impeach President Clinton, the highly disputed 2000 presidential election, and frequent congressional incivility interrupted only temporarily by the tragedy of September 11.[5] Less obvious but crucially important in this highly polarized context are the implications for congressional party leaders' roles and strategies, as well as the skills with which they exercise leadership. For, it is the formal party leaders who assert substantive and procedural roles for the parties inside Congress, and who are responsible for negotiating and bargaining with the president, and other contexts.

CONGRESSIONAL LEADERSHIP

Given the president's need for legislative support and prevailing conditions of American style party government—or conditional party government[6]—inside Congress, the roles and strategies that congressional party leaders develop, and the skills with which they lead their parties, potentially represent crucial elements in contemporary relations between the president and Congress.[7] Under contemporary conditions of party government, rank and file copartisans insist on active and strong party leadership that entails effectively coordinating copartisans' collective priorities and successfully delivering collective legislative products that promote their party's national reputation, especially in those policy areas deemed salient to winning the next election. These priorities and products may not reflect the preferences or policies of the president, even when the same party as the president's controls a chamber. If, as has more often than not been the case since 1968, the party of the House speaker or Senate majority leader does not also control the presidency, the leader becomes the *de facto* leader of the opposition competing with the president in trying to structure the strategic environment to advance their party's national reputation.[8] If the same party also controls the other chamber, then, the role is shared with the other chamber's leader. If the party of the House speaker or majority leader also controls the presidency, we expect an accommodative strategy.

Whether acting as opposition leader or accommodative partner, congressional leaders must contend simultaneously with several different institutional and other contexts comprising the leader's strategic context. Besides the president, they include the attentive public, the other party in the chamber, the other chamber—and, importantly, their chamber copartisans whose support they depend on for survival. These contexts will vary according to the specific legislative situation that he/she faces at any particular moment in legislative time.[9]

Table 7.1   Split-Party Control of the Congress and the Presidency, 1990–2003

	House		Senate			
	Majority Party	Majority Party Plurality	Majority Party	Majority Party Plurality	Presidency	Pattern of Control
102nd (1991–92)	Democratic	100	Democratic	12	Republican	Split
103rd (1993–94)	Democratic	82	Democratic	14	Democratic	Unified Democratic
104th (1995–96)	Republican	26	Republican	6	Democratic	Split
105th (1997–98)	Republican	19	Republican	10	Democratic	Split
106th (1999–2000)	Republican	21	Republican	10	Democratic	Split
107th (2001–2002)	Republican	9	Rep/Dem	0/2	Republican	Unified Republican/Split
108th (2003–2004)	Republican	24	Republican	2	Republican	Unified Republican

The extent to which congressional leaders will act for or challenge the president will depend on whether the party also controls the other chamber and/or the presidency, the president's public reputation and political skills exhibited on the particular issue, the results of the most recent elections, the size of the party's majority, the institutional equilibrium between competing power centers within the leader's chamber, the ideological and stylistic homogeneity of the party, how he/she achieved the leadership of the majority party, the leader's current reputation within the chamber, the party's public reputation and the current electoral context, and the salience of the specific issue. Inherently, in such fluid, unstable, environments, demands emanating from different contexts compete with one another and therefore suggest conflicting responses from leaders. Thus, a leader's party may push him/her in one particular direction—to act for or to challenge the president—but chamber copartisans, public opinion and/or the leader's personal goals might suggest another.

Contrary to contextualist interpretations,[10] congressional leadership is not predetermined: leaders have considerable discretion and scope.[11] Whether or not a Speaker or Senate majority leader decides on and then deploys a successful strategy depends very much on his/her individual skills, as well as the contextual factors themselves. Depending on effective selection and deployment of skills, as well as the specific configuration of the strategic environment that a leader faces on a specific legislative issue at a particular moment in time, different leaders will pursue different leadership styles and different governing strategies that reflect their goals and what they perceive can reasonably be accomplished.

By leadership skills, I mean the necessarily subjective perceptions and actions that individual leaders apply to inherently slippery strategic contexts (comprising opportunities, constraints, and information), with the assistance of their leadership teams, as part of the processes of defining policy issues in the public arena, shaping legislative agendas, structuring congressional decisions, persuading colleagues, and generally constructing legislative and political strategies designed to construct winning coalitions and enact the party's collective policy goals. Leaders' skills are necessarily individual because politicians are "goal seeking [as well as] . . . situation-interpreting individuals."[12] Different leaders have different individual strengths and weaknesses. The skills that congressional leaders seek to exercise include discernment of favorable and unfavorable situations/opportunities for exercising leadership; articulation and setting of clear legislative priorities; mobilizing and conciliatory skills employed with respect to the leader's chamber party and the attentive public; judicious timing of policy initiatives and actions; policy and political expertise; parliamentary skills; bargaining and conciliatory skills employed with respect to the president and the chamber minority; and overall understanding and evaluation of the strategic context faced by the leader and his/her chamber party.

In this chapter, I employ a "skills in context" approach[13] to examine the leadership styles and strategies of House Speaker Dennis Hastert (R.IL) and Senate Majority Leaders Trent Lott (R.MS) and Bill Frist (R.TN) in response to policy initiatives made by Presidents Clinton and Bush between 1999 and early 2003. Contemporary polarized politics, of course, provides the broader context of these leaders' styles and strategies, and their interactions with the president. I explore the leaderships of Hastert, Lott and Frist in respect of major legislation proposed by the Clinton and Bush presidencies between 1999 and 2003. The two central questions that concern this investigation are: how did these congressional party leaders use their skills and how effective were the strategies that they deployed both to challenge and act for the president? The clear implication of my approach is that the leadership exercised by these individuals in different situations was determined not only by context but also by their individual styles, skills and strategies.

LEADING THE HOUSE AND SUCCESSFULLY CHALLENGING THE PRESIDENT: THE GINGRICH PRECEDENT AND LEGACY

Before discussing Hastert, Lott, and Frist, it is instructive to make a few prefatory comments about Newt Gingrich, who at least in the early part of his speakership epitomized how a particularly activist congressional leader could successfully challenge and effectively circumscribe a president's scope of action two years into his term of office.

Most legislative leaders pursue a transactional rather than a transformational style. At the beginning of his speakership in 1995, Gingrich was a highly unusual transformational leader in the mold of nineteenth century speakers Clay, Stevenson, Polk and Reed.[14] Transforming leadership is more complex and more potent than transactional leadership. The transforming leader "recognizes and exploits an existing need or demand of a potential follower. But beyond that, the transforming leader looks for potential motives in followers, seeks to satisfy higher needs, and engages the full person of the follower."[15] As House Speaker, Gingrich was certainly the beneficiary of favorable contextual factors—including a deep reservoir of support and a strong team spirit within his party—but he was no passive agent either in the creation or exploitation of those conditions. He had the audacious ambition, imagination and leadership skills to seize the opportunities that the strategic environment presented. Disavowing Madisonian prescriptions and taking full advantage of the House's majoritarian rules, he declared himself a kind of prime minister in a parliamentary system and in 1995 effectively promoted his party's policy agenda using the iconic value of the *Contract With America* to galvanize his own party, deliver significant policy results and in the process marginalize President Clinton.[16]

Gingrich's actions in 1995 demonstrate how a congressional leader can for a time dominate the Washington environment given a favorable set of circumstances. It is far from clear that led by someone else—for example, Gingrich's predecessor, or his successor—congressional Republicans would have achieved the same policy decisions that they did with a president of the other party. Of course, it is important to add that following the budget *débâcle* of 1995–96, Gingrich had further missteps and President Clinton regularly bested the Republican leader and his party in a number of highly partisan confrontations.[17]

DENNIS HASTERT: PARTISAN LEADERSHIP UNDER SPLIT-PARTY AND UNIFIED GOVERNMENT

The strategic environment that faced Gingrich's ultimate successor as House speaker in 1999 was much less propitious than that which faced Gingrich in late 1994 and early 1995. Moreover, Dennis Hastert (R.IL) has proved to be no Newt Gingrich.

Under contemporary conditions of split-party government and polarized partisan politics, House speakers of a different party from the president can more effectively act as leaders of the opposition than their Senate counterparts—because House rules (control of the Rules Committee, the committee assignment process, floor agenda-setting powers, and so forth) facilitate majoritarian legislative strategies. House leaders from a different party from the president have every incentive to challenge a president of the opposing party by pursuing legislative strategies directed towards passing highly partisan measures and diluting bipartisan ones—in the hope that they may enhance their party's bargaining power in inter-branch and inter-cameral negotiations with a Senate more institutionally inclined towards bipartisanship, regardless of whether that chamber is controlled by the president's party or the same party as the House.

In the context of split-party government during the last two years of the Clinton presidency, then, Hastert pursued predominantly partisan legislative strategies on a series of major issues—the budget, campaign finance, managed care reform, and important aspects of foreign policy—in efforts to build a successful legislative record for his party and maintain or increase his party's majority in the House.

Neither the context in which Hastert became speaker in 1999 nor the prevailing conditions during the last years of the Clinton presidency were conducive to the kind of transforming leadership that Gingrich had demonstrated earlier. Although Clinton was damaged by the Lewinsky scandal, confounding party leaders' predictions and much historical experience, House Republicans had lost seats in the 1998 mid-term elections and subsequently resorted to regicide, deposing Gingrich in a successful *coup*. Instead of reaping the political dividends from Clinton's misdeeds, the booming economy, the first federal budget surplus for 30 years, and declining crime and welfare rolls, polls showed that the public regarded House Republicans' handling of the impeachment proceedings as blatantly partisan, sordid in parts, and illegitimate. Out of this mired context emerged Hastert, the congenial dealmaker, whose tactical skills and affable style was thought by his copartisans to suit better the party's contemporary needs than those of his more abrasive seniors, Majority Leader Dick Armey (R.TX) and Whip Tom DeLay (D.TX). Unlike the early Gingrich, the new leader would not try to change the world; rather he would avoid the hubris of a Gingrich and use his considerable more tactical and transactional skills and persistence to work with it and in the process deliver for Republicans long-sought tax cuts and more effective resistance to Clinton's efforts to spend more on popular domestic programs.

True to his style, in the early days of the 106th Congress (1999–2000) Hastert determined to construct the House Republican agenda that had been conspicuously absent from his party's 1998 election campaign. Eschewing Gingrich's revolutionary rhetoric and grand vision, he compiled an agenda that included bills relating to politically salient issues like social security and additional education spending that Clinton and other Democrats had emphasized in the recent elections, as well as familiar Republican issues such as tax reductions and missile defense.

As his predecessor found after 1995, Hastert quickly discovered that his scope for challenging the Democratic president was heavily circumscribed by his party's wafer-thin majority, particularly when issues came to the House floor that were very important to House Republicans and/or the attentive public. If, in his attempts to build a record for his party by working with the White House, he made concessions to the two dozen or so Republican centrists under pressure from their own reelection constituencies, he risked handing victories to the Democrats and the president and invoking the ire of Republican hard-liners—often led by Armey and/or DeLay, who typically objected to deals that compromised their conservative principles. Conversely, if Hastert bowed to the hard-liners, he risked committing House Republicans to strategies that handed new political victories to Clinton and made his party unpopular. Faced with these dilemmas, the amiable Hastert frequently adopted the line of least resistance: he sat on his hands or, like Gingrich, sided with the hard-liners with the result that Clinton was challenged but nevertheless got most of what he wanted. This was pretty much the story of the contest between House Republicans and Clinton over the FY 1999 budget.

Challenging the President: Partisan Politics and the FY 2000 Budget

Policy differences between the Democratic president and the Republican Congress were sharp, with Clinton and his congressional allies demanding higher spending in the context of an ever-growing budget surplus, and Republicans insisting on large tax cuts. As Republican centrists (and Democrats) demanded more spending from the growing surplus and conservative hard-liners insisted on tax cuts, Hastert chose not to lead from the front. Instead, he allowed committee chairs to sort out differences while appealing for party unity and agreeing to delay harsh decisions for the inevitably difficult appropriations process. The upshot was that in order to maintain House Republican unity Hastert ushered through a budget resolution that included substantial tax cuts over 10 years, increases in defense and education spending, maintained discretionary spending within existing caps, protected the Social Security Trust Fund but which, according to *Congressional Quarterly*, was not "realistic."[18] Predictably, during consideration of the 13 appropriation bills, Republican centrists and conservative hard-liners took advantage of their party's tiny majority to approve new spending above the budget caps. Hastert was accused of providing rudderless leadership and he and his party were left heavily exposed to another budgetary defeat at the hands of the president.[19]

In August 1999, Clinton threatened to veto the tax part of the budget. Hastert responded with a major publicity campaign that flopped and, ultimately, for the fourth time in five years, Clinton successfully outmaneuvered a Republican Speaker and his party in a budget confrontation. When Clinton vetoed the bill, Hastert did not even attempt to override it, and Republicans were forced into accepting an end-of-session reconciliation bill that gave the president most of the spending he wanted, deleted most of the conservatives' legislative riders, excluded Republicans' tax cuts and severely limited the prospects for tax cuts the following year.

Challenging and Acting With the President on Foreign Policy: Kosovo

On a number of other major policy issues that emerged during the last two years of the Clinton administration, Hastert moved to meet the president part way only to find his scope of action heavily circumscribed by conservatives in his Conference. In the Kosovo crisis of 1999, on his first important test on a major foreign policy issue, Hastert found himself pulled in different directions by the administration and different sections of his party, with the consequence that he and his party sent confusing signals to the president and the public and appeared divided and irresponsible. As the international crisis deepened in March 1999, DeLay initiated a party campaign to pin blame for U.S. involvement in peacekeeping on Clinton and to pre-empt the president's potential deployment of U.S. troops to Kosovo. As domestic and international pressure for intervention grew, Hastert was forced into conceding a floor vote to invoke Congress' constitutional prerogative to decide on whether monies should be authorized and appropriated. Two months later, as the conflict escalated and the president proposed using air combat and peace operations, Hastert stood by as DeLay, Armey, and Conference chair J.C. Watts (R.OK) publicly voiced their hostility to the president's action and DeLay mobilized the party's whip operation on a defense authorization bill to encourage party colleagues to voice their opposition on a series of floor votes.

When, however, Hastert was forced into allowing a floor amendment supported by most House Republicans, which would have prohibited the president from deploying U.S. ground troops to Kosovo, the Republican speaker responded to direct appeals from Clinton and Secretary of State Madeleine Albright and joined a bipartisan coalition to provide the Democratic president with some support. Then, when the crisis deepened further, Hastert worked with committee leaders to block party efforts to invoke the War Powers Resolution and to provide new funding for military operations against Serbia. Ultimately, with NATO aircraft bombing Serbia, efforts to block floor votes to trigger the War Powers Resolution were unsuccessful. Placed in the awkward position of supporting of his party or a Democratic president on what was a major aspect of U.S. foreign policy, Hastert supported the air war against Serbia, despite the opposition of most of his party, but then joined with most of his copartisans to oppose declaring war against Serbia and authorizing funding for U.S. ground troops, thereby supporting the efforts of most House Republicans to maximize embarrassment to Clinton. Inevitably, Hastert was left publicly defending a party that looked irresponsible and excessively partisan. Incapable of juggling the demands of the president and his own congressional party, he was again accused of providing weak and ineffective leadership.[20]

Challenging and Acting With the President: Gun Control and Managed Care

On two highly salient domestic issues—gun control after the 1999 Colorado school shooting and managed health care reform—Hastert found himself in a similar dilemma: on the one hand pressured by his copartisans to resist President Clinton's policy initiatives and on the other directed by his own instinct and popular pressure to meet the president part way. In response to the shootings in April 1999, President Clinton announced new gun control proposals. With an eye directed towards the 2000 elections, Hastert moved swiftly to address public concern and protect his party against charges of complacency. In what *Congressional Quarterly* called "one of the most remarkable political adjustments of recent congressional vintage,"[21] he announced publicly that he would seek new tighter controls, which historically had been blocked by congressional Republicans and their allies, the National Rifle Association. The Speaker then spent weeks negotiating a package of control proposals that shrewdly incorporated White House and Senate proposals, accommodated party constituencies, and added "poison pill" provisions anathema to many House Democrats. When Hastert took the package to the House floor, however, Armey and DeLay publicly refused to support his proposals.

As opinion polls showed continued strong support for Clinton's proposals, the president continued to press Hastert and the Senate for new controls. The speaker responded by cleverly allowing floor consideration of a "killer" floor amendment offered by senior Democrat John Dingell (D.MI) and purposefully choreographed a series of floor votes that allowed House Republicans to finesse competing constituencies. Although he voted for the watered-down bill, Hastert himself repeatedly supported moves to weaken new controls and the measure was ultimately defeated by a bipartisan coalition led by DeLay and supported by most Democrats who regarded it as too weak. *Washington Post* columnist Mary McGrory observed: "The hapless Hastert has an instinct for the right thing, but it is constantly stamped out by his fractious forces."[22]

Hastert and his party were placed in a similar position, with similar results, after President Clinton and the Democrats placed at the top of their agenda major new legislation to expand protections for the 161 million Americans enrolled in private managed health care insurance plans, which they had emphasized in the 1998 elections. Clinton had advocated enactment of a "patients' bill of rights" in his State of the Union address and again in March 1999 in a joint news conference with congressional Democrats. Despite considerable reservations, even downright opposition to the proposals from his party, Hastert declared a strong personal stake in the issue and was persuaded of the issue's political significance to his party (and the Democrats). As over gun control, he opted to negotiate a bill that would afford House Republicans political cover and enjoy party support. As intra-party negotiations dragged on, however, Hastert found himself outmaneuvered by strengthening support for a bipartisan bill offered by Congressmen Charlie Norwood (R. GA) and Dingell. Hastily, the Speaker appointed a party task force to develop a Republican alternative, which he reluctantly endorsed. When the legislation reached the House floor, however, almost 30 Republicans ignored their leader's pleas for unity and refused to support the leadership-backed bill, opting instead for the Norwood-Dingell bill. As the 2000 elections approached, Hastert listed agreement on the legislation as one of his top priorities but his own and his party's opposition to key proposals in it were sufficient to ensure that the legislation died in the House-Senate conference.

These case studies of Hastert's leadership point to some important qualifications in how we should expect House majority leaders to behave under contemporary conditions of split-party government and highly polarized congressional parties. Under such conditions and when "domestic" or "foreign" issues are very important to the majority party, we expect House majority leaders—at the behest of the majority in their party conference/caucus and party constituencies—to use the chamber's procedural tools and partisan legislative organization to pursue partisan strategies both to block legislation sought by the president and his/her partisan allies in Congress and to win chamber approval for their own party priorities. We also expect majority leaders to have strong incentives both to pass highly partisan measures and revise bipartisan measures in their chamber to reflect majority party preferences—both to enhance their party's bargaining positions *vis-à-vis* the more institutionally bipartisan Senate and to strengthen their hand in inter-chamber and inter branch negotiations. These dynamics explain well Hastert's actions on the FY 2000 budget and appropriations bills: notwithstanding the outcome of final congressional-presidential negotiations, highly polarized partisan issues usually fare well in the House. But, the other case studies—on Kosovo, gun control, and managed health care—also demonstrate the importance in the behavior of House majority parties and the conduct of congressional-presidential negotiations of the imagination, discretion, and skill exercised by a House leader. We see these factors at work both in Hastert discerning the need to placate public opinion and provide political cover for his party on highly salient policy issues promoted by the president's party, and in his pursuing compromise legislative strategies with a president of the opposing party.

Let us turn now to Hastert's leadership in the changed context of party control following George W. Bush's inauguration in the White House, and the subsequent shift in partisan control of the Senate following the defection of Senator James Jeffords (R.VT) in June 2001.

Acting for the President on a Party Priority: Tax Cuts

Notwithstanding the new president's non-existent coat tails and the tightness of the presidential election result, once he was inaugurated, Bush became his party's *de facto* legislative leader. Henceforth, House majority leaders would reasonably expect to receive presidential support for their agenda items and policy prescriptions and *vice versa.* Predictably, Bush made the party's long-sought income tax cuts the centerpiece of his legislative agenda—although his tones evoked a prime ministerial statement rather than the beginning of a negotiating process with the Congress. In his February 2001 announcement, the new president dismissed the clamor of party conservatives for deeper cuts and the concerns of centrists about the deteriorating budget and insisted that the Congress accept precisely the $1.6 trillion in cuts he recommended. "I want the members of Congress and the American people to hear loud and clear," he declared. "This is the right-size plan. It is the right approach, and I'm going to defend it mightily."

Hastert swiftly took up the president's initiative as opposition to the enormous size of the cuts was growing in the Senate. Opting for a highly partisan "take no prisoners" strategy while the president campaigned for his proposals in the country, he sought House approval for the measure before Congress passed a budget resolution. In a highly partisan floor debate in which Hastert emphasized the imminent danger of recession if the package was not agreed swiftly, and rejoicing in the fact that it was the first time since 1953 that his party had had the opportunity to enact a major bill requested by a Republican president, the president's program was rammed through the House with unanimous support of Republicans and barely a handful of Democrats. Within weeks, further tax cutting bills were promised and subsequently approved on partisan votes.

In June 2001, Hastert's strategic situation changed overnight when Jeffords defected and control of the Senate shifted to the Democrats. Henceforth, Hastert and his partisan colleagues in the House would become the president's principal legislative partner counterbalancing the influence of the newly Democratic Senate even though his party's majority was just nine. In this new context, the importance of a group of about two dozen House Republican centrists—successfully kept in line over tax cuts—would be significantly enhanced.

Acting for the President on a Presidential Priority: The "Faith" Initiative

In February 2001, Bush had proposed the administration's signature "faith-based" social services legislation—a set of assistance and tax proposals designed to provide religious charities with help in providing after-school activities, pre-release prisoner counseling, and mentoring programs for the children of prisoners, and to which the president declared himself personally committed. While even the 50-50 Senate proved much more wary about the proposals, Hastert pursued an essentially partisan strategy in the House that ignored his newly degraded strategic situation. In July 2001, the original legislation was significantly weakened in committee at the request of the White House, as fears of breaching the Constitution's church-state separation remained strong and the budget situation continued to deteriorate. A new controversy then erupted after a *Washington Post* article suggested that the administration would issue a regulation exempting religious groups from state and local anti-discrimination laws. As pressure from the president to pass the legislation increased, Republican leaders determined on swift partisan action: the Rules Committee refused an anti-discrimination amendment sponsored by Deputy Whip Mark Foley (R.FL). Foley and other centrists then organized a revolt that forced the Speaker first to postpone floor consideration and then to use all his powers to persuade the dissenters to accept a compromise that effectively emasculated the Administration's original proposal, which was then approved on a party-line vote.

Acting With the President on a Minority Party Issue: Managed Health Care Reform Revisited

The bruising experience of the "faith" initiative was soon followed by another over managed care. Following the shift in party control, a bipartisan coalition in the Senate won passage of a patients' rights bill while in the House a bill sponsored by Dingell, Norwood and Greg Ganske (R.IA) threatened Hastert and the president with loss of control of the House agenda. Bush threatened to veto both the Senate and Dingell-Norwood-Ganske bills, both of which enjoyed considerable bipartisan support in the House, and worked with Congressmen Ernie Fletcher (R.KY) and Collin Peterson (D.FL) to develop a new bipartisan alternative, which was accepted by most House Republicans. However, an intense effort to persuade Republican centrists to rally to the Fletcher-Peterson bill failed as support for the Ganske-Norwood-Dingell bill held. The president again threatened to veto the Ganske-Norwood-Dingell bill and in another embarrassing setback Hastert was forced to postpone a floor vote. However, following the White House's lead again, the Speaker resisted pressures from DeLay and other hard-liners to punish the centrists, and opted instead to rely on Norwood to broker a deal with the White House that ultimately succeeded in peeling off centrist support for the stronger Ganske-Norwood-Dingell bill.

Fearful of losing the rule on the bill, Hastert persuaded his leadership colleagues of the impossibility of forcing through the Fletcher bill and persuaded the Rules Committee to design a rule in which Ganske-Norwood-Dingell would form the basis for floor consideration but only Republican-sponsored amendments, including the Norwood-Bush compromise, would be permitted. In this structured context, Norwood-Bush was approved with most Republicans toeing the party line. In a series of skilful strokes, then, Bush and Hastert were able to reshape an issue that Democrats had exploited for years into legislation that would likely be enacted and for which their president and party could claim credit. In contrast to 1999, when partisan imperatives determined resistance to a Democratic president's initiatives and the bipartisan Dingell-Norwood bill, in 2001 Hastert quickly fell in behind his party's president once the White House had decided that they had to intervene. In the same spirit of party unity, once the bill passed the House, Hastert swiftly announced Norwood's appointment to a House-Senate conference committee whereas in 1999 the same speaker had denied him an assignment.

These case studies nicely illustrate the complexity of a House speaker's relations with two presidents in a variety of different strategic contexts over a relatively short space of time. A key variable in this relationship was, of course, the symmetry of partisan control—a contextual factor. But the complexity of the relationships goes well beyond partisan control of different institutions. It also includes the actions and the skills of leaders. Given the constraints imposed by copartisans in his own chamber, it seems unlikely that Armey, DeLay or another House leader would have avoided some of the losing battles with Clinton. Indeed, the number may have been greater. After George Bush's inauguration, Hastert came into his own as his transactional leadership style and substantial tactical, management, and consultative skills proved invaluable to his party's president. There were failures—most notably the "faith" initiative—but there were inherent intractable problems of substance involved in this issue. But there were also successes, notably tax cuts and managed care, where particularly in the latter case, Hastert—and the president—accommodated well to the new strategic context then shaped by Democratic control of the Senate; and, as a consequence, both were able to declare victory when defeat looked likely.

LEADING THE SENATE, TRANSACTING WITH THE PRESIDENT

Leading the Senate too has been affected by the highly polarized contemporary context of congressional politics—witnessed notably in senators' increasing recourse to filibusters or filibuster threats and Republicans' largely unsuccessful attempts to install party government.[23] However, the chamber's nonmajoritarian nature, the demands of individual senators and the minority party, and the weakness of Senate leadership have tempered partisan and policy polarization.[24] Former Senate majority leaders have variously described leading the Senate as like "trying to push a wet noodle" (Howard Baker—R.TN), "herding cats" (George Mitchell—D.ME), or "putting bullfrogs in a wheelbarrow" (Trent Lott—R.MS). As consequences, Senate majority leaders' capacity to pose exclusively partisan challenges to or deliver strong partisan support for the president is heavily circumscribed; and, concomitantly, a president's ability to influence a Senate majority of the same party is weaker than his/her ability to influence the House. So, whereas highly polarized partisan issues usually fare well in the House, the Senate's legislative products tend to have a strong bipartisan hue.

Trent Lott: Negotiating With the President Under Split-Party Government

Trent Lott (R.MS), Senate Majority Leader from June 1996 until Senator Jeffords' defection in June 2001, combined partisanship with pragmatism and a determination to try to run the Senate in a methodical and disciplined manner. Like Gingrich, he was an ambitious and partisan exponent of combative, hard-line, conservative positions. Lott's reputation, however, was not as a "bomb-thrower," rather a "politician first and a conservative second"[25]—that is, a leader who was sometimes willing to relegate his own conservative policy preferences and hard-line rhetoric to achieve legislative results.

Probably more than any congressional Republican, Lott was responsible for the impressive legislative record negotiated with President Clinton over the last 6 months of 1996 that both parties carried into the subsequent elections. Soon after he became leader and over the objections of Republican Whip Don Nickles (R.OK) and other hard-line conservatives, he persuaded Senate Republican hard-liners to abandon their uncompromising stances and cooperate with Senate Democrats and the Clinton White House on a raft of legislation that included the Kennedy-Kassebaum health insurance bill, welfare reform, as well as environmental, education, and an increase in the minimum wage reform. After the 1996 elections, Lott worked with the White House to win Senate ratification of a new chemical weapons convention and, as Gingrich became increasingly ineffective in the House, negotiated a bipartisan deal with the president on the FY 1998 budget that incorporated his party's preferences for less spending and tax cuts yet committed both parties to reducing the budget deficit over five years. The following year, Lott again resisted pleas from Republican hard-liners that he not make too many concessions and successfully reached another budget deal with the White House that won Senate approval despite the opposition of 20 Republican senators, including Nickles.[26]

Trent Lott: Challenging the President: the Budget, Education, and Gun Control

Yet, unsurprisingly, besides negotiating mutually beneficial legislative products with a Democratic president, Lott more typically challenged Clinton and aggressively promoted partisan Republican positions and goals. After the 1996 elections increased Senate Republicans' majority, he asserted his position as *de facto* opposition leader and adopted highly partisan strategies designed to seize the legislative initiative, especially after the Lewinsky scandal broke, and circumscribe the president's solid election victory. None of these partisan efforts were entirely successful but a number successfully kept the president's influence in Congress at bay.

Following the 1995-96 budget *débâcle*, Lott and his House counterparts succeeded in reaching an agreement with the president to balance the budget within seven years—not the 10 years the White House had wanted. A further effort in 1997 by Lott to win Senate approval for the party's cherished balanced budget constitutional amendment failed. Worse followed in June 1997. The Senate leader badly overreached when he attached a rider to a "must pass" supplemental appropriations bill providing disaster relief for flood victims and spending for peacekeeping operations in Bosnia. The maneuver was designed to deprive Clinton of another opportunity to close down the federal government during budget negotiations. The president threatened a veto and launched a highly successful public relations campaign that led to another congressional capitulation and considerable disquiet among Senate Republicans.

Similar attempts to challenge Clinton over education reform and gun control met similar fates. The president highlighted education reform in his February 1999 State of the Union address. Lott agreed to schedule a narrower bipartisan education flexibility bill but then, on the Senate floor, orchestrated a partisan strategy designed to block amendments offered by Senate Democrats, which would broaden the bill to incorporate Clinton's plan to hire 100,000 new teachers and other popular education proposals. Predictably, Senate Democrats retaliated by blocking any action on the bill until Lott agreed to allow debate on their amendments. Ultimately, the ed-flex bill was approved by the Senate almost unanimously but not before defeating Democratic amendments embodying Clinton's proposals and adopting Lott's amendment to allow states to spend money previously requested by the president and appropriated to employ new teachers for disabled programs. Only another veto threat from the president persuaded Senate Republicans to abandon Lott's amendment in conference.

Following the Colorado school shootings in 1999, Lott resisted debate on Clinton's new gun control proposals. However, as public opinion favored new restrictions the Senate leader was forced into accepting an open debate during which he was required to make major concessions to Democrats and Republican centrists. As a result, Lott himself was subject to intense criticism from Republican colleagues.

Acting for the President on Partisan Priorities: Cutting Taxes

With the inauguration of President Bush and the return to single-party Republican government in 2001, Lott's strategic role changed to that of promoting the priorities of a Republican president. However, the strategic context that he faced was in many ways similar to that before the elections: Bush had a flawed mandate, if any mandate at all; and the Senate was now tied 50-50 reinforcing the strategic position of the self-declared Republican centrists.

Days after Bush announced his centerpiece legislative proposals to cut taxes, Lott ignored public warnings from Senators Lincoln Chafee (R.RI) and Jeffords that the package was too expensive and would further increase the federal government's debt and confidently declared that the legislation would win Senate approval. However, while the House approved the president's package swiftly, Lott's attempt to ram through Bush's proposals relying only on Republican votes was stymied despite heavy lobbying of centrists from the White House and the president's defiant insistence on "right-sized" tax cuts. On the decisive amendment offered by a Democrat to cut the size of the proposed tax cuts and increase education spending, Chafee, Jeffords, and Senator Arlen Specter (R.PA) deserted their party. The final resolution gave the president only 75% of his request ($1.28 trillion), which he judiciously accepted. As if to underline inter-cameral differences, on the same day the House approved Bush's request to phase out estate taxes.

This brief discussion of Lott's leadership demonstrates both his skill as a partisan negotiator who comprehended his strategic context, bargained hard with Clinton but did not lose the deal; and his inclination to overreach—both in challenging a Democratic president and acting for a Republican president more forcefully than the strategic context allowed. On Bush's tax cuts and other priorities—the FY 2002 budget, missile defense, energy and the environment, abortion, and other issues—Lott followed the White House's gung ho partisanship, which seemed to assume that single-party government was a reality rather than a *façade* that concealed narrow margins between the parties. The consequences of overreaching partisan leadership in a nonmajoritarian chamber were demonstrated by winning bipartisan coalitions on the Senate floor and, most graphically, when Jeffords, a close friend of Lott, suddenly announced that he would leave the party to become an independent.

Bill Frist: Acting for the President—Tax Cuts

Lott's egregious comments in support of racial segregation at retiring Senator Strom Thurmond's (R.SC) 100th birthday party effectively put an end to him leading his party after Republicans regained their Senate majority in 2002. With strong support from the Bush White House and most Senate Republicans, the reluctant, softly spoken, but equally conservative, Bill Frist (R.TN) "emerged" as the new Senate leader. Frist was viewed as a more acceptable public persona for the party in the Senate, more closely identified with Bush's "compassionate" conservatism, and a more inclusive Senate leader who not only enjoyed close relations with the Bush White House (as National Republican Senatorial Committee chair and joint architect with Bush of the party's 2002 campaign) but could relate better to Senate centrists.[27]

Although only in the third year of his second term, the urbane Frist was known more for his policy interests than his mastery of the chamber's arcane procedures—Lott's *forte*. Predictably, in his first speech as majority leader, Frist emphasized "achievement as well as a cooperative spirit" and openly acknowledged the impossibility of strict party line voting and the need for bipartisanship: "Voting 51-lockstep on every vote is not practical and not realistic," he declared. "[W]e will hear both sides . . . [I]t won't be a railroading of one idea through." With both parties eager to complete the previous Congress' remaining business as swiftly as possible, Frist comfortably ushered through the delayed FY 2003 omnibus appropriations bill without cutting off debate, defeated Democratic attempts to increase homeland security and education spending, and delivered to the president a bill that closely followed Bush's spending ceiling. Unsurprisingly, he endorsed Bush's 2003 legislative agenda, including new tax cuts, and won Senate approval for the administration's largely symbolic bill to ban so-called "partial birth" abortions, albeit with language affirming a constitutional right to abortion.

Other attempts to act for the president were less successful—notably Frist's efforts to defeat Democratic filibusters to confirm Bush's nomination of conservative judges Miguel Estrada and Priscilla Owen to the U.S. Court of Appeals, to approve an amendment to the FY 2004 budget resolution allowing Senate drilling in Alaska's Arctic National Wildlife Refuge (ANWR), and to approve the president's so-called "faith" initiative. To win approval for the last measure, pivotal language that would have allowed religious groups to receive federal grants to operate food kitchens and shelters for the homeless was removed while additional social services spending was added, contrary to White House wishes.

Frist's efforts to assist his party's president soon led to the same intractable and recurrent problems of juggling different elements of his strategic context that the more experienced Lott had encountered. Faced by rising demands for new spending from Republicans and Democrats, and concerned at the increasing costs of the war against Iraq and an escalating budget deficit, in March 2003 Frist found himself in exactly the same position on Bush's emblematic tax cut proposals as his predecessor in 2001. On the Senate floor, two centrists and a mainstream Republican deserted their party to support a Democratic amendment that cut $100 billion from Bush's proposed tax cuts in the budget resolution. Five days later, and just a few hours after the White House sent to Congress a $74.7 billion emergency funding request to pay for the Iraq war, anti-terrorism and foreign aid, Republican centrists again joined with Democrats to reduce the president's tax cuts by half. Frist insisted on rerunning the vote the following day, but, as a *Washington Post-ABC News* poll showed, 65% of the public supported the Senate's action; the vote was the same.[28]

Worse followed: it soon transpired that Frist had been obliged to limit tax cuts to $350 billion to retain the support of two Republican dissidents for the budget resolution, but did not tell House leaders who then proceeded to win approval for $550 billion in cuts. Miffed at the impossible position in which Frist had placed them, Hastert and Majority Leader DeLay accused Frist of betrayal. Although Frist conceded his mistake, the damage was done, compounded by House leaders' decision to make the dispute public. Predictably, Frist's soft touch, non-confrontational, style and inexperience were criticized, especially by hardliners who speculated that Lott would have taken a firmer line with the dissidents. But the problems faced by the new Senate leader in trying to reconcile different contexts were hardly new. Ultimately, it was left to the president to resolve the dispute, which he did by judiciously claiming a major party victory even though he obtained only 48% of the tax cuts he requested.

THE PRESIDENT AND CONGRESSIONAL LEADERSHIP

In the contemporary context of polarized politics, the strategies and skills deployed by congressional leaders are important variables that influence the extent to which presidents win congressional approval for their programs, which in turn impact a president's relations with the Congress. Sometimes, as these case studies of Hastert, Lott, and Frist have shown, congressional leaders challenge the president; sometimes they act for him/her. When they do either, a complexity of contextual factors influences the strategies they deploy and the skills they utilize. The strategic environment in which congressional leaders seek to exercise leadership and interact with the president is multidimensional and dynamic. The configuration of partisan control over different branches and different chambers are only two, albeit important, variables—also crucial are parliamentary arithmetic, the profile of copartisans' policy preferences, the electoral context and/or public opinion, the relevant chamber's institutional characteristics, the president's public reputation, skills, and actions, the salience of a particular issue, and other factors. Moreover, the interactions among the strategic environment's component elements can change pretty rapidly—as, for example, after the 1996 and 1998 elections that reduced Republican majorities in the House, after Jeffords defection enhanced the impact of House Republican centrists, and after Bush entered the White House—especially after the 2002 midterm elections.

However, as these studies have shown, although extremely important, contextual factors alone do not determine congressional leadership strategies—or, therefore, the conduct of presidential congressional relations. Although none of the congressional leaders considered here "made politics" in Skowronek's sense,[29] as Gingrich did, the skills of discernment, judgment and action that they applied to inherently fluid strategic contexts that they encountered as congressional leaders clearly influenced events and outcomes. These skills helped determine when they should pursue partisan or bipartisan strategies, when to stand firm or compromise with the other party or the president, and so forth—and in consequence they themselves become elements in the multidimensional and dynamic strategic environment in which presidents and congresses interact within the contemporary separated system. Clearly, however, as these studies show, the very difficulties and dilemmas that Hastert, Lott and Frist—and Clinton and Bush—encountered in trying to exercise leadership in the contemporary polarized context also serve to demonstrate the importance of context. Leadership from both ends of Pennsylvania Avenue depends on leadership skills in context.

NOTES

1. The author gratefully acknowledges financial assistance under award LRG-35418 provided by the British Academy.

2. Anthony King, "A Mile and a Half Is a Long Way," in Anthony King, ed., *Both Ends of The Avenue* (Washington, DC: American Enterprise Institute, 1983), pp. 247–248.

3. See, for example, John H. Aldrich and David W. Rohde, "The Consequences of Party Organization in the House: The Role of the Majority and Minority Parties in Conditional Party Government" and Gary C. Jacobson, "Party Polarization in National Politics," in Jon R. Bond and Richard Fleisher, eds., *Polarized Politics: Congress and the President in a Partisan Era*, (Washington, DC: Congressional Quarterly Press, 2000), pp. 9–30 and 31–72; Jeffrey M. Stonecash, Mark D. Brewer, and Mack D. Mariani, *Diverging Parties: Social Change, Realignment, and Party Polarization* (Boulder, CO: Westview Press, 2003). Of course, party voting does not occur on all or, for that matter, most congressional issues but it does occur on those issues on which the respective parties seek to establish their national reputations; and there are more of those than there were 25 years ago. Even so, by international standards, party voting remains low: at the height of the so-called "Republican Revolution" in 1995 on only 32% of House votes did 90 percent of one party opposing 90 percent of the other party.

4. Keith T. Poole and Howard Rosenthal, "D-NOMINATE After 10 Years: A Comparative Update to *Congress: A Political-Economic History of Roll Call Voting,*" *Legislative Studies Quarterly* 26 (No. 1, 2001): 5–29.

5. Roger H. Davidson, "Senate Floor Deliberation: A Preliminary Inquiry" and Norman J. Ornstein, "Civility, Deliberation, and Impeachment" in Burdett A. Loomis, ed., *Esteemed Colleagues. Civility and Deliberation in the U.S. Senate* (Washington, DC: Brookings Institution Press, 2001): 21–42 and 223–40; Kathleen Hall Jamieson, "Civility in the House of Representatives: The 106th Congress." The Annenberg Public Policy Center, University of Pennsylvania, March 2001.

6. David W. Rohde, *Parties and Leaders in the Postreform House* (Chicago: University of Chicago Press, 1991).

7. Barbara Sinclair, *Legislators, Leaders, and Lawmaking. The US House of Representatives in the Postreform Era* (Baltimore: The Johns Hopkins University Press, 1995); Barbara Sinclair, "Leading the Revolution: Innovation and Continuity in Congressional Party Leadership," in Dean McSweeney and John E. Owens, eds., *The Republican Takeover of Congress* (Basingstoke, UK and New York: Macmillan/St Martins Press, 1998): 71–95; Barbara Sinclair "The Senate Leadership Dilemma: Passing Bills and Pursuing Partisan Advantage in a Nonmajoritarian Chamber" in Colton C. Campbell and Nicol C. Rae, eds., *The Contentious Senate. Partisanship, Ideology, and the Myth of Cool Judgment* (Lanham, MD: Rowman and Littlefield, 2001): 65–90; John H. Aldrich, *Why Parties? The Origin and Transformation of Party Politics in America* (Chicago: The University of Chicago Press, 1995); John E. Owens, "Late Twentieth Century Congressional Leaders as Shapers of and Hostages to Political Context: Gingrich, Hastert, and Lott," *Politics and Policy* 30 (June 2002): 236–281.

8. William F. Connelly and John J. Pitney, *Congress' Permanent Minority? Republicans in the US House* (Lanham, MD: Rowman and Littlefield, 1994): 24–26, 62–64; Daniel J. Palazzolo, *The Speaker and the Budget* (Pittsburgh, PA: University of Pittsburgh Press, 1992, pp. 91, 128–142; John E. Owens, "The Return of Party Government in the US House of Representatives: Central Leader-Committee Relations in the 104th Congress," *British Journal of Political Science* 27 (April 1997), p. 255.

9. David W. Brady and Craig Volden, *Politics and Policy From Carter to Clinton* (Boulder, CO: Westview, 1998); Charles M. Cameron, *Veto Bargaining. Presidents and the Politics of Negative Power* (New York: Cambridge University Press, 2000); George C. Edwards, *At the Margins. Presidential Leadership of Congress* (New Haven, CT: Yale University Press, 1989); Charles O. Jones, *The Presidency in a Separated System*. Washington, D.C.: The Brookings Institution, 1994; Mark A. Peterson, *Legislating Together. The White House and Capitol Hill From Eisenhower to Reagan*. Cambridge, MA and London: Harvard University Press, 1990; Sinclair, *Legislators, Leaders, and Lawmaking*: 296–302.

10. Joseph Cooper and David W. Brady, "Institutional Context and Leadership Style: The House From Cannon to Rayburn," *American Political Science Review* 75 (March 1981): 411–25; David W. Rohde and Kenneth A. Shepsle, "Leaders and Followers in the House of Representatives: Reflections on Woodrow Wilson's Congressional Government," *Congress and the Presidency* 14 (June 1987): 122–23; Barbara Sinclair, "Transformational Leader Or Faithful Agent? Principal Agent Theory and House Party Leadership," *Legislative Studies Quarterly* 24 (No. 3, 1999), p. 447.

11. John H. Aldrich and Kenneth A. Shepsle, "Explaining Institutional Change: Soaking, Poking, and Modeling in the US Congress" in William A. Bianco, ed., *Congress On Display, Congress At Work*. Ann Arbor and London: University of Michigan Press, 2000: 41; Palazzolo, *The Speaker and the Budget*, pp. 216–218; Ronald M. Peters, "Institutional Context and Leadership Style: The Case of Newt Gingrich," in Rae and Campbell, eds., *New Majority or Old Minority*, pp. 43–69; Randall W. Strahan, "Leadership and Institutional Change in the Nineteenth Century House," in David W. Brady and Matthew McCubbins, eds., *Party, Process, and Political Change in Congress. New Perspectives on the History of Congress* (Stanford, CA: Stanford University Press, 2002), p. 243.

12. Richard F. Fenno, "Observation, Context, and Sequence in the Study of Politics," *American Political Science Review* 80 (March 1986): 3–15.

13. Erwin C. Hargrove and John E. Owens, "Political Leadership: Skills in Context," in Erwin C. Hargrove and John E. Owens, eds., *Political Leadership in Context*. (Lanham, MD: Rowman and Littlefield, 2003).

14. Randall W. Strahan, 'Reed and Rostenkowski: Congressional Leadership in Institutional Time," in Allen D. Hertzke and Ronald M. Peters, *The Atomistic Congress. An Interpretation of Congressional Change* (Armonk, NY: M.E. Sharpe, 1992), pp. 199–230: 209, 208–217; Elaine K. Swift, "The Start of Something New: Clay, Stevenson, Polk, and the Development of the Speakership, 1789–1869," in Roger H. Davidson, Susan Webb Hammond, and Raymond W. Smock, eds., *Masters of the House. Congressional Leadership Over Two Centuries* (Boulder, CO: Westview, 1998), pp. 9–32.

15. James McGregor Burns, *Leadership* (New York: Harper and Row, 1978), p. 4.

16. Owens, "Late Twentieth Century Congressional Leaders," pp. 242–249; Randall W. Strahan and Daniel Palazzolo, "The Gingrich Effect," *Political Science Quarterly*, forthcoming 2004.

17. Owens, "Late Twentieth Century Congressional Leaders," pp. 249–255.

18. Andrew Taylor, "Unity and Wishful Thinking Yield GOP Budget Resolution," *Congressional Quarterly Weekly Report*, March 27, 1999, p. 751.

19. Carroll J. Doherty and Gebe Martinez, "GOP's Great Expectations For '99 Fade to Modest Hopes," *Congressional Quarterly Weekly Report*, May 15, 1999, pp. 1122–1123; David S. Broder, "Look Who's in the Driver's Seat," *Washington Post*, June 8, 1999, p. A19.

20. Editorial, "At a Time for Leadership, Hastert Abdicates," *Chicago Tribune*, May 2, 1999, p. A6; "Speaker Hastert, AWOL," *New York Times*, May 5, 1999, p. A24; "The House Republicans' Duck," *Washington Post*, April 30, 1999, p. A34.

21. Dan Carney, "House GOP Embrace of Gun Curbs Not Yet Lock, Stock and Barrel," *Congressional Quarterly Weekly Report*, May 29, 1999, p. 1267.

22. Mary McGrory, "Off Target At the GOP Corral," *Washington Post*, June 13, 1999, p. B1.

23. Barbara Sinclair, "Hostile Partners: The President, Congress and Lawmaking in the Partisan 1990s," in Bond and Fleisher, eds., *Polarized Politics*, p. 145; Sarah A. Binder, *Stalemate. Causes and Consequences of Legislative Gridlock* (Washington, DC: Brookings Institution, 2003), pp. 98–100.

24. Sinclair "The Senate Leadership Dilemma," pp. 114–125; Steven S. Smith and Gerald Gamm, "The Dynamics of Party Government in Congress," in Lawrence C. Dodd and Bruce I. Oppenheimer, *Congress Reconsidered*, 5th ed.(Washington, DC: CQ Press, 2001), pp. 265–266; John E. Owens, "Congress and Partisan Change," in Gillian Peele, Christopher J. Bailey, Bruce Cain, and B. Guy Peters, eds., *Developments in American Politics 3* (Basingstoke, UK and Chatham, NJ: Macmillan Press/Chatham House, 1999), pp. 46–57.

25. Dick Morris, *Behind the Oval Office: Winning the Presidency in the Nineties* (New York: Random House, 1997), p. 76.

26. Owens, "Late Twentieth Century Congressional Leaders," pp. 262–267.

27. Keith Perine, "Frist's Senate Voting Record Shows Blend of Partisanship and Pragmatism," *Congressional Quarterly Weekly Report*, January 4, 2003, p. 20.

28. Helen Dewar, "Senate Votes to Slash Bush's Tax Cut to $350 Billion," *Washington Post*, March 26, 2003, p. A1. Richard Morin and David Von Drehle, "Support For War Is Firm, Poll Finds: On the Home Front, Trimming Bush's Proposed Tax Cut Has 65 Percent Backing," *Washington Post*, March 30, 2003, p. A10.

29. Stephen Skowronek, *The Politics Presidents Make. Leadership from John Adams to Bill Clinton* (Cambridge, MA: Belknap Press, 1997).

CHAPTER 8

Presidential Strategies in the New Politics of Supreme Court Appointments

◆◆◆

Robert J. McKeever

The University of Reading

As the U.S. Supreme Court approached the end of its 2002–3 term, President George W. Bush and the United States Senate were locked in combat over judicial appointments to the Circuit Courts of Appeal. The Bush administration had adopted what might be termed the "Clarence Thomas" or "Godfather" approach to the nomination and confirmation process: it made the Senate an offer it thought it couldn't refuse. Just as President George H. Bush had nominated Justice Clarence Thomas in the belief that Senate Democrats could not refuse a member of one of their electoral constituent groups—African Americans—so too did George W. Bush offer the Senate women and minorities for the Circuit Courts of Appeal. Judge Priscilla Owen was nominated to the Fifth Circuit and Miguel Estrada to the D.C. Circuit. To both the president and Senate Democrats, however, the most important characteristic of these nominees was their conservative ideology. President Bush nominated them to continue the conservative counter-revolution on the federal judiciary and, as a result, Senate Democrats responded with a filibuster.

The Owen and Estrada battles are nothing new. They are merely the latest in a long war arising from what one Senator has called "the broken judicial confirmation process."[1] And if the spirit of partnership between White House and Senate has broken down over circuit court and even district court appointments, it should come as no surprise that appointments to the Supreme Court have become one of the most important and difficult strategic questions that the president has to consider in the modern era.[2]

This chapter analyzes why, when and how the Supreme Court appointment process became so contentious. This analysis is of more than historical interest—for the factors that caused the breakdown are equally the main determinants of the "new politics of Supreme Court appointments." This chapter then examines the choice of strategies and tactics available to the president when making a nomination to the Supreme Court in the contemporary system. It will argue that presidents who underestimate the constraints on their freedom of choice of Supreme Court justices, are least likely to achieve their overall goals for the federal judiciary.

THE BREAKDOWN OF THE JUDICIAL APPOINTMENTS SYSTEM

The final third of the twentieth century saw a dramatic and fundamental change in the politics of United States Supreme Court appointments. From 1930 until 1967, there had been twenty-three successful and largely problem-free presidential nominations to the Court. No nominees were defeated during that period and none came under serious attack in the Senate. Since 1967, however, out of nineteen nominations, five have been defeated and three others faced serious senatorial hostility (see Table 8.1).

In other words, we have moved from an era of uncontested Supreme Court nominations to one in which the president must anticipate a determined attempt to thwart his will, for "the possibility of refusal is ever present."[3] The obvious question that arises is what explains the transformation from the "old" to the "new" politics of Supreme Court appointments?

The Old Politics of Supreme Court Appointments

It is hard to see the old politics of Supreme Court appointments as anything other than bizarre or even perverse. There is no other area of shared presidential-

Table 8.1 Confirmation Votes 1967–1994

Easy Confirmation	Difficult Confirmation	Defeated
Marshall (1967) 69–11	Rehnquist (1971) 68–26	Fortas (1968) withdrawn
Burger (1969) 74–3	Rehnquist (1986) 65–33	Haynesworth (1969) 45–55
Blackmun (1970) 94–0	Thomas (1991) 52–48	Carswell (1970) 45–51
Powell (1971) 89–1		Bork (1986) 42–58
Stevens (1975) 98–0		Ginsburg (1987) withdrawn
O'Connor (1981) 99–0		
Scalia (1986) 98–0		
Kennedy (1987) 97–0		
Souter (1990) 90–9		
Ginsburg (1993) 96–3		
Breyer (1994) 87–9		

Source: L. Epstein et al, *The Supreme Court Compendium* (Washington, D.C.: Congressional Quarterly, 1994); K. Hall, ed., *The Oxford Companion to the Supreme Court of the United States*, (Oxford: Oxford University Press, 1992).

congressional activity in which Capitol Hill deferred so utterly to the White House; and no other where the usual rough-and-tumble of pluralist politics did not impinge. It is thus quite remarkable that in a matter as important for policy making as the composition of the third branch of the federal government, the Senate should simply concede near total discretion to the president.

It is not even as if that before 1930, there wasn't a history of Senate rejections of presidential nominees. Indeed, while there was no real pattern to it, the nineteenth century saw some one in three presidential nominees to the Court fail to be confirmed.[4] And again, in the early twentieth century, there was ideological opposition in the Senate to certain nominees and the intervention of interest groups. These came together in 1930, when President Hoover's nomination of John J. Parker was defeated 39–41 in the Senate, due to a blend of partisanship, Progressivism and pressure groups.[5]

Thereafter, however, the politics of judicial nominations entered a prolonged hibernation. Oddly, this occurred just as the Court reached its peak of political controversy in the form of the infamous judicial struggle against President Roosevelt's New Deal. As we shall see below, overt and controversial policy-making by the Court in final third of the twentieth century was precisely what initiated the new politics of appointments. In the 1930s, however, the reverse is true. Most probably this is because President Roosevelt's constitutionally dangerous Court-packing plan convinced the Senate that it should show greater deference to presidential prerogative in the matter of Court appointments.

Thus, no matter how controversial the nominee or even the Court's agenda, the Senate behaved quite atypically until the late 1960s. Take, for example, President Roosevelt's nomination of William O. Douglas in 1939. As something of a New Deal crusader, Douglas had made many enemies among conservatives and the business community, especially in his reforming role on the Securities and Exchange Commission. Yet despite literally hanging around the Senate Judiciary Committee's hearing room, anxious to testify on his own behalf, Douglas failed to persuade the committee that any testimony was required. And within two weeks of his nomination, the Senate confirmed Douglas with just four votes against.[6]

As late as the mid-1960s, well after the Warren Court had become controversial, Justices White (1962), Goldberg (1962) and Fortas (1965) were all confirmed by voice vote in the Senate. Yet Fortas was a famous friend and advisor of President Lyndon Johnson, thus raising separation-of-powers concerns, and he was seen as someone who would join the liberal-activist bloc on the Court. Shortly before his confirmation, *Newsweek* wrote:

> Fortas has no judicial experience. But Justice William O. Douglas—one of Fortas' teachers at Yale Law School—has been his judicial mentor and the new Justice is expected to fit right into Goldberg's spot in the Court's five-man activist bloc. In fact, he may be more effective than Goldberg.[7]

Yet the conservative members of the Senate Judiciary Committee treated Fortas very gently, even though they questioned him about recent major Court decisions on crime, reapportionment, and desegregation.[8]

It is clear then, that liberal judicial activism *alone* did not cause the modern transformation of the Supreme Court appointment process. The further ingredient required was a deterioration in the discourse and manners of the appointment process. As the Court continued on its activist path, endorsing increasingly contested civil rights and socio-moral policies, partisans gradually discarded the gentleman's club approach to Supreme Court appointments.

This manifested itself first just two years after the Fortas appointment, when President Johnson nominated the first black Supreme Court Justice, Thurgood Marshall. Marshall had an excellent pedigree for appointment to the Court: two years of service as Solicitor General, four years as a judge on the court of appeals for the Second Circuit and numerous appearances as a lawyer before the Supreme Court, most famously in *Brown v. Board of Education*. Yet, in key respects, his confirmation process differed from that of his modern predecessors. Moreover, it is hard to avoid the conclusion that race was the crucial factor which distinguished Marshall's treatment.

Most obviously, there was a Mason-Dixon Line divide on the Judiciary Committee which favorably reported Marshall's nomination, 11–5. The five minority Senators were the committee's five Southern members: James O. Eastland (D-Miss.), John L. McClellan (D-Ark.), Sam J. Ervin (D-N.C.), George A. Smathers (D-Fla.) and Strom Thurmond (R-S.C.). Secondly, while Senator Ervin's statement denied any race factor and attacked Marshall's likely activism, he did not conceal his scathing view of the Court's desegregation decisions and Marshall's role in them.[9] The most unfortunate aspect of the hearings, however, was the unpleasant line of questioning undertaken by Senator Thurmond. Having noted that much of Marshall's career had focussed on the interpretation of the Civil War amendments, Thurmond proceeded to fire off a relentless barrage of obscure questions about their passage and meaning. For example, one exchange went:

Sen Thurmond: Now, on the 14th amendment, what committee reported out the 14th amendment and who were its members?

Judge Marshall: I don't know sir.

Sen Thurmond: Why do you think the framers of the original version of the first section of the 14th amendment added the necessary and proper clause from article 1, section 8, to the privileges and immunities clause of Article IV, section 2?

Judge Marshall: I don't know sir.

Sen Thurmond: What purpose did the framers have . . . in referring to the incident involving former Representative Samual Hoar in Charleston, S.C., in December 1844, as showing the need for the enactment of the original version of the 14th amendment's first section?

Judge Marshall: I don't know.

Sen Thurmond: Did you understand the question?

Judge Marshall: Yes, sir.[10]

Since the Senator could not reasonably have expected Marshall to be able to answers the questions, his purpose was presumably to demonstrate that Marshall was too ignorant to be placed on the Supreme Court. However, it is the manner of the questioning which was unique in the modern history of the Court. And while Senator Thurmond's line of questioning was the most unpleasant, others subjected him to unprecedented aggressive questioning.[11] In short, for the first time in at least forty years, the Marshall hearings saw the gloves come off in the Senate confirmation process even if the eventual note was one-sided.

As so often is the case, once the genie is let out of the bottle, it is very difficult to persuade it to return. Southern Conservatives had taken a militant approach to Marshall's nomination and continued it when Justice Fortas was nominated to replace Earl Warren as Chief Justice. Having had an easy ride just three years earlier, Fortas was obliged to testify for twelve hours, over twice as long as any previous Supreme Court nominee.[12] The Judiciary Committee report noted that he was "closely interrogated" and was subjected to "sharp attack."[13] Although the Judiciary Committee reported the nomination favorably, a filibuster was launched in the Senate. Crucially, opposition came from Republicans as well as Southern Democrats and the filibuster held.[14]

The role of partisanship was confirmed when the Democrats took their revenge in defeating President Nixon's first two nominees to the Court, Clement Haynesworth and G. Harrold Carswell in 1969 and 1970, respectively.[15] By this time, then, the modern judicial confirmation had acquired two of the characteristics of "normal politics"—ideological and partisan opposition. Unsurprisingly, perhaps, other such characteristics eventually came into play, most notably, the participation of interest groups.

It is worth pausing at this point to note that both Presidents Johnson and Nixon must take some share of the blame for their failed nominations. Johnson was open to the charge of cronyism in nominating Fortas to be Chief Justice (and indeed, Homer Thornberry as associate justice). He also chose this strategy when he was, in effect, a lame-duck president and thus he clearly overrated his ability to secure support from the Senate for problematic nominees.

President Nixon could hardly be blamed for the defeat of Clement Haynesworth, although his presidential campaign attacks on the Court could only further politicize the confirmation process. However, his decision to try to force the third-rate Carswell on a Democrat-controlled Senate involved a rather surprising underestimation of the degree to which ideological and partisan considerations now constrained the confirmation process.

After the bruising battles over Fortas, Haynesworth, and Carswell, Presidents Nixon and Ford adopted a relatively cautious approach to judicial nominations. Nixon nominated the eminently confirmable Lewis Powell and Harry Blackmun, although he did produce ideological and partisan opposition by his nomination of William H. Rehnquist. President Ford, with no mandate and facing a Democrat-controlled Senate, wisely nominated a well-respected and moderate Republican, John Paul Stevens, to his only vacancy. The situation quietened further in the 1970s, because President Carter had no Supreme Court vacancy to fill.

What re-kindled the fires was the arrival of the Reagan administration, armed with a clear goal of completing the judicial counter-revolution that had stalled under Nixon. Equally important was the fact that the new administration had the most detailed and thorough system for identifying and nominating the kind of judges they wanted to see on the federal courts. This same system, with some modifications, is essentially the same one that has been used by subsequent presidents. Where administrations have differed, however, is in their strategic and tactical decisions.

The Reagan administration, under the leadership of Attorney General Edwin Meese, fully appreciated the extent to which the Supreme Court makes social policy. They also fully appreciated the extent to which a judge's ideological and interpretive inclinations determine judicial policymaking. Logically enough, the administration established an elaborate screening process for potential nominees to the federal courts, in an effort to ensure that, as far as possible, their judicial choices would decide cases in the way desired by the administration.

However, the fact that the Reagan administration had a highly visible counter-revolutionary strategy produced an equally robust response from the opposition. Senate Democrats were not merely determined to stop the more extreme Reagan nominees, they worked in tandem with forces outside of Congress. This was the next major development in the new politics of Supreme Court appointments: the massive involvement of interest groups.[16]

It had always been possible for groups and individuals to testify at Senate hearings on Supreme Court nominations. But this had only occurred in a sporadic and insignificant manner. Thus, those testifying against Fortas in 1968 were only four in number: the National Organization for Decent Literature, the Liberty Lobby, the Council Against Communist Aggression and the Conservative Society of America.[17] The Democrats, however, showed a greater sensitivity to the power of groups, when a significant number of union and civil liberties groups testified against Haynesworth.[18] Nevertheless, this was essentially the re-appearance of the same coalition that had helped to defeat John Davis in 1930. In that sense, the great interest group explosion was still to come.

Surprisingly, in view of the charges of racism leveled against him, Carswell faced no greater number of groups against him than Haynesworth, although the National Organization for Women (NOW) made its first appearance at a Judiciary Committee hearing for a Supreme Court nominee. Yet more significant than group opposition in the defeat of Carswell was the bipartisan committee formed against him and led by Senator Church (D-Idaho) and Senator Javits (R-NY).[19] Although a unique institutionalization of bipartisan opposition to a Supreme Court nomination, this represents a potent reminder to presidents that, as in many legislative battles, it is extremely difficult to prevent at least a small number of Senators of the presidential party from joining the opposition if the nomination is a contentious one.

Also surprising is that the nomination of William H. Rehnquist in 1971 did not generate more interest group opposition. Certainly the union-civil rights duet made its by now regular appearance, but while women's groups appeared in greater number than before, not all took a stand for or against Rehnquist.[20] The ACLU did not testify but it did break tradition by taking a public stand against a nominee for the first time.[21] The anti-Rehnquist cause failed to generate strong support outside the core liberals in the Senate and thus Democrats split 30–23 in favor of confirmation.[22]

As noted above, it was the arrival of the Reagan administration that brought the next qualitative change in the confirmation process. Yet it began cautiously by nominating Sandra Day O'Connor. The pressure for a woman to be nominated had been growing in the 1970s and, charged with being unsympathetic to the cause of women's rights during the 1980 campaign, the candidate Reagan was forced into virtually promising to make his first nominee a woman. This, of course, also had the effect of disarming opposition amongst the Democrats, who saw themselves as the champions of gender equality. It also helped that O'Connor was perceived as a moderate conservative. So, through wisdom or pressure, the Reagan administration's first nominee was confirmed with little fuss.

That all changed with the twin nominations of Justice Rehnquist as Chief Justice and Antonin Scalia as associate justice in 1986. It came to a climax the following year with the failed nomination of Judge Robert Bork. The Reagan administration had good reason to be bold and to nominate two leading conservatives in 1986: double nominations can be difficult for the opposition, which has to decide whether to divide its forces and attack both nominees or concentrate their fire on just one. In this case, the likely target was Rehnquist but for all the liberal opposition to him, he had been confirmed with only 26 votes against in 1971. Finally, the Republicans had a majority in the Senate. Despite an impassioned opposition from most Democrats in the Senate and a wider array of opposition groups testifying against Rehnquist at the hearings, he was approved with "just" 33 votes against.

The following year, the Reagan administration showed that it could be foolhardy, as well as astute in these matters. The advantages of 1986 were gone: the Democrats had captured the Senate, Bork was a sole nominee, and he was highly controversial. Moreover, if approved, he would replace Justice Powell, who was viewed as a moderate and the key swing vote in many closely decided cases, including that of abortion. In nominating him, the administration lost sight of the strategic nature of Supreme Court nominations in the modern era.

It was even more foolish when, having seen Bork rejected by 55–45, the administration went for the combination of a "spite candidate" and a "stealth candidate."[23] President Reagan reacted to the defeat of Bork by promising to send up another nominee that the liberals would dislike as much as Robert Bork. However, he chose a little known member of the D.C. Circuit court, Douglas Ginsburg, in part because he lacked the voluminous history of legal commentary that had made Bork such a visible target. Ironically, it was the very lack of a record that had the media scurrying around trying to find something out about the new nominee and the result was that Ginsburg had been known to smoke marijuana at Harvard parties. The administration had little choice but to withdraw his candidacy and nominate instead the moderate conservative judge, Anthony Kennedy. Kennedy was easily confirmed.

President George H. Bush had similar goals to the Reagan administration. Even more than President Reagan perhaps, President Bush wanted to prove his support for the socio-moral agenda of the Christian right by appointing Supreme Court justices who could help to advance that agenda. The Bush administration was also acutely aware that it could easily see its nominee "Borked" by the Democratic majority in the Senate if it chose an extreme conservative. It therefore adopted a most astute strategy. The first vacancy would go to a moderate conservative, who was also a stealth candidate: in the end it was David H. Souter who fitted the bill. The second vacancy was virtually promised to the conservative interest groups that focussed on the Court and hence could be much more conservative than Justice Souter was. Even here, however, the administration was canny: it chose a black arch conservative, Judge Clarence Thomas, to fill Thurgood Marshall's seat, thus throwing liberal Senators and interest groups off-balance.

The strategy appeared to be working well until out of the blue came allegations that Thomas had sexually harassed a female colleague years ago. From the point of view of the administration's strategy, this was simply bad luck. Anita Hill had never made these allegations public before, so no amount of searching the Thomas record would have uncovered them. The charges gave his opponents the ammunition they needed, but the Bush strategy proved just robust enough to withstand the onslaught. Thomas was confirmed 52–48.

President Clinton chose to avoid confirmation battles, even though the Democrats had a majority in the Senate at the time of his two nominations. By nominating well-respected moderate liberals in 1993 and 1994, Clinton avoided any costly clashes with Republicans. Clinton was to come in for criticism from some liberal quarters for being too ready to do deals on federal court appointments with Senate Republicans, especially after they took control of the Senate.[24] Yet Clinton well understood the constraints he was operating under and adapted his strategy accordingly. This is sound, if not spectacular, management of scarce political resources.

Politics As Usual?

The period since 1967 has seen three key developments in the judicial appointments process:

1. A much more oppositional Senate.
2. A vastly increased role for interest groups.
3. Greater attentiveness from the media and the public to the point where these may be significant as factors in their own right.

It is immediately obvious that these are the same major features that characterize the normal legislative process in the United States. Yet there are other aspects of the new politics of Supreme Court nominations that distinguish the process from "politics as usual." Two in particular merit attention:

1. The Senate is still more deferential in the matter of Supreme Court appointments than it is in any other major area of congressional activity. The fact is that some of the attitudes of the old politics of appointments remain. The most important of these is a recognition that the president has the right to nominate someone of his own political and jurisprudential persuasion. This is partly due

to the simple fact that the Constitution gives the president the initiative in the appointments process; and partly the realist perception that if the Senate rejects a nominee *merely* because of ideology, the president is unlikely to nominate someone who is more ideologically attuned to the Senate.

2. The second is that in "politics as usual," both sides are willing to engage in at least some—and often a lot of—bargaining and compromise. However, with a legislative bill, that negotiation may best be undertaken after the bill is first introduced. Both sides are thereby permitted to adopt a tough position at the outset of the consideration of a bill, but then gradually assume a much more conciliatory position. This is not the case with a Supreme Court nominee. Once the president has announced the name of his candidate, there will be a straight up-or-down vote. No further bargaining or compromise is possible.

These two features distinguishing the new politics of judicial appointments from "politics as usual" are just as important for presidents to bear in mind as are the post-1967 developments. Taken together, they suggest that the president faces a choice of fairly clear paths to take when filling a Supreme Court vacancy.

PRESIDENTIAL STRATEGIES IN THE NEW POLITICS OF SUPREME COURT APPOINTMENTS

First, it is a well-established fact that presidents have to prioritize their agenda if they wish to be successful. They have to establish how much importance they attach to a particular goal and how far they are willing to expend their limited political resources in achieving it. Part of that calculation is a determination of the degree to which they are willing to compromise on the scope of the basic goal to be achieved.

Most of this fundamental aspect of presidential agenda setting applies to the appointment of a new Justice of the Supreme Court. True, the president does not have the option of leaving a Supreme Court vacancy off his agenda altogether: the position must be filled. However, the president can make an autonomous judgement as to the other aspects noted above: how important is the appointment to the president's overall agenda and how much is he willing to compromise on the outcome?

Here, a president faces two basic choices. He may decide that the appointment merits a high place on his agenda and that it is therefore essential that he achieve his goal to the fullest possible extent. In short, he is prepared to fight and to devote substantial resources to achieving victory. The alternative is to give a lower priority to the appointment, to be willing to compromise and settle for something less than total victory.

The history of post-1967 nominations yields example of both approaches, although most presidents have chosen the former strategy. President Johnson had an unusually clear idea of the individual he wished to put on the Court. He had gone to considerable lengths in 1965 first to persuade Justice Goldberg to leave the Court in order to create a vacancy and second to persuade his close friend and advisor Abe

Fortas to accept nomination. Thus, when the Chief Justiceship became vacant, there was only one candidate in the president's mind: Fortas.

The Reagan administration developed a similar preoccupation with appointing Judge Robert Bork to the Court. Bork was probably the pre-eminent advocate of the administration's belief in originalist jurisprudence. He was seriously considered for nomination in both 1981 and 1986, although the administration was aware that Bork's controversial views would make him more difficult to confirm than other possible nominees. Although there were sound tactical reasons for not nominating Bork for these earlier vacancies, the fact is that in 1987 the chances of getting him confirmed were even more remote. The president was into the final quarter of his tenure, the liberal opposition had warmed up with the campaign against Justice Rehnquist the previous year, and, most important of all, the Democrats had recaptured the Senate in November 1986.

In short, both Johnson in 1968 and Reagan in 1987 allowed their obsession with appointing a particular individual to cloud their usually sound political judgement. Although both presidents faced difficult political odds at the time of their failed nominations, they probably could have secured confirmation of someone of their ideological persuasion who didn't have the baggage carried by Fortas and Bork. Both presidents, then, were guilty of inflexibility.

The Bork nomination aside, the Reagan administration shared with the Nixon and George H. Bush administrations, a clear vision of the kind of Supreme Court Justices they wanted. Nixon wanted strict constructionists and Southerners, the former to end the liberal tide on the Court and the latter to aid the national electoral strategy of the Republican party. The Reagan and Bush administrations wanted to see the reversal of key liberal judicial decisions, on issues such as abortion, affirmative action, federalism and church-state relations, and generally to see the end of judicial activism and its replacement with originalist interpretation.

Although Nixon achieved only moderate success in his campaign, the Reagan and Bush administrations got much closer to their goals. Nixon's only clear success was the appointment of Rehnquist. Justice Blackmun turned out to be almost as liberal and activist as the Warren Court majority and Chief Justice Burger and Justice Powell were usually moderately liberal. Thus, all three were in the majority in *Roe v. Wade*.

The Reagan-Bush appointees, with the notable exception of Justice Souter, have turned out to be mostly, if not wholly, what their nominating presidents wanted. Combined with Chief Justice Rehnquist, Justices O'Connor, Scalia, Kennedy, and Thomas constitute the most frequent voting bloc in cases decided by a 5–4 split. And although the bloc has not held together on the issue of the basic right to abortion and some Establishment Clause cases, these appointees have put an end to liberal judicial activism.

How were the Reagan and Bush administrations able to accomplish this? First, both administrations were exhaustive in their search for a list of potential nominees. The committees established to do this were innovatory, well organized, and thorough. This enabled them both to identify the kind of judges deemed desirable and to discover factors that might adversely affect a nominee's confirmability.

Secondly, the administrations were successful because they were flexible within certain ideological parameters and tactically astute. As noted above, when candidate Reagan was boxed in on the issue of gender equality, the administration turned it to its advantage. While it felt obliged to nominate a woman to the first Supreme Court vacancy, it also realized that even a very conservative woman nominee would be extremely difficult for liberals to oppose. It was they after all who had originally put pressure on Reagan to appoint a woman.

The same is true of Justice Thomas. President George H. Bush, when faced with the retirement of the one and only black American to sit on the Court, was under considerable pressure to fill the vacancy with another. This, however, was turned against liberal opponents by the nomination of the arch-conservative Clarence Thomas. Although the confirmation battle over Justice Thomas is now notorious, it shouldn't be forgotten that until the allegations by Professor Anita Hill emerged, the attempt to "Bork" Clarence Thomas was clearly failing. Even with the full support of civil rights groups, the liberal coalition was struggling to win over moderate Democrats, particularly Southerners, whose black constituents were delighted with Thomas's nomination. Without the truly unforeseeable Hill allegations, the Senate majority confirming Justice Thomas would have been a comfortable one.

The Scalia-Rehnquist nominations of 1986 presented a somewhat different set of tactical considerations. Most obviously, there were two nominees to be confirmed. The administration chose two very conservative nominees, both of whom would merit opposition from liberals on ideological grounds. However, ideology alone is not deemed a sufficient grounds for legitimate opposition. Something extra is required. For Fortas, it was cronyism and doubts over financial ethics. The latter also applied to Haynesworth. For Carswell, it was racism and sheer incompetence. For Bork, it was that his ideology placed him "outside the mainstream." For Douglas Ginsburg, it was character, because he had smoked marijuana as a law professor. For the opposition to Justice Thomas, as noted above, it was character, because of the allegations of sexual harassment.

Antonin Scalia was vulnerable to none of these "special" issues. Moreover, as the first Italian-American to be nominated to the Supreme Court, liberal opponents would be sensitive to the dangers of offending the pride of many of their supporters. Understandably, liberals decided to concentrate their fire upon Rehnquist. Now there were some "special issues" here, involving civil rights abuses going back to the early 1960s. However, these had been aired and deemed insufficient to deny confirmation in 1972. Without any new evidence of "special issues," there was little hope that moderate Senate Democrats would vote against Rehnquist's elevation to the position of Chief Justice.

There is also evidence in the Reagan-Bush years that they had some appreciation of when caution was advisable. After the Bork-Ginsburg debacle, the administration turned to the moderate conservative Anthony Kennedy, in major part because he was eminently confirmable. President George H. Bush was more astute from the start. Recognizing the fact that he faced a Democrat-controlled Senate and that the Bork-Ginsburg-Kennedy nominations had cost the Reagan administration dearly in terms of political resources and standing, Bush decided to go with a moderate nominee for his first vacancy, while promising conservative groups to nominate their preferred candidate for a second vacancy.

David H. Souter was indeed easily confirmed, but of course took up a place on the liberal wing of the Court, confounding both the administration and the nominee's opponents. Does this suggest that Bush won a battle but only at the cost of losing the war? It's possible. On the other hand, the "defeat" could be explained by an overreliance on the word of Souter's sponsor, John Sununu, and a concomitant failure to research the potential nominee thoroughly enough. Once the president believed that he would achieve his main goal of getting his first nominee easily confirmed, he took for granted that a Sununu protégé would be sufficiently conservative. In this way, the strategy of nominating a stealth candidate for the Court backfired. But the failure was one of the most basic kind that no administration should make: a failure to know your nominee.

All the presidents discussed in this section had a clear idea of who they wanted to put on the Court and, with the exception of the Souter vacancy, they were prepared to expend considerable political resources on getting their nominees confirmed. Yet they met with mixed success. We will discuss the lessons to be learned from this below.

First, however, it is important to look at the presidents who chose not to provoke their opponents: Presidents Ford and Clinton. Although we have only two cases in this category, it is worth noting that while Ford made his nomination from a position of weakness, Clinton made his from a position of strength. Ford was an unelected president, serving out the remainder of President Nixon's second term. He thus had few political resources to begin with and even fewer after he had pardoned his disgraced predecessor. He was the lame-duck president par excellence. His nominee to fill Justice Douglas's seat in 1975 would also have to be confirmed by a heavily Democrat Senate. Wisely, Ford made no attempt to continue Nixon's counter-revolutionary strategy and instead nominated a moderate and highly respected Republican judge, John Paul Stevens. Senate Democrats clearly appreciated the spirit of the nomination and he was confirmed by a vote of 98–0. Of course Justice Stevens became one of the Court's liberals, but it is doubtful if Ford could have succeeded with a known conservative of the Rehnquist kind. Moreover, given the radical liberalism of some of Justice Douglas's views, Ford could at least be assured that Justice Stevens might well nudge the Court in a more conservative direction on at least some issues. Under the circumstances, Ford made the most of a weak hand.

More intriguing, though, is the approach taken by President Clinton. His vacancies appeared early in his presidency, when presidential resources are usually considered to be at their height. Moreover, he had a solid Democrat majority in the Senate. Finally, after years of conservative Republican appointees, liberal Senators and interest groups were anxious to put some of their own on the Court.

Surprisingly, perhaps, President Clinton took an approach more akin to that of President Bush with his first vacancy, but applied it to both his nominations in 1993 and 1994. Clinton undoubtedly wanted to put liberals on the Court, but he selected moderates rather than the liberal equivalents of Robert Bork. Thus one name frequently mentioned for the Court was the governor of New York, Mario Cuomo.

However, while Governor Cuomo was the ideal choice as far as liberals were concerned, he was both controversial and frankly loathed by many conservatives. As an aide to Senator Orrin Hatch commented, the nomination of Mario Cuomo would have led to a confirmation bloodbath.[25] In 1993–1994, Clinton might well have emerged victorious from such a struggle, but it would have been at the cost of deflecting attention from his legislative priorities.

President Clinton therefore negotiated his candidates for the Court before he nominated them. This involved ensuring that key Republican players, such as Senator Hatch, the ranking member on the Senate Judiciary, found his nominees acceptable. Indeed, Senator was positively enthusiastic about the nominations of both Ruth Bader Ginsburg (1993) and Stephen Breyer (1994). Both have established themselves on the liberal wing of the Court and have voted more or less as any more extreme liberal would have voted. In other words, by choosing to avoid conflict, Clinton was able to get most of what he wanted from his Court opportunities and did so without expending his political resources.

LESSONS FOR PRESIDENTS (AND OTHERS)

The broad picture which results from this is that the nomination and confirmation of Supreme Court Justices is, in many respects, similar to "politics as usual." On the other hand, opposition to presidential nominees in the Senate is by no means routine and requires special circumstances or unusual provocation by the president. Both of these characteristics need to be carefully considered by the president when he is selecting a Supreme Court nominee.

Scholarship on the legislative process strongly suggests that reliance upon partisanship to obtain passage of presidential legislation is a mistake. Laws are usually passed by bipartisan coalitions that are far larger than minimum–majority size.[26] Moreover, this holds true under conditions of both unified and divided government. Keith Krehbiel, drawing upon David Mayhew's work, asserts that "unified and divided governments are essentially indistinguishable from one another in terms of their propensities for gridlock, or conversely, for producing important legislative enactments."[27]

Another well-established axiom of American politics is that "presidential power is the power to persuade"[28] and, in particular, the power to persuade members of the opposition party to vote for your bills in the legislature. "Politics as normal," therefore, clearly counsels the president to approach Supreme Court nominations in a bipartisan spirit. This includes the willingness to bargain and compromise with those not yet fully persuaded.

Here, however, a distinctive feature of the nomination process kicks in: any bargaining and compromise must be done before the nominee is announced. A presidential bill may be sent to Congress in its most desired form, but neither president nor Congress seriously expects it to be passed without amendment, probably of a major kind. This facility is not available in the case of presidential nominations that go to the Senate requiring an up-or-down vote.

Some, however, would assert a much more important feature which distinguishes senatorial consideration of a Supreme Court nominee from that of a presidential bill: that is, that the president is accorded, or at least may claim, near-total deference to his right to choose.[29] Presidents may therefore be tempted to ignore potential opposition to their choice of nominee, in the expectation that an insufficient number of those otherwise opposed will abandon the deference norm. Yet what the history of modern nominations shows, if nothing else, is that there are an increasing number of reasons why Senators feel themselves empowered to reject presidential nominees to the Supreme Court and the federal courts in general. Ideological opposition to the nominee is the most important, but policy values, partisanship and interest group opposition may also be significant in any given political context.[30]

This analysis therefore yields several axioms that may be used by the president when selecting a nominee to the U.S. Supreme Court:

Axiom 1:   Presidents do not need to battle their opponents in the Senate in order to further their goals in relation to judicial policy and the role of Court in the political system. A president can avoid provoking his Senate opponents by avoiding flamboyant or controversial selections. It is particularly inadvisable to make spite nominations.

Axiom 2:   Presidents can count on the unanimous support of members of their own party in the Senate when they nominate an uncontroversial candidate, but they will almost certainly lose some of those votes where their nominee is seriously provocative to the opposing party.

Axiom 3:   Presidents can count on a large number of votes from the opposition party in the Senate when they nominate an uncontroversial candidate.

Axiom 4:   Presidents can count neither on the unanimous support of their own party nor on a significant number of votes from the opposition party if they propose a controversial nominee.

Axiom 5:   Presidents who make a controversial nomination will almost certainly face a confirmation battle that they are as likely to lose as they are to win.

Axiom 6:   A nominee perceived as controversial on ideological grounds may be made sufficiently uncontroversial by offsetting the ideological extremism with a positive ethnic or gender appeal. An Anglo-Saxon, male, ideologically extreme nominee is the least likely of all to secure nomination.

Axiom 7:   The best way to avoid making a controversial, unconfirmable nomination is to negotiate with the opposition in advance.

If we return now to the situation facing President George W. Bush in the summer of 2003, it can be seen that that the administration is tempted to ignore these axioms and provoke a confirmation battle which it could well lose. Earlier in 2003, the *Washington Post* carried the following report:

White House aides have developed a strategy for filling a future vacancy on the Supreme Court that calls for nominating an ideological conservative even if it increases the chances that the person would not be confirmed, administration officials said.

. . . advisers to the President see no necessity to try to head off Democratic opposition by offering a moderate nominee . . . The officials said they are more likely to choose someone inclined to more conservative interpretations of the Constitution and take their chances with the Senate, where Republicans hold a majority of 51–49.

This aggressive attitude was partly inspired by an apparent belief that the Democrats intended to oppose whoever the President nominated, so the administration might as well choose a full-blown conservative.[31]

The passage quoted contains several fallacies. First, the Democrats are not likely to oppose whomever the president nominates. Indeed, such would be the relief of the Democrats if the nominee was not an extremist that the president would encounter little effective opposition. The second fallacy is the seeming willingness to rely upon a majority of 51–49. Ideologically controversial nominees unite the opposition and fracture the majority party. It is unlikely that the president could hold Republican defections to a mere handful if an ideological extremist were to be chosen. The third probable mistake is to dismiss the need to head off opposition, that is, the need to bargain and negotiate in advance. The mere unwillingness to countenance discussion with the opposition party is guaranteed to make a confirmation battle more certain and more dangerous.

Moreover, the reported list of conservatives' favored candidates for nomination suggests a failure to learn the lessons of recent confirmation history. Names mentioned include J. Harvie Wilkinson, chief judge of the 4th Circuit Court of Appeals; J. Michael Luttig, also from the 4th Circuit; Solicitor General Theodore Olson; Edith Jones, from the 5th Circuit; and Samuel Alito, from the 3rd Circuit. Of these, only Jones and Alito possess an off-setting characteristic.

Contrast this with the candidate that conservatives are opposed to: White House Counsel Alberto A. Gonzales. First, he is not an extremist. As conservatives are keen to point out, he seems at least somewhat moderate on issues such as abortion and affirmative action. He would likely be in the mold of Justice O'Connor or Kennedy. Secondly, he would be the first Hispanic to be nominated to the Supreme Court, that is, the best off-setting characteristic possible.

The question arises as to why a president who is willing to bargain and compromise on issues such as tax-cuts and school vouchers would choose to adopt an absolutist approach over Supreme Court nominations? Part of the answer could be that the imperatives of the new politics of Supreme Court appointments have still to be fully appreciated.

NOTES

1. Senator John Cornyn (R-Tex.), "Second Judicial Nominee Targeted," WashingtonPost.com, April 30, 2003.
2. R. E. Hartley and L. A. Holmes, *The Increasing Senate Scrutiny of Lower Federal Court Nominees, Political Science Quarterly*, 117 (2002), pp. 259–278.

3. J. D. Felice & Herbert F. Weisberg, "The Changing Importance of Ideology, Party, and Region in Confirmation of Supreme Court Nominees, 1953-1988," *Kentucky Law Journal*, 77 (1988–89), pp. 509–530.

4. Henry J. Abraham, *Justices, Presidents, and Senators: A History of the U.S. Supreme Court Appointments from Washington to Clinton* (Lanham, MD: Rowman and Littlefield, 1999), p. 28.

5. Abraham, *Justices, Presidents, and Senators*, pp. 30–31.

6. Epstein et al, *The Supreme Court Compendium* (Washington, D.C.,: Congressional Quarterly, 1994), p. 288.

7. *Newsweek*, 9 August 1965.

8. Fortas Hearings, 5 August 1965.

9. Judiciary Committee Report, August 21, 1967, p. 11.

10. Senate Judiciary Committee Hearings on the Nomination of Thurgood Marshall to the U.S. Supreme Court, 19 July, 1967, p. 164.

11. For example, Senator Eastland noted that when Marshall was on the court of appeals, he had written an opinion which had cited the work of Herbert Aptheker. Eastland then asked: Well, now, of course, I don't want to leave the impression that you have ever been a communist or anything like that, but did you know that at the time you cited this work that, the author of that book, Herbert Aptheker, had been for many years an avowed Communist and was the leading Communist theoretician in the United States?, ibid. p. 176.

12. Report of the Senate Judiciary Committee on the nomination of Abe Fortas as Chief Justice, 20 September, 1968, p.1.

13. Ibid. p. 8.

14. Abraham, *Justices, Presidents, and Senators*, p. 218.

15. Of the Democrat opposition to Haynesworth, Stephen Ambrose wrote: "The real objection was Haynesworth's conservative philosophy, and beyond that the Democrats' desire to have some revenge for the Fortas rejection." *Nixon: The Triumph of a Politician, 1962–72* (New York: Simon & Schuster, 1989), p. 315.

16. Gregory A. Caldeira and Jerald R. Wright, "Lobbying for Justice: The Rise of Organized Conflict in the Politics of Federal Judgeships," in Lee Epstein, ed., *Contemplating Courts* (Washington, DC: CQ Press, 1995).

17. Fortas Hearings, 1968, p. iii. At his 1965 hearings, only the Liberty Lobby appeared against him, Fortas hearings, 1965, p. iii.

18. Those against were: the AFL-CIO; the UAW; the Textile Workers Union; the Leadership Conference on Civil Rights; the NAACP; the ADA; the Committee for a Fair, Honest and Impartial Judiciary; the Black American Law Students Association; and several leading black members of the House of Representatives, Haynesworth Hearings, 1969, pp. iii–iv.

19. *Congressional Record*, vol.116, Pt 8, 91st Congress, 2nd Session, 1970.

20. Rehnquist/Powell Hearings 1971, pp. iii–v. NOW spoke against both Powell and Rehnquist, but the National Women's Political Caucus only made a general plea for women to be nominated to the Court, pp. 421–423.

21. Abraham, *Justices, Presidents, and Senators*, p. 269.

22. Abraham, *Justices, Presidents, and Senators*, p. 270.

23. On the former, see Peter G. Fish, "Perspectives of the Selection of Federal Judges: Spite Nominations to the United States Supreme Court," *Kentucky Law Journal*, 77 (1988–1989), pp. 545–576. On the latter, see for example, Robert J. McKeever, *Courting the Congress, Politics*, 11 (no., 1991) pp. 26–33.

24. "Washington Focus: Law and Judiciary," *Congressional Quarterly Weekly Report*, April 10, 1999, pp. 845–847.

25. Interview with Manus Cooney, 4th November, 1996.

26. K. Krehbiel, *Pivotal Politics: A Theory of US Lawmaking* (Chicago: University of Chicago Press, 1998), p. 6.

27. Krehbiel, *Pivotal Politics*, pp. 52–53.

28. Richard Neustadt, *Presidential Power*.

29. Donald Songer, "The Relevance of Policy Values for the Confirmation of Supreme Court Nominees," *Law & Society*, 13 (Summer, 1979): 927–948, 928.

30. See, for example, Jeffrey A. Segal, Albert D. Cover and Charles M. Cameron, "Senate Confirmation of Supreme Court Justices: The Role of Ideology in Senate Confirmation of Supreme Court Justices," *Kentucky Law Journal* 77 (1988–89), pp. 485–507; Songer, "The Relevance of Policy Values For The Confirmation of Supreme Court Nominees"; Felice & Weisberg, see fn. 3; Gregory A. Caldeira, "Commentary on Senate Confirmation of Supreme Court of Supreme Court Justices: The Roles of Organized and Unorganized Interests," *Kentucky Law Journal* 77 (1988–89), pp. 531–538.

31. *Washington Post*, 19 January, 2003, p. A04.

CHAPTER 9

George W. Bush:
Policy, Politics, and Personality

◆ ◆ ◆

James P. Pfiffner
The School of Public Policy
George Mason University

During his time in office, President George W. Bush demonstrated impressive leadership skills.[1] He was able to overcome the lack of a mandate in the 2000 election and convince Congress to pass a large tax cut. He continued to press his policy agenda when the terrorist attacks of 9-11 transformed his presidency and reoriented its focus. The war on terrorism in Afghanistan was prosecuted effectively, with the Taliban being overthrown and Al Qaeda driven out of the country. The broader success of the war was mixed, however; as of the summer of 2003 Osama Bin Laden was not captured, the terrorist threat of Al Qaeda was not eliminated, and Afghanistan remained unstable.

In an impressive display of political leadership, in 2002 President Bush was able to overcome the skepticism of the professional military in the United States, the opposition of much of the world, and the lack of support from the UN Security Council and take the United States to war with Iraq in order to depose Saddam Hussein. The war ended within three weeks, though the attempt to install a legitimate successor government was to take much longer. Over this period, President Bush has exhibited several patterns of behavior that provide some insight into his policy choices. He has shown a preference for moral certainty over strategic calculation; a tendency for visceral reaction rather than reflection; a preference for clarity rather than complexity; a bias toward action rather than deliberation; and a preference for the personal over the structural or procedural.[2] Bush exuded confidence and moral certainty and exhibited no evidence of self doubt or ambivalence about major decisions.

Even though many presidential options are constrained by the established structure of the office and by environmental demands on the president, the Bush presidency illustrates the impact of personality on the major policies of a presidency.[3] The first section of this chapter will examine President Bush's bias for action and impatience with procedural delay. The second section will address his moral certainty and its implications. The third section will look at the consequences of his personal approach to politics and policy formation. The conclusion will note the positive and negative implications of each of the president's tendencies. It must be noted that few inside accounts of the Bush presidency have been made public so far, thus these observations are based on public documents and are therefore necessarily tentative.

This chapter will not attempt to analyze President Bush from a psycho-biographical perspective such as that of James David Barber's framework of presidential character.[4] And from evidence so far available, his advisory system does not seem to fit easily into the frameworks developed by Richard Tanner Johnson or Alexander George.[5] Bush's White House does not even seem to fit either the strong chief of staff or the spokes-of-the-wheel models of White House staff organization.[6] The purpose of this chapter is merely to point out patterns of presidential behavior and relate these patterns or tendencies to important policies of the administration.

A BIAS FOR ACTION

As president, George W. Bush demonstrated decisiveness and an impatience for unnecessary delay. In contrast to President Clinton, who wanted to analyze every issue thoroughly and ensure that all angles had been examined, often in long drawn out meetings, President Bush preferred to act decisively and intuitively. In his words, "I just think it's instinctive. I'm not a textbook player. I'm a gut player."[7] He felt that one part of his role as president was "to force decisions, and to make sure it's in everybody's mind where we're headed."[8]

In the aftermath of the terrorist attacks on the United States of 9-11, President Bush often exhibited impatience in leading his administration and the military to develop and implement the U.S. response. Though he sometimes felt the military's response to his direction was too slow, he understood the instinctive conservatism of military leadership. "It's very important to realize how do you balance the military's desire to cover all contingencies at least once, maybe sometimes twice—they're relatively risk-adverse and they should be, after all they're dealing with people's lives—versus the need to, for whatever reason, to show action."[9] Of course the president was also making decisions of life and death, but he also felt the political need to show the public that he was acting. As he told King Abdullah of Jordan in late September of 2001, "We're steady, clear-eyed and patient, but pretty soon we'll have to start displaying scalps."[10]

In late September, during the planning stages for the war in Afghanistan, when National Security Advisor Condoleezza Rice explained to the president that the military was not yet ready to insert troops into Afghanistan because the search and rescue (CSAR) capacity was not yet in place, Bush responded, "That's not acceptable." Rice explained the difficulty of establishing bases, getting equipment in place, and coordinating with foreign governments. At a meeting with the principals, Vice President Cheney expressed a different perspective. "The president wants to avoid putting any artificial constraints or timelines on our military action. Let's do it right.

Let's not do something stupid for PR purposes." Later Bush reflected on his impatience and the role of Condoleezza Rice: "Sometimes that's the way I am—fiery. On the other hand [Rice's] job is to bear the brunt of some of the fire, so that it takes the edge off a little bit. And she's good at that."[11]

Bush's bias for action also reflected his perspective on political capital. He felt that his father had not fully used the tremendous political capital he enjoyed after the Gulf War in 1991 when his public approval was at historic highs; he was determined that he would not make the same mistake.[12] Bush 43 wanted to use his political capital to achieve large goals. "I will seize the opportunity to achieve big goals. There is nothing bigger than to achieve world peace."[13] If he did not use his time wisely, Bush felt that history would not be kind to him. "History will be the judge, but it won't judge well somebody who doesn't act, somebody who just bides time here," he told Japanese Prime Minister Koizumi in the fall of 2001.[14] Impatience and a bias for action do not necessarily mean a lack of determination or perseverance, which Bush demonstrated in pursuit of tax cuts and other administration priorities.

In January of 2003 when other members of the UN Security Council wanted to give the inspectors in Iraq more time to search for weapons of mass destruction, President Bush was convinced that inspections would not work and was impatient for U.S. military action to depose Saddam Hussein. "Time is running out on Saddam Hussein. He must disarm. I'm sick and tired of games and deception. And that's my view of timetables."[15] At a news conference, Bush declared, "Any attempt to drag the process on for months will be resisted by the United States. . . . This just needs to be resolved quickly."[16]

The positive side of a bias for action is that a president has a better chance to get things done in a city where new initiatives can often be delayed until enough opposition develops to stop them entirely. This was one of the problems with President Clinton's health care proposals in 1993 and 1994. The potential down side of a bias for action includes premature decisions, a failure to examine the full implications of decisions, and the use of information before it is fully vetted or examined. The following sections will illustrate some of the positive and negative aspects of a bias for action.

Early Decisions on War With Iraq

In an interview in the summer of 2002 Bush reflected on the nature of the coalition to fight the war on terrorism in Afghanistan, but his words also foreshadowed his impatience with the process of gaining international approval and the UN Security Council resolution for confronting Iraq.

> Well, you can't talk your way to a solution to a problem. . . . I believe in results. . . . It's like earning capital in many ways. It is a way for us to earn capital in a coalition that can be fragile. And the reason it will be fragile is that there is resentment toward us. . . . Well, we're never going to get people all in agreement about force and the use of force. But action—confident action that will yield positive results provides kind of a slipstream into which reluctant nations and leaders can get behind. . . ."[17]

According to State Department director of policy and planning, Richard Haas, in the summer of 2002 President Bush had already made up his mind that war with Iraq was inevitable (barring capitulation by Saddam Hussein). "The president made a decision in the summer of 2002. We all saluted at that point. That is the way it works."[18] Haas said that he raised the issue of war with Iraq with Rice, ". . . I raised this issue about were we really sure that we wanted to put Iraq front and center at this point, given the war on terrorism and other issues. And she said, essentially, that that decision's been made, don't waste your breath."[19] The president may have made up his mind even earlier. In March 2002 the president told Condoleezza Rice when she was in a meeting with several senators, "F____ Saddam. We're taking him out."[20]

Though Secretary of State Colin Powell convinced Bush to go to the UN and orchestrated the unanimous UN Security Council passage of Resolution 1441, the president ordered troops to the Gulf region in December 2002, shortly after the resolution was passed.[21]

A bias for action and impatience with large bureaucracies can be a useful trait in a president, as long as the president has an effective advisory system that fully lays out the consequences of immediate action. In the decision making process leading up to the war with Iraq, the president may not have fully considered the arguments against the war that were made by Secretary of State Colin Powell (or potentially others) because he had seemingly already made up his mind. As indicated by State Department official Richard Haas, administration officials did not feel free to present opposing arguments to the president or his immediate aides because they were convinced that the decision had already been made. One former Bush staffer said of the Bush White House, "No one's allowed to second-guess, even when you should."[22] This does not mean that the decision to go to war with Iraq was wrong or that Bush would have made a different decision about war had his aides not perceived that he had already made up his mind; it merely means that he probably did not get the full range of frank advice from his advisers that he might have.

The Use of Forged Documents in the Arguments for War

Another example of President Bush's tendency to act instinctively and his impatience with details was the use by the United States government of forged documents to bolster the argument for war with Iraq. On September 24, 2002 the government of Britain charged that Iraq had tried to buy significant amounts of nuclear material from Niger. That information was used in a closed hearing of the Foreign Relations Committee of the Senate to help convince Senators to vote for the resolution giving President Bush the authority to take the United States to war with Iraq. Several months later, in his State of the Union speech on January 28, 2003, President Bush said "The British government has learned that Saddam Hussein recently sought significant quantities of uranium from Africa."[23]

The problem was that the documents used as evidence were forged and not authentic. The letter-head of one letter was from the military government that had been replaced before the 1999 date on the letter, and the signature on the letter indicated the name of a foreign ministry official who had left the position in 1989. The forgery was made public on March 7, 2003 by Mohamed El Baradei who was director of the International Atomic Energy Agency who reported the findings to the UN Security Council.[24]

Why would President Bush use documents of such dubious provenance? The issue was not minor; it was a question of convincing Congress to approve a resolution to let the president make the final decision about going to war. The State of the Union address presented the country with the prospect of war with Iraq, and the assertion that Saddam Hussein was developing nuclear weapons was one of the strongest arguments the administration had that regime change in Baghdad was necessary. Even though there may have been other, more credible evidence that Saddam was developing weapons of mass destruction, the use of forged documents to make the public argument for war with Iraq, if exposed, would undercut U.S. credibility with foreign nations.

There were reports that top CIA officials had serious reservations about the authenticity of the documents that were the basis for Bush's statements.[25] What could explain the president's willingness to use the dubious documents in a public argument for war with Iraq? The president could easily have demanded that the CIA carefully examine the documents before including an account of them in his State of the Union address, but seemingly he did not. Most likely the account fit well with the president's judgments about Iraq, and he did not want to wait for the time it would take to subject the documents to careful scrutiny. It is also possible that the CIA felt pressure (justified or not) not to press arguments that might be interpreted as unfavorable to the administration's arguments about Saddam Hussein.[26]

The president's willingness to use the documents as a basis for his public argument for regime change in Iraq without demanding that they be examined carefully by U.S. intelligence experts illustrated his tendency to act instinctively and quickly rather than after careful deliberation and examination of the evidence.

Another example of the president's use of incorrect information in his arguments without careful examination occurred when President Bush was responding to reporters' questions about the conclusiveness of evidence that regime change in Iraq was necessary. On September 7, 2002, at Camp David Bush said, ". . . when the inspectors first went into Iraq and were denied, finally denied access, a report came out of the Atomic—the IAEA—that they were six months away from developing a weapon. I don't know what more evidence we need."[27] The IAEA report, however, said that ". . . the IAEA has found no indication of Iraq having achieved its program goal of producing nuclear weapons or of Iraq having retained a physical capability for the production of weapon-usable nuclear material or having clandestinely obtained such material."[28] The report did say that before the 1991 Gulf War Iraq had been 6 to 24 months away from creating a nuclear capacity.

The downside of President Bush's impatience and self-reported dependence on his instincts, rather than careful analysis, was that at times he might make public statements that later turn out to be not true. This can be damaging to the nation's credibility, especially in making decisions about going to war. Stephen Hess, former Eisenhower White House staffer, scholar, and expert on the Presidency, said,

". . . what worries me about some of these [statements in the fall of 2002] is they appear to be with foresight. This is about public policy in its grandest sense, about potential wars and who is our enemy, and a president has a special obligation to getting it right."[29] A president's effectiveness can be compromised if a bias for action pushes out the need to ensure the accuracy of important statements.

The Early Start of the Ground War in Iraq

President Bush's decisions on the commencement of the ground war in Iraq were criticized by some in the professional military as premature. There had been an ongoing disagreement between some military officers and the civilian leadership in the Department of Defense over the number of troops necessary for a successful military campaign in Iraq. During planning for the war in the fall of 2002 Secretary of Defense Donald Rumsfeld repeatedly overruled military planners and insisted that the number of ground troops planned for the war be reduced.[30]

In the immediate lead-up to the war, U.S. troops were in ships in the Mediterranean Sea waiting for permission from Turkey to use their ports and roads so that the United States could open up a second front in the north of Iraq for the push to Baghdad. When Turkey's parliament denied access to U.S. troops, a decision had to be made as to whether to delay the onset of the ground war until the troops (and other troops from the United States) were in staging areas in Kuwait or to begin the war shortly after the bombing of Saddam's bunker on March 19.

President Bush decided to move quickly with a "rolling start," counting on the reinforcements to move into Iraq later rather than waiting for all the forces to be ready before beginning the attack. The first two weeks of the war saw U.S. troops successfully drive to Baghdad, but with extended supply lines that were vulnerable to attack and troops who were exhausted from battle who could not be immediately replaced with fresh troops. The willingness of U.S. generals to make their critical views known publicly through recently retired high level military leaders was unusual during war time. Retired General Joseph P. Hoar, commander of the U.S. Central Command (including Iraq) from 1991–1994, wrote ". . . the civilians wanted the war done in a new, leaner way to justify their vision of the 'transformation force' expected to be in place by 2010 . . . the concept of risk in a military operation is not solely about winning and losing, it is also about the cost. In this case, the cost will be measured in American lives."[31]

After another week of combat, however, American troops were successful in occupying Baghdad. With relatively few American deaths (about 100 to that point), the president's decision to move quickly was seemingly vindicated. Whether the decision was a stroke of brilliance or a tactical error can only be judged definitively in historical perspective. The point is that President Bush had a bias for action and was decisive in his judgments about military strategy.

President Bush's early decision about war with Iraq, his willingness to accept at face value documents of dubious authenticity to support his arguments for war, and his decision to move ground troops quickly into Iraq, may have been related to his own moral certainty and his judgment about the necessity for regime change in Iraq.

MORAL CERTAINTY AND UNIVERSAL RHETORIC

President George W. Bush's style of political leadership exhibited a confidence and moral certainty that helped the nation deal with the aftermath of the terrorist attacks on the World Trade Towers and the Pentagon. In such situations, the rhetoric of moral certainty is clearly an asset. Bush's moral certainty reflected his deeply held religious beliefs which were evident in his public and private lives. His moral certainty was also reflected in his conviction that the United States was in the right and did not have to defer to other nations. His ideas about the implications of the uniqueness of U.S. military power and the moral imperatives that led from his values were formally expressed in the National Security Policy of the United States. This section examines these dimensions of President Bush's leadership; it concludes with an evaluation of the positive and negative aspects of each of them.

President Bush's Religious Beliefs

Ever since his life-altering decision to stop drinking in 1986, George Bush's Christian convictions have played a major role in his life.[32] He regularly participated in Bible study groups and spoke, sometimes publicly, about his faith. In contrast to some other presidents who expressed religious beliefs, Bush clearly was a person who took his faith very seriously in his personal and public life. In 1993, the year before running for governor, Bush said that only those who believed in Jesus could get into heaven.[33] This was in an interview with a Jewish reporter, not a private religious meeting; it thus was intended to have political significance.

According to a Bush friend, Bush told him when he was Governor of Texas, "I believe God wants me to run for president."[34] During his campaign for the presidency George W. Bush often mentioned his Christian religious values, and when asked in a Republican debate in Iowa (December 13, 2000) to name his most admired "*political* philosopher," (emphasis added) he responded "Christ, because he changed my heart."[35] Bush's faith led him to believe that human history (and presumably politics) are governed by the intentions of God. "Events aren't moved by blind change and chance. Behind all of life and all of history, there's a dedication and purpose, set by the hand of a just and faithful God."[36]

The president's approach to religion was evident in the White House where he opened cabinet meetings with a prayer. The pervasiveness of the president's approach to his Christian faith was reflected when a new speech writer, David Frum (who happened to be Jewish), first entered the West Wing and heard the words, "Missed you at Bible study," directed at his boss, Michael Gerson. Frum said that Bible study in the Bush White House, ". . . was, if not compulsory, not quite *uncompulsory*, either" (emphasis in original) and was "disconcerting to a non-Christian like me."[37] Although this incident might be seen as minor, it illustrated the assumption that at least some White House staffers were expected to share not only the President's religion, but also to conform to the prevailing White House staff religious practices, that is, attending regular prayer breakfasts.

President Bush's religious convictions were consistent with his lack of ambivalence about war and his willingness to take actions unpopular in much of the world.[38] His religious beliefs may also have led to his moral certainty, his disdain for hesitation, his avoidance of ambiguity, and his lack of self doubt. According to historian Richard Brookhiser, "Practically, Bush's faith means that he does not tolerate, or even recognize, ambiguity: there is an all-knowing God who decrees certain behaviors, and leaders must obey."[39]

Condoleezza Rice, commenting on her advisory role, said of Bush "He least likes me to say, 'This is complex.' "[40] Bush's impatience with complexity was accompanied by the firm conviction that the United States was special in the world and that it had a mission to stand up for moral values and confront evil. Other states did not merely have different interests than the United States, some of them pursued evil goals and had to be confronted, militarily if necessary. Bush's faith that history is guided by God and conviction that the United States was fighting for God-given values may have made it easier for him to embrace war as one of the instruments of history.

Universal Values and "Unilateralism"

During the campaign for the presidency, George W. Bush's tendency was toward disengagement from the rest of the world, compared to the Clinton administration. He felt that China was the strategic competitor of the United States rather than the strategic partner that Clinton sought. He felt that the U.S. was too engaged in the Middle East peace process, and he thought that the U.S. should reconsider its commitment to peacekeeping in the Balkans. He rejected the Clinton administration's attempt to foster a reconciliation between North and South Korea. Bush did not seem to be inclined to an aggressive foreign policy. In commenting on foreign relations during the presidential debates, he said, "It really depends on how our nation conducts itself in foreign policy. If we're an arrogant nation, they'll resent us. If we're a humble nation, but strong, they'll welcome us."[41] With his support of increased military spending and reservations about an active foreign policy, Bush seemed to echo Theodore Roosevelt's advice to "speak softly but carry a big stick."

But the terrorist attacks of 9-11 on the United States ended his reluctance to be assertive in foreign policy, ". . . my vision shifted dramatically after September the 11th because I now realize the stakes. I realize the world has changed."[42] No longer would the United States be a "humble nation," but one chosen by God to lead the world: ". . . our nation is chosen by God and commissioned by history to be a model to the world of justice and inclusion and diversity without division."[43] It would be the mission of the United States to extend the universal values of America to the rest of the world. "As I said in my State of the Union, liberty is not America's gift to the world. Liberty is God's gift to every human being in the world. . . .We're called to extend the promise of this country into the lives of every citizen who lives here."[44] The pursuit of regime change in Iraq was part of President Bush's vision of extending liberty to the rest of the world.

Bush's moral clarity was based on strong convictions. In discussing the war on terrorism, he stated:

There is a human condition that we must worry about in times of war. There is
a value system that cannot be compromised—God-given values. These aren't
United States-created values. There are values of freedom and the human condition and mothers loving their children. What's very important as we articu-
late foreign policy through our diplomacy and military action, is that it never
look like we are creating—we are the author of these values.[45]

Bush clearly felt that his foreign policy decisions were always in pursuit of these values. At one level the president was indicating that the United States was subject to
God's will; on the other hand, he was implying that the United States knew God's
will and was the instrument of God's will.

Critics of the administration argued that Bush's vision of America's place in the
world led to a unilateral approach to international relations and undercut multilateral cooperation with other nations. President Bush's tendency to see the United
States as unique and uniquely powerful led to the rejection or abandonment of a
number of treaties or proposed international agreements by his administration.
These included:

Antiballistic Missile Treaty (signed with the USSR in 1972)

Kyoto accord on global warming (1997)

Treaty on Anti-Personnel Mines (1997)

Comprehensive Test Ban Treaty (rejected by the Senate 1999)

Biological Weapons Control Treaty (Biological and Toxin Weapons Convention) protocol to verify and enforce the 1972 treaty on biological weapons
(2001)

Small-arms Control Agreement (2001)

UN Conference Against Racism (2001) (U.S. refused to participate)

Rights of Woman (CEDAW: Convention on the Elimination of All Forms of
Discrimination Against Women (2002)

International Criminal Court (2002)

The "Agreed Framework" with North Korea, negotiated by the Clinton administration

Each of these active or proposed treaties or conventions undoubtedly had problems from the U.S. perspective, and some were also rejected by the Clinton administration. But collectively, from the perspective of other countries, it could easily
look like a pattern of contempt for international agreements and an unwillingness
of the Bush administration to work with other countries on mutual problems. Often
the potential agreements were seemingly dismissed out of hand without efforts by
the administration to propose alternative ways to address the intent behind the
agreements.

In the buildup to war with Iraq the Bush administration further demonstrated
its rejection of multilateral approaches by arguing that the UN would be irrelevant
if it did not ratify the U.S. approach to Iraq. And when Germany and France were
unwilling to endorse the U.S. decision to go to war with Iraq, they were dubbed the

"Old Europe" by Donald Rumsfeld. When it was obvious that a second resolution to authorize war with Iraq would not be ratified by the UN Security Council, the United States abandoned its efforts for a resolution and went to war against the expressed wishes of most of the members of the Security Council. Bush exhibited impatience with and sometimes a disdain for diplomacy. In response to a question about the Middle East, Bush said: "Look, my job isn't to try to nuance. My job is to tell people what I think."[46]

Bush rejected any criticism of his approach as being unilateral. ". . . If you want to hear resentment, just listen to the word unilateralism. I mean, that's resentment. . . . which I find amusing."[47] In responding to a European leader's complaint that the United States did not sufficiently take into account European perspectives, Bush stated his views on coalitions: "Well, that's very interesting. Because my belief is the best way that we hold this coalition together is to be clear on our objectives and to be clear that we are determined to achieve them. You hold a coalition together by strong leadership and that's what we intend to provide."[48]

President Bush's approach to nations which disagreed with his priorities was often that they were beyond the pale. As he said in January 2003, "Either you're with us or you're with the enemy. Either you're with those who love freedom or you're with those who hate innocent life."[49] The President's approach to other nations was sometimes resented by them. Fareed Zakaria, former editor of *Foreign Affairs*, argued in March 2003 that President Bush was undermining good will for the United States throughout the world. "Having traveled around the world and met with senior government officials in dozens of countries over the past year, I can report that with the exception of Britain and Israel, every country the administration has dealt with feels humiliated by it."[50]

The president seemed to ignore his observation in the second presidential debate that U.S. arrogance could easily lead to resentment. But others' opinions may not have bothered the president as foreign opinion about the United States shifted from sympathy and support (immediately after 9-11) to suspicion and hostility (preceding war with Iraq). In dismissing the voices of dissent on the UN Security Council, President Bush declared that the United Nations was irrelevant to the U.S. decision to go to war with Iraq, "This is not a question of authority, it is a question of will."[51]

National Security Strategy of the United States, the "Bush Doctrine"

Bush's moral convictions and belief in the special role of the United States was expressed most thoroughly and authoritatively in the 2002 document, "The National Security Strategy of the United States of America." The document articulated what Henry Kissinger called a "revolutionary" revision of U.S. policy away from the containment and deterrence strategy of the Cold War era and addressed a new emphasis on terrorism and rogue states.[52]

The policy doctrine began with a declaration that the U.S. model of government is universal and has triumphed:

The great struggles of the twentieth century between liberty and totalitarian-ism ended with a decisive victory for the forces of freedom—and a single sustainable model for national success: freedom, democracy, and free enter-prise. . . . These values of freedom are right and true for every person, in every society. . . . [53](p. 1)

The document also declared that the United States would act preemptively or to prevent any challenge to it, ". . . America will act against such emerging threats be-fore they are fully formed." (p. 1) And it issued a warning to rival military powers: "Our forces will be strong enough to dissuade potential adversaries from pursuing a military build-up in hopes of surpassing, or equaling, the power of the United States." (p. 22) Thus the declaration was aimed not just at rogue states but at any future "potential adversary" of the United States.

Bush noted the dominant position of the United States in military power, "The United States possesses unprecedented—and unequaled—strength and influence in the world," (p. 3) and said it would use its power, ". . . the United States will use this moment of opportunity to extend the benefits of freedom across the globe." (p. 2) America would not wait to be attacked, "the United States cannot remain idle while dangers gather." (p. 11) But rather ". . . we will not hesitate to act alone, if necessary to exercise our right of self defense by acting preemptively against such terrorists. . . ." (p. 6) or "rogue states" determined to acquire weapons of mass destruction.

It is one thing for a nation to argue in an *ad hoc* manner that, as a matter of na-tional security or self interest, it intends to attack another nation that it believes is threatening. But it is quite another thing to elevate preemptive war to a matter of high principle and formal national security doctrine. A war is considered preemp-tive when a state attacks another state that is poised to attack it, thus preempting the anticipated attack. But preemptive war easily slides into preventive war when the potential threat is in the future; it is just a matter of how imminent the threat is perceived to be. The warning in the U.S. statements that other nations should not use preemption as an excuse for aggression is not likely to be heeded by other na-tions and may encourage or legitimate their use of preventive wars. As Brent Scow-croft, national security adviser for Presidents Ford and Bush 41, said:

> It is not clear to me what advantage there is in declaring it publicly. It has been common knowledge that under some circumstances the U.S. would pre-empt. As a declaratory policy it tends to leave the door open to others who want to claim the same right. By making it public we also tend to add to the world's perception that we are arrogant and unilateral.[54]

Positive and Negative Consequences of Moral Certainty

The positive side of President Bush's moralistic and Manichaean view of the world is the moral clarity it brings to U.S. policy.[55] His certainty and conviction enhanced his leadership during the war on terrorism. But the drawbacks in elevating the principles of the war on terrorism (e.g. preemption) to the explicit strategic policy of the United States are that the stated principles do not apply as well to the many nation states in the world and make consistent application of the principles difficult. The drawbacks of such an approach may entail several potential problems:

1. Other states may use the same justification for preemptive wars in their own interests.
2. If the U.S. does not apply the doctrine consistently, it may be seen as bluffing and not serious.
3. Other states might take the U.S. declaration as a serious threat and react militarily.

These drawbacks can be seen in case of North Korea. In 2001 the Bush administration rejected the Clinton administration's "The Agreed Framework" because North Korea was not fully adhering to its side of the agreement to stop nuclear weapons development in exchange for fuel and food aid. In January 2002 President Bush included North Korea in the "axis of evil" that the United States had to oppose. In June at West Point he said that the U.S. would act preemptively against its enemies, and in September he elevated preemption to formal U.S. national security doctrine. And during the same year the Bush administration prepared for war against one of the "axis of evil" states, Iraq.

Thus when in late 2002 and early 2003 North Korea expelled the UN inspectors who were monitoring its nuclear plants and announced its withdrawal from the nuclear nonproliferation agreement, the United States was put in a difficult position. While it was moving against Iraq, which did not yet have nuclear weapons, it was faced with the reality of North Korea which had several nuclear weapons and threatened to begin to build more of them in the near future. The administration's reaction was that this did not constitute a crisis, and after saying that it would not negotiate with North Korea, it began to move back to the Clinton position of offering aid in exchange for an agreement to stop nuclear weapons development. The actions of North Korea could well have been a rational response to the new U.S. strategic doctrine of preemption along with its inclusion in the "axis of evil" that Bush had declared.

Declarations of universal values in pursuit of U.S. foreign policy goals are sometimes useful, as they were in the war on terrorism. But writing them into policy could cause problems, especially when applied to other nation states. The Bush administration wanted to use the principles to move against Saddam but did not want to use them against North Korea. Nor did it want North Korea to conclude that the United States was serious about its declared principles and likely to attack North Korea. The U.S. also had to deal with other nation states which did not fully adhere to the ideals articulated in its policy pronouncements. For instance Pakistan was an undemocratic, nuclear power, but it was closely allied with the United States and was crucial to the war on terrorism. Saudi Arabia and other Middle East states were also not democratic but nevertheless were important allies of the United States.

VIEWING THE WORLD IN PERSONAL TERMS

One of the attractive sides of President Bush was his personal approach to people. Many Americans saw him as a "regular guy" in contrast to his father who was often perceived as distant or out of touch (regardless of the validity of such perceptions). The president often gave nicknames to members of his administration or the press and kidded them during breaks in formal appearances. In sharp contrast to his father, the younger Bush clearly enjoyed campaigning, and his active campaigning was seen as one of the reasons for the Republicans' congressional victories in the 2002 elections. In the White House Bush often used humor to defuse tense situations and put his aides at ease.[56] While his personableness was always an asset, Bush's tendency to take politics personally was sometimes an asset and sometimes a drawback.

For instance, President Bush held former President Clinton in contempt and seemed to turn away from some policy options merely because they were associated with Clinton.[57] In the campaign he said that China should be considered our strategic competitor rather than our strategic partner, as Clinton had said. Bush quickly rejected the Clinton administration's "Agreed Framework" attempt to smooth relations between North and South Korea and did not try to amend (by seeking stronger enforcement) and build on them. Most striking was Bush's contempt for Clinton's response to terrorist attacks on the U.S. embassies and the U.S.S. *Cole*. Clinton had launched cruise missiles at an al Qaeda camp in Afghanistan; the missiles arrived too late, and the camp was empty.[58] Bush admitted, however, that he did not attempt any action or serious planning before 9-11.

Bush's instinctive reaction to events, his decisiveness, and his personal orientation were illustrated in the aftermath of the terrorist bombing in New York City. Senators from states affected by the 9-11 bombings came to visit Bush in the Oval Office on September 13, 2001, and Senator Charles Schumer (D-NY) told Bush of his personal experience of the bombings and his fear for his daughter; he then asked the president for $20 billion in aid for New York. While many presidents might have given a temporizing answer and have it staffed out, President Bush replied, "New York really needs twenty billion? You got it."[59] Later legislators from New York complained when the funds were not soon forthcoming.

In addition to President Bush's interpersonal skills, he often saw the world in personal terms. Perhaps the most famous example of this was President Bush's decision after several meetings that he could trust Russian Premier Putin. After his first meeting with Putin, Bush said, "I looked the man in the eye. . . . I was able to get a sense of his soul."[60] Later in the summer of 2001, Putin told Bush about a cross of his mother's that held great sentimental value to him. Bush was very impressed at the religious symbol, and when Putin later showed the cross to Bush, Bush concluded that he could be trusted. "We had a very successful meeting. And I had convinced him that I no longer viewed Russia as an enemy, and I viewed him, on a personal level, as somebody with whom we could deal."[61]

In reassuring President Musharraf in November 2001 that the United States would not abandon its commitment to Pakistan after the war in Afghanistan was over, Bush told him, "Tell the Pakistani people that the president of the United States looked you in the eye and told you we wouldn't do that."[62] U.S. policy in the Middle East seemed to change significantly in the spring of 2002 when Bush decided that Yassar Arafat was personally responsible for the continued suicide bombings and had to go before peace could be seriously pursued. Bush subsequently decided not to continue to press the Israelis about their settlements in the West Bank and called Ariel Sharon a "man of peace." When Premier Schroeder of Germany was running for reelection in the fall of 2002, he criticized U.S. plans for war in Iraq and said that Germany would not participate in an unauthorized attack. President Bush took Schroeder's statements personally and refused to call him with the traditional congratulations after his victory in the elections.

At one point during the fall of 2001 there were warnings of another terrorist attack, possibly targeting the White House, and the question of whether the president should leave the White House came up. Remembering some criticisms of his decision not to return to Washington immediately after the 9/11 attacks, Bush declared: "Those bastards are going to find me exactly here. And if they get me, they're going to get me right here." Vice President Cheney put the issue into less personal terms, "This isn't about you. This is about our Constitution," and the continuity of government. And so Cheney decided to go to a "secure, undisclosed location."[63]

While President Bush was often effective in using personal politics in international relations, for example in getting President Putin to accept the U.S. withdrawal from the ABM treaty, there were also drawbacks. Bush's declaration, "I loathe Kim Jong Il!,"[64] may have heightened tensions with North Korea, convinced it that cooperation with the United States was hopeless, and hardened its determination to restart its nuclear program in earnest. Personalizing interstate disputes also may reduce options for compromise and coming into agreement without embarrassment for one leader or the other. During the 1962 Cuban Missile crisis John Kennedy was careful not to push Khrushchev into a corner from which he could not extricate himself without losing face. Don Greg, former ambassador to South Korea was doubtful about U.S. reactions to North Korea's leader. "I believe it is counterproductive to treat Kim in a derisive or disdainful manner. . . .Now we are filled with legitimate doubts, but reasonable certainty about Kim's potential cannot be reached through ridicule."[65]

Early in the war on terrorism President Bush said that he wanted U.S. forces to capture Osama bin Laden "dead or alive." But as time passed and it became likely that Osama had escaped Afghanistan, his name was seldom heard in public statements by the administration.[66] He was soon replaced as the face of terror with Saddam Hussein. In the fall of 2001 Bush said "After all, this is the guy who tried to kill my dad."[67] Personalizing international disputes reduces the range of options available to presidents and may make it more difficult to respond to changing circumstances.

While President Bush often reacted to international relations in personal terms, he also depended on people, rather than structures or processes, in his advisory system. "If I have any genius or smarts, it's the ability to recognize talent, ask them to serve and work with them as a team."[68] Bush administration national security decision making did not seem to resemble any of the three models set out by Richard Tanner Johnson or Alexander George: formalistic, competitive, or collegial.[69]

Bush resisted the formal policy development processes favored by the Eisenhower and Nixon administrations.[70] He did not seem to relish the competitive approach that FDR often used.[71] One might argue that he favored the collegial model because of the high value he put on teamwork. But important aspects of the collegial model as analyzed by George included the creative dimensions of bringing differing perspectives to bear on the major questions facing an administration in a crisis. While President Bush may have welcomed differing perspectives on some aspects of implementation of his policy choices, reports do not seem to indicate that he welcomed vigorous give-and-take about fundamental policy direction.

The fact that some in the professional military in the summer of 2002 went public with their reservations about war with Iraq was one indication that they did not feel he was fully considering the consequences of possible war.[72] That Brent Scowcroft and James Baker of the first Bush presidency wrote op-ed pieces against war with Iraq was an indicator that in their judgment, the case against war had not been fully considered.[73] According to Bush aides, there never was a full-scale debate or discussion in a formal NSC meeting over whether or not to go to war with Iraq.[74] The president did hear the case against war with Iraq in the summer of 2002, but it did not come through a formal process but rather personally from Colin Powell.

Powell's role was particularly important for President Bush. Powell was the only person in the administration with sufficient stature and clout to be able to present an alternative perspective to the hard line point of view of Cheney, Rumsfeld, and Deputy Secretary of Defense Paul Wolfowitz. Rice arranged for Powell to see the president to make his case, but she did not see it as her role to make a strong case herself in opposition to the other principals. In a dinner with the president on August 5, 2002, Powell laid out the arguments against war with Iraq but also the arguments for going to the United Nations for a resolution if the president chose war.[75] Although Bush was not persuaded by Powell's reservations about war with Iraq, he did decide to go to the UN for a resolution about Iraq. Whether these presidential decisions were wise or not, it was only Powell who could have made the case credibly to the president.[76]

Thus President Bush's approach to the world and his style of decision making were personalistic in nature rather than procedural or structural. The advantages of his personal approach to international relations were his ability to form personal bonds with some foreign leaders that smoothed relations with their nations. The disadvantage of such a personal approach is that once disagreements become personalized, it is more difficult to reach a reconciliation if changing conditions warrant it. A personal approach to decision making can work well if the right people have the confidence of the president and can present opposing views and alternatives. The disadvantage to depending on individuals for this function is that it is highly dependent on having the right individuals always available.

CONCLUSION

The conclusion of this chapter is that presidential personality makes a difference in an administration's policy priorities and achievements. It is true that presidents are constrained in important ways by the structure and organization of the White House, and they face compelling environmental pressures to act in certain ways. It is also true that new presidents are stepping into a stream of policy development and governmental commitments that they cannot change at will. But the argument of this chapter has been that George W. Bush's personality—as exhibited in his bias for action, his moral certainty, and his personalistic approach to politics—has made important differences in his policy choices and thus in the direction of the United States government.

His bias for action led to his early decisions about war in Iraq, his willingness to use suspect documents to argue for it, and his decisions to begin the war with a "rolling start." His moral certainty, based in part on his religious beliefs, led to his conviction that God had chosen the United States to "extend" universal values throughout the world, sometimes through war. His personalistic approach to politics led to easing relations with Russia and aggravating relations with North Korea.

The consequences of these traits in a president are neither uniformly advantageous nor detrimental. They are, however, problematical. A bias for action can short circuit bureaucratic or political resistance; but it can also lead to premature decisions. Moral certainty can lend rhetorical support and firm leadership when there is unanimity of purpose; but it can shut off a full debate when there is serious doubt about a course of action. A personal approach to politics can facilitate cooperation with others (persons or nations); but it can also narrow options and forestall reconciliation under changed circumstances. Whether these personality traits are harnessed in the service of good policies depends on the wisdom of the president.

NOTES

For help in developing this chapter the author would like to thank Fred Greenstein, Jason Hartke, Hugh Heclo, Don Kash, Bob Karlson, Arnauld Nicogossian, and Colleen Shogan.

1. For treatments of President Bush's leadership skills, see: Bob Woodward, *Bush At War* (NY: Simon and Schuster, 2002); David Frum, *The Right Man* (NY: Random House, 2003); Don Kettl, *Team Bush* (NY: McGraw-Hill, 2003); Fred Greenstein, "The Leadership Style of George W. Bush," paper prepared for delivery at the conference on "The Bush Presidency: An Early Assessment," Princeton University, 2003); and Michael Kinsley, "The Power of One," *Time* (21 April 2003), p. 86.

2. See the insightful analysis by Nicholas Lemann, "Without a Doubt," *New Yorker* (14&26, October 2002), p. 164. David Frum, a former Bush speechwriter, wrote in an admiring book about the president, "He is impatient and quick to anger; sometimes glib, even dogmatic; often uncurious and as a result ill informed; more conventional in his thinking than a leader probably should be. But outweighing the faults are his virtues: decency, honesty, rectitude, courage, and tenacity." David Frum, *The Right Man* (NY: Random House, 2003), p. 272.

3. For analyses of environmental constraints on presidents, see Hugh Heclo, "The Changing Presidential Office," in James P. Pfiffner, ed. *The Managerial Presidency* (College Station, TX: Texas A&M University Press, 1999), pp. 23–36; Terry Moe, "The Politicized Presidency," in John Chubb and Paul E. Peterson, eds. *The New Direction in American Politics* (Washington: Brookings, 1985); Karen Hult and Charles Walcott, *Governing from the White House: From Hoover to Johnson* (Lawrence, KS: University Press of Kansas, 1997). For analyses of the importance of personality in politics, see Fred I. Greenstein, *Personality and Politics* (Chicago: Markham, 1969); Fred I. Greenstein, *The Presidential Difference: Leadership Style from FDR to Clinton* (NY: Free Press, 2000).

4. James David Barber, *The Presidential Character: Predicting Performance in the White House*, 4th ed. (Englewood Cliffs, NJ: Prentice Hall, 1992).

5. Richard Tanner Johnson, *Managing the White House* (NY: Harper and Row, 1974). Alexander L. George, *Presidential Decisionmaking in Foreign Policy* (Boulder, CO: Westview Press, 1980); Alexander L. George and Juliette L. George, *Presidential Personality and Performance* (Boulder, CO: Westview Press, 1998).

6. See *The Modern Presidency*, 3rd ed. (New York: Bedford St. Martin's Press, 2000), pp. 44–84; "The President's Chief of Staff: Lessons Learned," *Presidential Studies Quarterly* (Winter 1993), pp. 77–102.

7. Woodward, *Bush at War*, p. 137.

8. Woodward, *Bush at War*, p. 144.

9. Woodward, *Bush at War*, pp. 144–145.

10. Woodward, *Bush at War*, p. 168.

11. Woodward, *Bush at War*, pp. 157–158.

12. For an analysis of Bush's first year in office and his perspective on political capital see James P. Pfiffner, "The Transformation of the Bush Presidency," in James P. Pfiffner and Roger H. Davidson, *Understanding the Presidency*, 3rd ed. (NY: Longman, 2003), pp. 453–471.

13. Woodward, *Bush at War*, p. 339.

14. Woodward, *Bush at War*, p. 282.

15. White House news release (14 January 2003), "President Bush Discusses Iraq," White House web site.

16. Karen DeYoung, "Bush: UN Must Act Fast," *Washington Post* (1 February 2003), p. 1.

17. Woodward, *Bush at War*, p. 341. The interview took place in the summer of 2002 in the context of a discussion about attacking Iraq. Bush was reflecting about the coalition against al Qaeda, but also seemed to be referring to potential war with Iraq.

18. Richard Wolffe and Tamara Lipper, "Powell in the Bunker," *Newsweek* (24 March 2003), p. 31. See also Jim Hoagland, "How He Got Here," *Washington Post* (21 March 2003), p. A37. See also Nicholas Lemann, "How It Came to War," *New Yorker* (31 March 2003), p. 36, Haas said: "The moment was the first week of July [2002] when I had a meeting with Condi [Condoleezza Rice].

19. Nicholas Lemann, "How It Came to War," *New Yorker* (31 March 2003), p. 36.

20. Michael Elliot and James Carney, "First Stop Iraq," *Time* (31 March 2003), p. 173.

21. President Bush's intentions for war in Iraq were also reflected by Vice President Cheney's statement in August that UN inspections would be useless. "A return of inspectors would provide no assurance whatsoever of his compliance with UN resolutions. . . . On the contrary, there is a great danger that it would provide false comfort that Saddam was somehow

'back in his box'." Bob Woodward, *Bush at War* (NY: Simon and Schuster 2002), p. 344. For an analysis of the Bush administration's decision to go to war in Iraq, see James P. Pfiffner, "Assessing the Bush Presidency," in Mark J. Rozell and Gary L. Gregg, eds. *Considering the Bush Presidency* (NY: Oxford University Press, forthcoming).

22. Howard Fineman, "Bush and God," *Newsweek* (3/10/03), p. 22.

23. See Dana Priest and Kaaren DeYoung, "CIA Questioned Documents Linking Iraq, Uranium Ore," *Washington Post* (22 March 2003), p. A30; and Seymour M. Hersh, "Who Lied to Whom?" *New Yorker* (31 March 2003), pp. 41–43.

24. Dana Priest and Kaaren DeYoung, "CIA Questioned Documents Linking Iraq, Uranium Ore," *Washington Post* (22 March 2003), p. A30; and Seymour M. Hersh, "Who Lied to Whom?" *New Yorker* (31 March 2003), pp. 41–43. It is hard to understand how mere incompetence could have allowed the reference to forged documents get into the president's State of the Union speech. One former intelligence official said, "Someone set someone up." (Hersh, p. 43).

25. Walter Pincus and Dana Milbank, "Bush Clings to Dubious Allegations About Iraq," *Washington Post* (18 March 2003), p. A13.

26. See James Risen, "C.I.A. Aides Feel Pressure In Preparing Iraqi Reports," *New York Times* (23 March 2003), p. B10.

27. Dana Milbank, "For Bush, Facts Are Malleable," *Washington Post* (22 October 2002), p. 1, A22.

28. Milbak, "For Bush, Acts Are Malleable," p. A22.

29. Dana Milbank, "For Bush, Facts Are Malleable," *Washington Post* (22 October 2002), p. A22.

30. According to Seymour M. Hersh, "On at least six occasions . . . he [Rumsfeld] insisted that the number of ground troops be sharply reduced." "Offense and Defense," *The New Yorker* (7 April 2003), p. 43. See also Joseph P. Hoar, "Why Aren't There Enough Troops in Iraq?" *The New York Times* (2 April 2003), p. A29; Bernard Weinraub with Thom Shanker, "Rumsfeld's Design for War Criticized on the Battlefield," *The New York Times* (1 April 2003), p. 1; Jonathan Weisman, "Rumsfeld and Myers Defend War Plan," *Washington Post* (2 April 2003), p. A19.

31. Joseph P. Hoar, "Why Aren't There Enough Troops in Iraq?" *The New York Times* (2 April 2003), p. A29

32. See Richard Brookhiser, "The Mind of George W. Bush," *Atlantic Monthly* (April 2003), p. 63.

33. Howard Fineman, "Bush and God," *Newsweek* (10 March 2003), p. 27.

34. Jackson Lears, "How a War Became a Crusade," *New York Times* (11 March 2003), p. A29.

35. Bob Allen, "Faith formed a wedge in primary politics, observers say," *Baptist Standard* (24 April 2000), accessed at www.baptiststandard.com/2000/. When he was asked to explain his answer further, Bush said that it would be hard to explain to someone who was not Christian. "When you turn your heart and your life over to Christ, when you accept Christ as the Savior, it changes your heart and changes your life."

36. Laurie Goodstein, "A President Puts his Faith in Providence," *The New York Times* (9 February 2003), p. wk4.

37. David Frum, *The Right Man* (NY: Random House, 2003), pp. 3–4.

38. Garry Wills, a scholar of American politics as well as religion, observed: "His [Bush's] calm assurance that most of the world and much of his nation is wrong comes from an apparent certainty that is hard to justify in terms of geopolitical calculus. It helps, in making that

leap, to be assured that God is on your side. One of the psychological benefits of this is that it makes one oppose with an easy conscience those who are not with us, therefore not on God's side. They are not mistaken, miscalculating, misguided or even just malevolent. They are evil." Garry Wills, "With God on His Side," *New York Times Magazine* (30 March 2003), p. 29.

39. Richard Brookhiser, "The Mind of George W. Bush," *The Atlantic Monthly* (April 2003), p. 63.

40. Nicholas Lemann, "Without a Doubt," *New Yorker* (Oct 14&26, 2002), p. 177.

41. "The Second 2000 Gore-Bush Presidential Debate: October 11, 2000," Commission on Presidential Debates, p. 2 of transcript downloaded from www.debates.org. Bush also said ". . .I'm going to be judicious as to how to use the military. It needs to be in our vital interest, the mission needs to be clear, and the extra [sic] strategy obvious. (By "extra strategy" he probably meant "exit strategy." Or the transcript may have had a typographical error.)

42. Quoted in Karen DeYoung, "Bush: UN Must Act Fast," *Washington Post* (1 February 2003), p. 1.

43. Speech to B'nai B'rith, 28 August 2002. Quoted in Martin E. Marty, "The Sin of Pride," *Newsweek* (10 March 2003), p. 32–33. See also, "God and Country Home Search Page Science Site Index Main Start Page, http://www.geocities.com/petrerroberts.geo/Relig-Politics/GGGWBusyh.html.

44. White House Website, "Presidential Remarks 2/10/03," news release at Opryland Hotel in Nashville, TN (3/11/03).

45. Woodward, *Bush at War*, p. 131.

46. Quoted in George Will, "When 'nuance' excuses terror," *Jewish World Review* (11 April 2002), accessed at www.jewishworld.com.

47. Woodward, *Bush at War*, p. 341.

48. Woodward, *Bush at War*, p. 281.

49. Bill Sammon, "Bush defends 'different strategies.'" *The Washington Times* (4 January 2003), (accessed at: http://dynamic.washtimes.com/twt-print.cfm? ArticleID=20030104-67215576). See also, Remarks at the New Jersey Army National Guard Aviation Support Facility "I had made it clear to the world that either you're with us or you're with the enemy, and that doctrine still stands." Kryn P. Westhoven, Public Affairs Staff, "Bush: 'We're in it for the long haul'" (www.dix.army.mil/PAO/post092702/bush.htm).

50. Fareed Zakaria, "The Arrogant Empire," *Newsweek* (24 March 2003), p. 29.

51. "President Says Saddam Hussein Must Leave Iraq Within 48 Hours: Remarks by the President in Address to the Nation," (17 March 2003), transcript posted on White House website (accessed 15 April 2003). Punctuation of the sentence is as it appears on the White House transcript.

52. Henry Kissinger, "Our Intervention In Iraq," *Washington Post* (12 August 2002), p. A15.

53. *The National Security Strategy of the United States of America*, (www.whitehouse.gov/nsc/print/nssall.html). The page numbers in the text refer to the pages in the downloaded document.

54. Michael R. Gordon, "Serving Notice of a New U.S., Poised to Hit First and Alone," *New York Times* (27 January 2003), p. 1, A11.

55. A counter example to Bush's penchant for moral clarity and disdain for nuance was his response to stem-cell research. After consulting a team of advisers, his policy resolution called for a compromise among his important constituencies. The religious right wanted a

complete ban on stem-cell research, while several prominent Republicans, including Senators Orrin Hatch and Bill Frist and Nancy Reagan, favored scientific and medical research using stem-cells. Bush compromised by allowing research on already existing stem-cell lines. See the discussion in Richard Brookhiser, "The Mind of George W. Bush," *Atlantic Monthly* (April 2003), p. 62.

56. See Richard Brookhiser, "The Mind of George W. Bush," *The Atlantic Monthly* (April 2003), p. 60.

57. See David Frum, *The Right Man* (NY: Random House, 2003), Chapter 2, "The Un-Clinton," pp. 12–30.

58. President Bush derisively called such actions "pounding sand." (Woodward, *Bush at War*, p. 123) "The antiseptic notion of launching a cruise missile into some guy's, you know, tent, really is a joke," Bush told Bob Woodward. "I mean, people viewed that as the impotent America. . . . a flaccid, you know, kind of technology competent but not very tough country that was willing to launch a cruise missile out of a submarine and that'd be it." (Woodward, *Bush at War*, p. 38) On the other hand, Bush admitted that before the terrorist attacks on New York and the Pentagon, he had done little to avenge previous attacks or prevent new ones. "There was a significant difference in my attitude after September 11. . . . [before 9/11] I was prepared to look at a plan that would be a thoughtful plan that would bring him [Osama bin Laden] to justice, and would have given the order to do that. . . . But I didn't feel that sense of urgency, and my blood was not nearly as boiling." (Woodward, *Bush at War*, p. 39).

59. Richard Brookhiser, "The Mind of George W. Bush," *The Atlantic Monthly* (April 2003), p. 68.

60. Nicholas Lemann, "Without a Doubt," *The New Yorker* (Oct. 14&21, 2002), p. 173.

61. Woodward, *Bush at War*, p. 120.

62. Woodward, *Bush at War*, p. 303.

63. Woodward, *Bush at War*, p. 270.

64. (Woodward, *Bush at War*, p. 340.

65. Don Gregg, "Kim Jong Il: The Truth Behind the Caricature," *Newsweek* (3 February 2003), p. 13.

66. Woodward, *Bush at War*, p. 100.

67. John King, "Bush calls Saddam 'the guy who tried to kill my dad'," CNN.com (27 September 2002).

68. Woodward, *Bush at War*, p. 74.

69. Richard Tanner Johnson, *Managing the White House* (NY: Harper and Row, 1974). Alexander L. George, *Presidential Decisionmaking in Foreign Policy* (Boulder, CO: Westview Press, 1980); Alexander L. George and Juliette L. George, *Presidential Personality and Performance* (Boulder, CO: Westview Press, 1998).

70. Eisenhower said: "I know of only one way in which you can be sure you've done your best to make a wise decision. That is to get all of the people who have partial and definable responsibility in this particular field, whatever it may be. Get them with their different viewpoints in front of you, and listen to them debate. I do not believe in bringing them in one at a time, and therefore being more impressed by the most recent one you hear than the earlier ones." Quoted in John P. Burke and Fred I. Greenstein, *How Presidents Test Reality* (NY: Russell Sage, 1991), p. 54.

71. President Bush conducted NSC meetings in the wake of the terrorist attacks to deliberate about the U.S. response and strategy. Contrasting views would be presented, but Bush did not encourage spirited debate over important issues. For instance, recalling one meeting when Rumsfeld became upset about the CIA seeming to dominate war planning, Bush said "That's the kind of discussion that frustrates me, because I like clarity." He did not pursue the disagreement and settle it; he told Rice, "Get this mess straightened out." Woodward, *Bush at War*, p. 244.

72. See James P. Pfiffner, "National Security Decision Making and the War with Iraq," Paper prepared for presentation at the conference on "The Presidency, Congress, and the War on Terrorism: Scholarly Perspectives." University of Florida (February 7, 2003).

73. Baker, III, James A. 2002. "The Right Way to Change a Regime." *The New York Times*, 8/25/02, p. wk9; Scowcroft, Brent. 2002. "Don't Attack Saddam." *The Wall Street Journal*, 8/15/02, p. A12.

74. Jim Hoagland, "How We Got Here," *Washington Post* (21 March 2003), p. A37.

75. Woodward, *Bush at War*, pp. 333–334.

76. Strictly speaking, Powell was not playing the role of "devil's advocate" because he really believed the arguments he was making. (See Alexander George, *Presidential Decisionmaking in Foreign Policy* (Boulder, CO: Westview Press, 1980), pp. 169–174. Despite his ability to persuade the president, or probably because of it, Powell was resented by many White House staffers; their leaks undercut him as did calls for his resignation by conservative pundits. (Woodward, *Bush at War*, pp. 14, 223–225, 345.) President Bush seemed to recognize Powell's efforts and was willing to be persuaded by some of his arguments, but he was condescending in his praise for Powell. When asked about Powell's contribution to the administration, President Bush admitted that Powell was a "diplomatic person who has war experience." Then he said, "Let me think about Powell. I got one. He was very good with Musharraf. He single-handedly got Musharraf on Board." (Woodward, *Bush at War*, p. 342.) Bush's faint praise for Powell was reminiscent of President Eisenhower's response to a reporter's question about Vice President Nixon's contributions to his administration, "If you give me a week, I might think of one. I don't remember." Quoted in Tom Wicker, *One of Us: Richard Nixon and the American Dream* (NY: Random House, 1991), p. 224.

CHAPTER **10**

The New National Security Strategy and the Old National Security Council

John Hart
Australian National University

> The major institutions of American national security were designed in a different era to meet different requirements. All of them must be transformed.

So begins the final chapter of President Bush's national security strategy document published in September 2002.[1] Following a wide-ranging statement of the rationale for new strategic priorities, this last section of the paper foreshadows major changes in the key institutions of U.S. national security consequent upon the changed international environment, the collapse of the Soviet Union, the end of the cold war, the rise of global terrorism, and the events of September 11, 2001.

The president's strategy document outlines a fundamentally new approach to national security policy in which traditional concepts of deterrence and containment give way to the doctrine of preemption in the fight against the new enemy—terrorism, weapons of mass destruction, and those states that harbor terrorists.[2] "America is now threatened less by conquering states," it notes, "than we are by failing ones. We are menaced less by fleets and armies than by catastrophic technologies in the hands of the embittered few."[3] Given the magnitude of the policy shift outlined in the document, it is more than appropriate to highlight the need for institutional adaptation to the new global environment and the new strategic priorities, and the last chapter of the paper does just this by considering the role of the armed forces, the need to strengthen the CIA's intelligence capabilities, new approaches to international diplomacy within the State Department, and improvements in financial management, recruitment, and retention in the Pentagon.

182

Whether or not the specific changes that the president calls for in the armed forces, the CIA, the State Department and the Pentagon amount to a transformation may be a matter of opinion, but to students of presidential decision-making and America's national security institutions, the more significant question arising from the last chapter of *The National Security Strategy of the United States of America* is why it says nothing at all about the pivotal coordinating institution at the apex of national security decision-making, the National Security Council.

The document itself gives no clue about why the National Security Council has been omitted from the purview of the last chapter and why, by implication, it is not included in those "major institutions of national security" that "must be transformed."

It may, of course, just be that the present incumbent of the Oval Office is more than satisfied with the role of the National Security Council and with the manner in which it performs its statutory duty "to advise the President with respect to the integration of domestic, foreign and military policies relating to the National Security"[4] and sees no need for NSC system to adapt. This would not be an unreasonable assumption given that, although there has been considerable criticism of the NSC system during its 56-year life, most of it has come from academic observers and the world of think tanks rather than from presidents themselves. Of all the presidents, John F. Kennedy has probably been the one who has shown most concern about the NSC and, strongly influenced by the arguments of Senator Jackson's subcommittee reports,[5] he made significant changes to the NSC model he inherited from Eisenhower.[6] President Carter established a review of the NSC as part of his Reorganization Project, but there was little presidential response to the content of the report and its recommendations.[7] And, of course, President Reagan was forced to institute a major review of the NSC—The Tower Commission—as a result of the Iran-Contra episode, but that review actually validated the NSC system, rather than criticized it, even though Iran-Contra amounted to, in the words of Professor Koh, "a nearly successful assault upon the constitutional structures and norms that underlie [the] postwar national security system."[8]

It is interesting to note what the Tower Commission (consisting of Senator John Tower, former Senator and former Secretary of State Edmund S. Muskie, and President Ford's National Security Adviser Brent Scowcroft) had to say about the NSC system because its perspective, which is a very presidential one, explains clearly why most presidents have been comfortable with the NSC and, specifically, why President Reagan did not have to respond to the institutional implications of Iran-Contra in any major way. The structure and function of the NSC, says the Tower Commission, is basically what presidents choose to make it and ought to remain what presidents choose to make it:

> Our review validates the current National Security Council system. Different Presidents have utilized that system in very different ways, in accordance with their individual work habits and philosophical predilections. On occasion over the years it has functioned with real brilliance; at other times serious mistakes have been made. The problems we examined in the case of Iran/Contra caused us deep concern. But their solution does not lie in revamping the National Security Council system.

That system is properly the President's creature. It must be left flexible to be molded by the President into the form most useful to him. Otherwise it will become either an obstacle to the President and a source of frustration; or an institutional irrelevance, as the President fashions informal structures more to his liking.[9]

Another possible explanation for the omission of any discussion of the NSC in the Bush national security strategy document is similar to the reason given by the Clinton administration when it announced its National Performance Review in September 1993 and almost entirely excluded the Executive Office of the President from the "reinventing government" exercise—that the White House is "regularly reinvented with each change of administration."[10] Studies of the evolution of the NSC tend to support the view that presidents are able to and do modify national security decision-making process in response to both changing political forces and presidential management needs,[11] suggesting that the NSC system serves the needs and interests of presidents, as they see those needs, rather well. President Bush may well have thought that he had already transformed the NSC when he issued a presidential directive on the organization of the National Security Council system within three weeks of taking office.[12]

Finally, the reason for the omission of the NSC might be nothing more profound than the argument that the NSC is an arm of the president and that the president is its presiding officer so that, had the NSC been included in the scope of the "institutional transformation" chapter, it would have signaled that the president was calling for his own transformation and highlighting his own shortcomings with regard to national security advice.

But, given that the Council serves as both the principal formal advisory body to the president on national security policy and the major policy coordination mechanism, and that its statutory membership—the president, vice president, secretary of state, secretary of defense, chairman of the Joint Chiefs of Staff, and the director of central intelligence—constitutes the core of U.S. national security decision-makers, the role of the NSC ought to be considered in any reassessment of the national security policy-making system. Although presidents, generally, have been uncritical of the NSC system and even though the current president excludes it from his call to transform *all* national security institutions, none of the possible explanations above for why the NSC was excluded from the Bush national security strategy statement is strong enough to deflect academic observers from continuing to explore the issue of how the NSC adapts to changing conditions and circumstances.

THE EVOLUTION OF THE NSC AND ITS CRITICS

The story of the evolution of the National Security Council system has been told many times and the main themes of development of the NSC are well known.[13] In essence, the NSC began its life as a body intended to ensure a more collective form of decision-making in national security affairs as a reaction against the highly personal and ad hoc style of President Roosevelt during World War II. The Council was written into the National Security Act of 1947 largely through the efforts of James Forrestal, the then Secretary of the Navy, who had been impressed by the collegial decision-making practiced by the British Committee of Imperial Defence and advocated a similar model be adopted in the U.S. He also saw the National Security Council as a way of protecting the interests of the Navy by giving it back what it had lost by no longer having a seat in the president's cabinet as a consequence of the establishment of a single Department of Defense. President Truman was not sympathetic to the creation of the NSC but it was, in the words of Anna Kasten Nelson, "a creature of compromise"—part of the price he had to pay to win support for his plan to unify the armed forces under a single Defense Department.[14]

As things turned out, the Council never did constrain the president in the way that some of its advocates had hoped. Truman was adamant that the NSC was only an agency for considering policy options and that all final decisions were his.[15] Efforts to physically locate the NSC in the Department of Defense were thwarted, as were attempts to give the Council statutory powers that would have compelled the president to take decisions in the Council. Moreover, Truman attended very few of the Council's meetings in its early days and only warmed to this new institutional mechanism when the Korean War broke out and he found it to be a useful source of policy coordination and advice.

Largely because the National Security Council has not functioned in the way that its proponents had hoped, the workings of the Council itself have not generated much concern amongst political scientists. Rather, most of the attention that has been given to the NSC has been directed at the evolution and operation of the Council's staff. Since the Eisenhower administration, the Council's staff has been the principal focus of the NSC system and, in effect, the NSC became, according to I. M. Destler, "an umbrella for the emergence of a presidential foreign policy staff."[16]

The other principal institutional development of the NSC system has been the power of the president's national security adviser—a position established by President Eisenhower that effectively downgraded that of the statutorily established Executive Secretary of the NSC. In creating the post and putting the national security adviser in charge of the NSC system, Eisenhower provided the foundation for the subsequent centralization of power and authority in the hands of Henry Kissinger and Zbigniew Brzezinski during the Nixon and Carter presidencies.[17]

The growth in the size of the NSC staff and its effects on the function of the NSC, the unaccountable power of the national security adviser, and the abuse of staff power which led to the Iran-Contra affair under President Reagan, have, in the past, been the major targets of the critics of the NSC system. The Iran-Contra episode now appears as an isolated aberration—nothing comparable has occurred during the presidencies of any of Reagan's successors. Neither the Tower Commission report, nor that of the congressional committees set up to investigate Iran-Contra, led to any major changes in the NSC system, even though the joint report of the House and Senate committees found a "seriously flawed policy making process"[18] and criminal indictments were brought against three NSC staffers responsible for Iran-Contra. The power and prominence of Henry Kissinger or

Zbigniew Brzezinski has not been replicated by any subsequent national security adviser—all their successors have been more constrained and less publicly flamboyant—and critical concern about the role of the national security adviser has abated. During the 1970s, a number of bills were introduced in Congress to make the national security adviser's appointment subject to the Senate confirmation and in 1980 the Senate Foreign Relations Committee held hearings on the issue, but there was no further action on the part of Congress.

The growth in the size of the NSC staff has, however, continued to be a source of concern and criticism, and it is pertinent to consider recent comment in this respect because it has relevance to the current operation of the NSC under the present administration. A brief prepared by the joint Brookings Institution and Center for International and Security Studies National Security Council Project in 2000 estimated that the true size of the NSC staff consists of 225 personnel, including about 100 substantive professionals, a considerable increase over the ten or so professionals on the NSC staff in the early 1960s.[19] Moreover, the authors of the brief argued that the NSC "has become more like an agency than a presidential staff" having developed "its own press, legislative, communication, and speechmaking offices [and] conducts ongoing relations with the media, Congress, the American public, and foreign governments." They criticize the NSC for being immersed in policy detail and giving insufficient attention to coordinating the policy process. They say that the NSC staff is overly bureaucratized with rigid procedures that make it less flexible and less adaptable, and that the short-term focus of its work means that the "immediate [is] crowding out the important."[20] The nature of the criticism of the NSC from Daalder and Destler, in a brief that was obviously written for the benefit of the president-elect, echoes the complaints about the NSC system from the Jackson subcommittee at the end of the 1950s. Moreover, the essence of the recommendations in 2000 were much the same as those emanating forty years ago—that the size of the NSC staff should be drastically reduced and that the organization and structure of the staff should be rationalized. Both the Jackson subcommittee and the Brookings National Security Council Project believed that large staffs and overly complex organization hampered the function of the NSC.

While the Daalder/Destler brief for the National Security Council Project had a lot to say about size and organization of the NSC staff, it says absolutely nothing about the functioning of the Council itself. Indeed, the Council, as distinct from the staff system that supports it, has never been the subject of any systematic analysis, with the exception of a small body of work which formed part of the Eisenhower revisionism literature in the 1980s and was designed to counter the criticism of the Eisenhower NSC system made by the Jackson subcommittee. The thrust of this research examined NSC meetings to show that genuine deliberation took place and that the NSC was the principal forum for the formulation and implementation of national security policy in the Eisenhower administration—a finding on which not all Eisenhower revisionists are in agreement.[21] Nevertheless, with this small exception, the Council itself has been ignored by NSC scholars and very little is known about the way the Council itself operates and whether or not the Council adequately fulfills its functions mandated by the National Security Act.

The other significant silence in the literature on the NSC is the question of the extent to which the structure and organization of the NSC system are matched to the strategic framework within which U.S. national security policy is formulated. Even if, during the Cold War years, there was an implicit assumption that the NSC system was congruent with the strategy of containment and deterrence so that the question did not have to be put, that question now becomes a relevant one in light of the new national security strategy outlined in the Bush administration's *National Security Strategy* document.

THE NATIONAL SECURITY COUNCIL AND NATIONAL SECURITY STRATEGY

The above discussion was intended to identify three areas in which one might usefully think about the future of the National Security Council system, namely the ongoing concern about the size and structure of the NSC staff, the hitherto neglected question of the role of the Council itself, and the silence on the relationship between the form of the NSC system and the strategic framework for national security. These questions are triggered directly by the publication of President Bush's *National Security Strategy* document and specifically by its assertion of the need to transform all the major institutions of American national security, even though it does not include the National Security Council amongst those institutions to be transformed. These questions raise issues about the institutional design of the NSC and, although the answers to those questions may not necessarily suggest anything as major as a transformation of the NSC, they might usefully point to aspects of the NSC system that need to adapt to changing circumstances. The principal changed circumstance is President Bush's new national security strategy.

The Consequences of the New National Security Strategy

National security strategy has changed because, as the document says starkly, "[w]ith the collapse of the Soviet Union and the end of the Cold War, our security environment has undergone profound transformation."[22] One consequence of that changed security environment is the end of balance-of-power politics and the declining utility of the doctrine of deterrence. Instead, *The National Security Strategy* document recognizes that "the United States possesses unprecedented and unequaled strength and influence in the world" and asserts that this strength must be used in pursuit of America's strategic goals.[23] The old balance-of-power[24] and deterrence, it might be argued, favored the mode of deliberation that the National Security Council was designed to achieve—that is, careful judgment about policy options based upon well-developed staff work to ensure that all choices had been considered and that all potential options were presented to the members of the Council in a balanced way. The classic example of how the old balance-of-power environment allowed time for NSC deliberation was the Cuban missile crisis where both sides demonstrated reluctance to use force before all other possibilities had been exhausted. In this crisis, the NSC, or rather the Kennedy variant of it—the Executive Committee of the National Security Council known as ExComm—worked, as far as we know, on the basis of advice presented to it by the NSC staff and, even though, the events of October 1962 were a crisis, the time-frame, conditioned by the balance-of-power and deterrence, allowed the NSC process to work reasonably successfully.[25] That constraint imposed by balance-of-power and deterrence strategies disappears under the Bush doctrine and, in any future conflict between the United States and its adversaries, and impetus to use force preemptively presents a different set of parameters within which the NSC system must operate.

How well the deliberative processes of the NSC can work in these new conditions when, presumably, there will be less emphasis on constraint and more on decisive and speedy action is difficult to answer. The assumption is that the NSC process will be expected to move faster and that, if the commander in chief is now operating under conditions of permanent war, one needs to question how the deliberative processes of the NSC, particularly the "staffing out" of policy proposals, will work. We know very little about how the NSC functions as a "crisis-manager" and particularly how crisis and confrontation between the U.S. and its adversaries affects the ability of the NSC staff to work through and prepare policy options in a satisfactory manner.

The recent book by Bob Woodward at least presents an impression of the NSC as a crisis-manager during the war in Afghanistan in 2001 and, although his coverage of the NSC at work does not pretend to offer the systematic and analytically rigorous approach that political scientists would use if they had the benefit of such privileged access, it, nevertheless, offers some morsels that constitute data of a kind. Woodward records, in varying degrees, the conduct of 40 NSC meetings and 12 principals (the Council minus the president) meetings between September 11th November 13th 2001.[26] There is no evidence in the book that deliberations at the almost-daily and sometimes twice-daily meetings were based upon papers prepared by the staff and available to all members of the Council, although that is not to say that the staffing process became irrelevant during the war period or that members of the Council did not receive the benefit of staff deliberation in some other way. But there is evidence in Woodward's book that, on two occasions, the staff had not adequately prepared the Council for issues that came before it. At a meeting of the NSC on 24th September President Bush raised the issue of how humanitarian aid for Afghanistan can be coordinated with the military action. "Can we have the first bombs we drop be food?" he asked. It clearly caught the Council off-guard and unprepared. As Woodward reports: "The surprise for [Condoleezza] Rice was when the President raised the issue of humanitarian aid. It had not really been discussed among the principals, the deputies or sub deputies. What was this? Where was it coming from?"[27] Similarly, at an NSC meeting on the 4th October, President Bush asked a question about who would run Afghanistan after the war was over. Again, the NSC was unprepared. Woodward records: "We should have addressed that, Rice thought. Her most awful moments were when the president thought of something that the principals, particularly she, should have anticipated."[28]

The second problematic aspect of the new national security strategy is that it encompasses a number of strategic goals that are presently handled by other coordinating bodies in the Executive Office of the President, which raise questions about the jurisdiction of the NSC and its relationship to those other EOP entities. Presumably, the National Economic Council would have a stake in the commitment to disrupt the financing of international terrorism, and the emphasis on free trade in chapter VI of the document as a central strategic aim would necessarily involve the Office of the United States Trade Representative.

The most serious problem of overlapping jurisdiction, however, derives from the centrality of the war against terrorism in the strategy document and the subsequent establishment of the Homeland Security Council and the Office of Homeland Security as new units within the Executive Office of the President.[29] Initially, the president opted for this coordinating mechanism within the EOP as his response to the events of September 11, but in mid-2002 he had a change of heart and announced the establishment of a Department of Homeland Security.[30] This did not involve the abolition of the EOP Homeland Security Council or the Office of Homeland Security, and what now exists at the highest level of American government is a fully-fledged cabinet-level department to develop and coordinate Homeland Security policy matched by a presidential staff agency and a formal Council which also coordinates homeland security policy and operates alongside the National Security Council, which also has responsibilities in the same area.

The president now has an assistant for national security in the White House working alongside an assistant for homeland security together with a secretary of a new Department of Homeland Security. The division of labor in this arrangement is far from clear and so too is the logic of retaining a coordinating presidential agency when a coordinating department has been statutorily established. It has been complicated even further by the subsequent creation of the president's Homeland Security Advisory Council and four senior advisory councils by an executive order signed on March 21, 2002.

There is now a plethora of units responsible for advice and/or policy coordination in the area of homeland security within the executive branch and, more significantly, two senior presidential agencies with highly elaborate staff structures and organization. The potential for jurisdictional battles over "turf" has already been recognized and the need to link these two bodies has been flagged.[31] The future of the National Security Council may well be affected by existence of a separate Homeland Security Council and potential jurisdictional rivalry in such a critical policy arena could be costly.

The future of the Executive Office of the President may well also be affected by these developments. The major rationale behind the EOP is that it provides the president with a staff capacity to assist in the management and coordination of executive branch business especially where policy issues transcend the jurisdiction of any one department or agency. Yet the existence of a number of separate coordinating mechanisms within the EOP that have overlapping jurisdictions themselves raise fundamental questions about the future of the presidential branch of government in the USA.

The Consequences for the Council

We know little about the dynamics of the National Security Council under President George W. Bush, but we do know that, in his administration, the membership of the Council has been expanded. The notion that the Council's statutory membership—

the president, vice president, secretary of state, and secretary of defense, assisted by the director of central intelligence and chairman of the Joint Chiefs of Staff—are the only participants at NSC meetings is no longer so. President Bush formally added the secretary of the Treasury to the NSC (as a non-statutory regular attendee) when he issued his first national security Presidential Directive just after taking office. He also included the national security adviser (seemingly as a member rather than as a staff official who services the Council). Two additional White House staffers, the chief of staff and the assistant to the president for economic policy, have been given the right to attend any NSC meeting,[32] and the attorney general and the director of OMB are invited to meeting when matters within their jurisdiction are being discussed. It is clear from Woodward's account of NSC meetings, although he does not systematically record those attending each meeting, that the meetings rarely consisted of just the formal statutory members and sometimes the meetings included people other than those mentioned in the extended list above. For example, it appears that the deputy national security adviser regularly attends and speaks at Bush NSC meetings and Woodward records others being present even when their principals were in attendance such as General Tommy Franks and Cofer Black of the CIA.

The enlargement of the NSC poses the question of how the dynamics of Council meetings are affected by the number of attendees. Social psychology research on group dynamics has established the fact that size matters in group meetings,[33] but it is just one of many variables and, in any case, the theory of group dynamics is not easily testable in the context of current presidential decision-making. We do not know the extent to which large NSC meetings constrain the ability of participants to express controversial views to the president, but there is clearly some evidence provided by Bob Woodward that Secretary of State Colin Powell was constrained by the formal NSC on one occasion and requested (unusually for him) a private meeting with the president in order to get his views across.[34] And, so long as the most senior members of the Council have the opportunity of privately putting their views to the president, that is likely to upset the smooth functioning of the Council. At this stage, one can do little more than pose the hypothesis that the larger the size of the NSC, the more likely it is that key participants, particularly those who find themselves in a minority or even isolated, will seek to make an end-run around the group and thus undercut the formal advisory mechanism.

Powell's position in the Bush administration, and the known rivalry between the State Department and Defense Department,[35] also raises questions about how the new national security strategy, with its emphasis on preemption, affects the balance of opinion between the voices of militarism and the voices of diplomacy. The strategy itself predisposes military responses rather more than did the containment and deterrence strategies of the past, and there have been instances in the Bush NSC meetings where there has been an imbalance in favor of those representing the military side of the equation at NSC meetings. It needs to be asked whether the voice of the State Department is overwhelmed and outnumbered in these enlarged NSC meetings. (It may well be overwhelmed at Homeland Security Council meetings as well simply because the State Department has no formal representation on that body.)

Although critics hammer away at the increasing size of the National Security Council staff and its effect on the work of the NSC system, they have paid no attention to the increasing membership of the Council and what effect size has on Council deliberations. It may just be that the expanded NSC, brought about in part by the changed national security environment, adversely affects the quality of advice that the president receives. This ought to be known, but the behavioral dynamics of NSC meetings have never been an object of systematic study. The reason why is fairly obvious and it is unlikely that even the most scholarly of presidents would open up the NSC to outside observers, but those who specialize in the study of the National Security Council urgently need to bring the Council itself into their analysis of the workings of the NSC system.

The Consequences for the NSC Staff

Arguments about the adverse impact of the expanding size of the NSC staff that have been advanced by observers such as Daalder and Destler are obviously relevant to the future of the NSC, but it should be noted that they pre-date the *National Security Strategy* document and stand independently of the changed national security environment. What the National Security Strategy does impact upon is not staff size, although if Daalder and Destler criticisms are valid, size is still an important factor, as much as the existing structure of the staff. The NSC staff is presently structured around 21 divisions: six of them are regionally focussed (Europe and Eurasia, Western Hemisphere, East Asia, South Asia, Near East and North Africa and Africa), eleven of them are functionally based (e.g., Human Rights, International Finance, Defense Strategy, Counter-Terrorism, Arms Control, and Intelligence and Counterintelligence), and four of them are operational (Counselor, Legal Advisor, Legislative Affairs, and Public Affairs). Given the centrality of countering global terrorism in the *National Security Strategy* document, the regional-based organization of six of the NSC directorates no longer makes much sense. It must create overlapping jurisdiction with the functionally-based directorates and it is less relevant to the global nature of the major problems that the National Security Council deals with. A reduced staff and a functionally-based director are structure is needed to bring the NSC staff structure in line with the thrust of the new national security strategy.

THE PRESIDENT AND THE NSC

There is some evidence in Bob Woodward's account of the management of the war in Afghanistan that the fit between the old National Security Council and the new National Security Strategy may go beyond those issues briefly identified above. What Woodward has to say about the approach of the president himself to national security decision-making raises fundamental questions about the role of advisory and coordinating mechanisms in helping the president reach decisions. "Bush's leadership style bordered on the hurried" we are told. "He wanted action, solutions."[36] And then the most disconcerting revelation in the whole book: "During the interview, the president spoke a dozen times about his 'instincts' or his 'instinctive' reactions, including his statement, 'I'm not a textbook player, I'm a gut player.' " Woodward comments: "It's pretty clear that Bush's role as politician, president and commander in chief is driven by a secular faith in his instincts—his natural and spontaneous conclusions and judgments. His instincts are almost his second religion."[37] That seems more at odds with the old National Security Council than anything within the new national security strategy itself.

NOTES

1. *The National Security Strategy of the United States of America* (Washington, DC: The White House, 2002), p. 29.
2. A separate paper dealing specifically with weapons of mass destruction was issued in December 2002. See *National Strategy to Combat Weapons of Mass Destruction* (Washington, DC: The White House, 2002).
3. *Ibid.*, p. 1.
4. 50 U.S. Code 15, Sec. 402.
5. The Senate Government Operations Committee's Subcommittee on National Policy Machinery, chaired by Senator Henry Jackson in 1959 and 1960, was highly critical of the NSC during the Eisenhower administration. For a full account of the Subcommittee's critique of the NSC see Henry Jackson (ed.), *The National Security Council: Jackson Subcommittee Papers on Policy-Making at the Presidential Level* (New York: Praeger, 1965).
6. See John Hart, *The Presidential Branch: From Washington to Clinton* (Chatham, NJ: Chatham House, 1995), p. 72.
7. The essence of the Carter review of the NSC can be found in a subsequent journal article by the author of the report. See Philip A. Odeen, "Organizing for National Security," *International Security* 5 (Summer 1980): pp. 111–129.
8. Harold Hongju Koh, *The National Security Constitution: Sharing Power After the Iran-Contra Affair* (New Haven, CT: Yale University Press, 1990), p. 2.
9. President's Special Review Board, *Report of the President's Special Review Board* (Washington, DC: U.S. Government Printing Office, February 26, 1987), p. I–3.
10. Report of the National Performance Review, *From Red Tape to Results: Creating a Government that Works Better and Costs Less* (Washington, DC: U.S. Government Printing Office, 1993), p. 139
11. For recent evidence, see, particularly, Amy B. Zegart, *Flawed By Design: The Evolution of the CIA, JCS, and NSC* (Stanford, CA: Stanford University Press, 1999), ch. 3, and William Newmann, "Causes of Change in National Security Processes: Carter, Reagan and Bush Decision Making on Arms Control," *Presidential Studies Quarterly* 31 (March 2001): pp. 69–103.
12. National Security Presidential Directive—I, "Organization of the National Security Council System," (Washington, DC: The White House, February 13, 2001).
13. For a summary, see Hart, *The Presidential Branch*, pp. 67–80.
14. Anna Kasten Nelson, "National Security I: Inventing a Process (1945–1960)," in Hugh Heclo & Lester Salamon, eds., *The Illusion of Presidential Government* (Boulder, CO: Westview Press, 1981), p. 231.
15. The president wrote in his memoirs: "I used the National Security Council only as a place for recommendations to be worked out. Like the Cabinet, the Council does not make deci-

sions. The policy itself has to come down from the president, as all final decisions have to be made by him. A 'vote' in the National Security Council is merely a procedural step. It never decides policy." See Harry S. Truman, *Years of Trial and Hope 1946–1952* (New York: Doubleday, 1956), p. 59.

16. I. M. Destler, "National Security Advice to U.S. Presidents: Some Lessons from Thirty Years," *World Politics* 29 (No.2, 1977), p. 146.

17. I elaborate on this point in John Hart, "Eisenhower and the Swelling of the Presidency," *Polity* 24 (Summer 1992), pp. 686–689.

18. See U.S. 100th Congress 1st Session, *Report of the Congressional Committees Investigating the Iran-Contra Affair* (Washington, DC: Government Printing Office, 1987), pp. 11–22.

19. Ivo H. Daalder & I. M. Destler, "A New NSC for a New Administration," *Policy Brief Number 68* (Washington, D.C.: The Brookings Institution, November 2000), accessed at http://www.brook.edu/dybdocroot/comm/policybriefs/pb068/pb68.htm

20. *Ibid.*

21. For an overview see Hart, *The Presidential Branch*, p. 71.

22. *The National Security Strategy of the United States of America*, p. 13.

23. *The National Security Strategy of the United States of America*, p. 1.

24. The Bush document tends to use the term 'balance-of-terror' to describe what was conventionally known as the 'balance-of-power' (see, for example, *The National Security Strategy of the United States of America*, p. 13—"Having moved from confrontation to cooperation as the hallmark of our relationship with Russia, the dividends are evident: and end to the *balance of terror* that divided us . . ." It uses the term "balance-of-power" in a new way to describe a kind of equilibrium to be reached in global politics after the United States has achieved the strategic goals outlined in the strategy document. See, for example, p. 1— "The great strength of this nation must be used to promote a balance of power that favors freedom."

25. I choose this example notwithstanding Richard Pious' argument in "The Cuban Missile Crisis and the Limits of Crisis Management," *Political Science Quarterly* 116 (Spring 2001): pp. 81–105, that Kennedy's response to the crisis was "as much about presidential power stakes, prestige, and reputation as it was about the balance of nuclear terror." He does not specifically say that the balance of power was irrelevant and I do not think that my usage of the concept in this context is contradicted by his argument.

26. Bob Woodward, *Bush at War* (New York: Simon & Schuster, 2002).

27. Woodward, *Bush at War*, p. 130.

28. Woodward, *Bush at War*, p. 195.

29. They were established by Executive Order 13228 signed by President Bush on 8th October 2001. The elaborate structure of the Homeland Security Council, which closely follows the structure of the NSC, was detailed in Homeland Security Presidential Directive-1 issued on October 29th 2001.

30. On June 6th 2002.

31. See, for example, William W. Newman, "Reorganizing for National Security and Homeland Security," *Public Administration Review* 62 (September 2002), pp. 132–133.

32. On the expansion of the foreign policy responsibilities of the chief-of-staff see David B. Cohen, Chris J. Dolan and Jerel A. Rosati, "A Place at the Table: The Emerging Foreign Policy Roles of the White House Chief of Staff," *Congress and the Presidency* 29 (Autumn 2002): pp. 119–149.

33. See Paul 't Hart, Erick K. Stern & Bengt Sundelius, "Foreign Policy-Making at the Top: Political Group Dynamics," in Paul 't Hart, Erick K. Stern & Bengt Sundelius (eds.), *Beyond Groupthink: Political Dynamics and Foreign Policy-Making* (Ann Arbor, MI: University of Michigan Press, 1997), p. 12.

34. *Bush at War*, p. 332.

35. See Glenn Kessler, "State-Defense Rivalry Intensifying, *The Washington Post,* April 22, 2003, p. A1.

36. Woodward, *Bush at War*, p. 256.

37. Woodward, *Bush at War*, p. 342.

CHAPTER 11

Old Wars, New Wars, and the American Presidency

◆◆◆

G. Calvin Mackenzie
Colby College

Wars reshape landscapes: physical, geopolitical, and institutional. No nation is the same at the end of a war as it was at the beginning. Nor is any arrangement of authority or power. Among all the acts of sovereignty—taxation, eminent domain, incarceration, execution—none reaches so broadly nor sears so deeply as the act of war.

The twentieth century development of the American nation state was driven by many causes: abundant natural resources, immigration, a fierce entrepreneurial spirit, and so on. But war, too, played a central role. America's wars turned it from a dormant and distant nether land into a colossus of international relations. Wars ignited scientific discovery and economic modernization. And they forced together citizens of different races and classes in pursuit of common goals.

Those wars also altered the role of government in American society and redefined the relationships among political institutions. The federal government was stronger at the end of the century than at the beginning in relation to the states. The presidency and the federal bureaucracy were stronger relative to the Congress. Wars played a major part in those evolutions.

We focus here on just one piece of this evolution: the role and operations of the American presidency. And we pose two questions. First, how and in what ways have the wars of the twentieth century affected the presidency? Second, how will the emerging war on terror, what President George W. Bush has called "the first war of the twenty-first century," affect the presidency in our time?

A caveat. In the second part of this undertaking, there are many unknowns. The war on terrorism, presumably, is in its nascent stages. Will it be long or short, a sidebar to American life or a centerpiece, a success or a failure or a draw? We know none of these things. Much of what follows is therefore necessarily speculative, an attempt to derive the lessons from America's earlier war experiences and apply them to those that lie ahead. But we shall also try to note how this new war may be different from earlier wars, and how its effects on the American presidency may be as well.

TOTAL WAR AND THE AMERICAN PRESIDENCY

War posed a daunting challenge to a largely undeveloped presidency in the first half of the twentieth century. The responses of Presidents Woodrow Wilson and Franklin Roosevelt in shouldering the burdens of war altered public perceptions of the presidency, enlarged the structure and changed the operations of that institution, and accumulated in ways that have permanently transformed the role of the president in the American political system. A brief overview of these presidents at war suggests the nature and magnitude of those changes.

World War I

On May 7, 1915, a German U-boat off the coast of Kinsale, Ireland sunk the Lusitania, a large British ocean liner, with a single torpedo. More than 1,200 people died in the attack, including 124 American citizens. Were such an event to occur today, one can quickly imagine the response: a hasty National Security Council meeting, a televised presidential speech to the nation explaining the need for a military response against the perpetrating country, the launching of American warplanes loaded with precision-guided and highly lethal weapons from a nearby aircraft carrier or overseas base.

But in 1916, no such response was forthcoming. The administration in Washington sent a note of protest to the German government through normal diplomatic channels. There was no National Security Council meeting because there was no National Security Council. There was no televised speech to the nation because there was no television (nor broadcast radio either). And there was no military response from nearby forces because there were no nearby forces. Indeed there were few forces anywhere capable of responding against the powerful German war machine. Woodrow Wilson was simply incapable of a military response to a clear act of provocation.

America in the second decade of the twentieth century was not a country prepared for a "great war," not militarily, not organizationally, not institutionally, and not philosophically. Woodrow Wilson recognized this and was little disposed during much of his first term to change it. When war broke out in Europe, Wilson could imagine little direct role for his own country. "His general idea," Wilson's confidante Colonel Edward House noted in his diary, "is that if the Allies were not able to defeat Germany alone, they could scarcely do so with the help of the United States because it would take too long for us to get in a state of preparedness."[1] Wilson was not even certain that the Army was capable of quelling a pro-German uprising among American citizens were the U.S. to go to war against Germany.[2]

All of the available evidence supports the President's doubts. The American navy in 1914 ranked third or fourth in size among the world's navies. But that was largely a meaningless ranking. The only modern navies were those of Britain and Germany. America's navy depended heavily on outmoded battleships that could not match the big guns of the more modern dreadnoughts. Germany had wreaked havoc all over the north Atlantic with its U-boat fleet; the American navy had no significant submarine force.

But the Navy was the sparkling gem of America's armed forces. The Army paled in contrast. There are no reliable comparisons of the world's armies in 1914, but most estimates place the American army somewhere around twentieth in size, smaller than Portugal's and smaller than those of several of the Balkan states.[3] In the month in which Congress declared war on Germany, the American Army could muster only 5,791 officers and 121,797 enlisted men.[4] Nor was it a modern fighting force in any sense. Most of its senior officers had entered service before the Spanish-American War; the last Civil War veteran had retired in 1915. Most of its fighting experience, such as it was, had been on the frontier in the Indian Wars and in brief skirmishes with Mexico.

The elements of the Army were largely autonomous, and internal strife was normal. The War Department was as old-fashioned and balkanized as the Army itself. General Leonard Wood noted in his diary on May 21, 1917 that "when the department touched anything it touched it with the dead, cold hand of inefficiency."[5] Army units were dispersed around the country, and in China, Puerto Rico, and the Panama Canal Zone. As military historian John Patrick Finnegan has noted, "It had neither tanks nor gas masks. There were only seven hundred and forty-two field pieces and forty-three heavier guns in the country, with an inadequate supply of ammunition. The Army possessed less than two thousand machine guns, and they were mostly out-of-date. The air arm consisted of hopeful plans and some handfuls of ill-assorted flying machines."[6]

Prior to the war, the sad state of the Army had been of little concern to official Washington. Congress was consistently niggardly in its appropriations. The administration, in these days before the centralization of the federal budgeting process, could do little to loosen the purse strings. But it seemed indisposed to do so in any case. The War Department's annual report for 1913 even justified the small size of the Army, noting that Americans were "a peaceful and unmilitary people."[7]

Woodrow Wilson concentrated much of his effort on keeping America out of the war. His highest hope was to act as peacemaker, bringing the belligerents together to end the war through a negotiated settlement. The slogan of his re-election campaign in 1916 was "He kept us out of war."

Wilson's actions in the years after war broke out were driven by the intersection of three great forces. One was his natural pacifism, his deep distaste for war. (His nemesis, Teddy Roosevelt, constantly called him the "pacifist professor.") A second was his perception that the American people shared that distaste, especially for European wars. The third was his realistic appraisal of the limited capacity of American armed forces to participate effectively in a war that was being fought across a large and submarine-infested ocean.

The failure of diplomacy and the growing number of German assaults on American shipping eventually eroded the first two of these deterrents to military action. But the third was an enduring reality. When the events of early 1917 forced Wilson to give up his dream of peace making and prepare for war, he faced several daunting challenges.

The first was to bring the American people along with him. He was fortunate in this regard that the majority of Americans, after accumulated violations of American neutrality, were beginning to lean in that direction, for he had none of the instruments of modern mass communication to lead a public relations effort and no White House communications office to help shape and implement one. Wilson was a gifted orator, widely regarded as one of the best ever to inhabit the White House. But few Americans ever heard him speak since that could only occur within hearing distance of his voice. Wilson was forced to rely, in forging public support for the war, on the leaders of the Preparedness Movement and on the elements of the Democratic Party that stood with him.

After the war began, the government took on unprecedented roles in shaping popular support. To lead a massive propaganda effort, Wilson issued an executive order creating the Committee on Public Information (CPI). CPI disseminated a steady stream of vigorous defenses of the war effort to news outlets and opinion leaders. To protect the president's message by stifling dissent, Congress passed several laws, each at the President's urging: the Espionage Act of June 1917, the Trading with the Enemy Act of October 1917, and the Sedition Act of May 1918. Uncertain of the reach of his persuasive powers, Wilson sought instead to use the force of law to forge public support for the war.

The larger challenge was preparing the Army to fight a war and mobilizing the economy to meet the Army's material needs. In each of these activities, the President started from scratch. The Army was too small and there was no meaningful recruitment procedure in place. For most of American history, volunteers had staffed military units, and Wilson seriously contemplated a volunteer approach to raising the strength of the Army. But he noted the unsuccessful British experience with volunteer forces in the early years of the war and opted instead for a program of conscription. To allay widespread suspicion of federal power, the program Wilson submitted to Congress in April 1917 placed responsibility for drafting conscripts in the hands of more than 4,600 local draft boards.

Conscription quickly became one of the largest programs ever undertaken by the national government of the United States. By war's end, 24 million men had registered for the draft, nearly 45% of the country's male population. More than 2.7 million were drafted; combined with enlistees, the total number of men in the Army during the war was 4.27 million. Another half million served in the Navy. Though American participation in the war lasted less than two years, 5% of the population served in uniform.[8]

Getting soldiers was, of course, only part of the task the country faced. They had to be organized and trained, equipped, and delivered to the battlefield where they had to be supplied and sustained and replaced. This required a reorganization of the government in Washington and broad contributions from the civilian economy across the country. Wilson's inclination in dealing with the economy was to rely on voluntary cooperation. When that failed, he turned to coercion, seeking and receiving from Congress the legislative tools he needed. The federal government began to build shipyards and munitions plants. Wherever necessary, it took control of the railroads. To ensure that markets would produce and deliver the consumables that the Army required, the Lever Act of August 1917 authorized the federal government to set prices for foodstuffs and to regulate their production and distribution. It created two powerful new agencies: the U.S. Food Administration and the U.S. Fuel Administration.

Some newspapers called these interventions in the market "state socialism." But they were accepted with little opposition in the country and the Congress as necessary ingredients of this still-novel task of war making.

Perhaps the most difficult chore facing Wilson was putting the federal government itself on a war footing. The government's competence to run a war was barely detectable when Wilson called on the Congress to declare one in April of 1917. And the presidency itself was barely competent to lead one. The president had no professional staff, no formal role in the budget process, little direct command on the cabinet departments and line agencies of the bureaucracy, and no power to reorganize them. He was commander-in-chief, but a hide-bound War Department was rarely in the grasp of his leadership tools.

Initially Wilson had little choice but to cajole, wheedle, nag, and otherwise persuade the agencies of the government to get themselves in shape to manage the war. The president's role in determining organizational needs was formalized in May 1918 when Congress passed the Overman Act, providing the president with sweeping authority to reorganize government agencies. The end of the war was only a few months away at this point, and Wilson used his new reorganization authority sparingly. But the Overman Act established a powerful precedent for presidential reorganization authority that has lingered, with much debate, into our own time.[9]

All of this activity required the federal government to raise and spend unprecedented sums of money. A national income tax had been established by constitutional amendment just before the war. But it had not yet replaced the country's traditional reliance on excise and customs duties as the primary source of national revenue. That would change dramatically under the groaning burden of war finance.

In the fiscal year immediately preceding America's entry into the war, the entire federal budget had been $800 million. By fiscal 1918, the government would be spending nearly twice that amount every month. The best estimates are that the direct costs of the war were $35.5 billion—roughly equal to the total cost of the first hundred years of running the national government.[10]

These unprecedented costs required an unprecedented response. Some of the war was funded through Liberty Loans and other bond drives. But much of the funding came through increased taxation, and heavy reliance on the new income tax. In fiscal 1916, income taxation provided 16% of all federal revenues; by fiscal 1918, it was providing 60%.[11]

The transformation of America's military condition in the years from 1916 through 1918 was little short of miraculous. But when the war ended, the military quickly demobilized and soon shrank almost to its prewar proportions. By 1929, the strength of the regular army stood at 130,000 men.[12] Most of the war agencies disappeared just as quickly. What did not disappear so quickly, however, were the war's other legacies.

The First World War, though short in duration, was deep in impact—on American life and American government. It revealed in stark ways what a determined executive, with re-engineered institutions and popular support, could accomplish. It stretched the capacities of national financial management and revealed its flaws. The creation of the annual budget, and of a Bureau of the Budget to assist the president in preparing it, followed soon after the war and was one of its lasting bequests. The direct intervention of powerful federal agencies in the economy was justified as a temporary expedient of war, but it laid the groundwork for subsequent and more enduring interventions a decade later when the economy failed.

In two other ways, the war left its most significant legacies. World War I certified America's new role as a great power. Americans did not especially warm to that role and wasted no time shedding its military artifacts. To many Americans, impotent neighbors to the north and south and broad oceans to the east and west were still all the protection the country needed from the hostile intentions of potential adversaries. But World War I showed how quickly and effectively America could make the transition from peace to war and how formidable a foe it could be once engaged. The American national security state may not have been born with the First World War, but it was surely conceived then.

Equally significant was the impact of the war on the American presidency. Woodrow Wilson was the dominant figure of his time in America, as presidents had been only rarely in the past. The war elevated him to that status. But the legacy was institutional as well as personal. The war magnified the president's role as commander-in-chief, but also as diplomat-in-chief, as a director of the national economy, and as manager of the federal bureaucracy. The recommendations for strengthening presidential management capacities from President Taft's Commission on Economy and Efficiency, issued in 1912 and largely ignored, were soon dusted off and enacted in law to provide some of the institutional support these new roles required. Wilson's supine successors dissipated much of the momentum the war had yielded, but when the next national emergency arose, an economic emergency, the momentum for institutional development in the presidency was quickly reinstated.

World War II

In World War I, Congress had to confront a hard reality. It simply could not legislate flexibly or fast enough to meet the rapidly evolving demands of war management. It possessed no great expertise on that topic, nor did it have any institutional capacity for managing complex and inconstant enterprises like a foreign war. So it adopted a practice that it had rarely used in the past: the delegation of broad discretionary powers to the president. The Lever Act and the Overman Act are prime examples; but there were many others as well.

What precisely did this mean for the future of legislative-executive relations and, more broadly, for the Constitution? "How," the constitutional scholar Edwin S. Corwin asked, "in view of the scope that legislative delegation takes nowadays, is the line between delegation and abdication to be maintained?"[13]

But the danger to constitutional government from an expanding executive was little in evidence in the years that led up to World War II. The popular reading of this history is that the country was isolationist, the Congress reflected the prevailing sentiments of the country, and only the aggressive and farsighted leadership of Franklin Roosevelt saved the United States from its own faulty instincts. The real story is quite different.

No doubt Roosevelt saw the risks to America and to democratic freedom from the dictators in Europe and Japan, perhaps with notable foresight. But from the time he signed the Neutrality Act in 1935 until the early months of 1941, he acted with circumspection and caution in pushing for war preparedness or in offering support to beleaguered allies.

The American armed forces had demobilized after World War I and had remained small and unmodernized in the two decades that followed. As Sean Dennis Cashman notes in his history of the war:

> In May 1940 the War Department reported that the army could field only 80,000 men and had equipment for fewer than 500,000 combat troops. As to aircraft and qualified crews, America had but 160 pursuit planes, 52 heavy bombers, and only 260 fully trained pilots.[14]

Job One for Roosevelt was the reconstruction of American military strength. But that was no simple task, economically or politically. The effects of the Depression still lingered across the country and while military spending created jobs, it also burdened the country's overstretched revenue sources. And, in the absence of a clear and consensual national security goal, it was difficult to build political support for military mobilization. Only after the German invasion of Poland in September 1939 and Nazi military successes in the following spring, did the political environment begin to change sufficiently for Roosevelt and the Congress to move forward with an ambitious mobilization effort. Appropriations for the Army grew to $8 billion in 1940 (from $500 million in 1939) and $26 billion in 1941.[15]

Despite repeated invitations from Prime Minister Winston Churchill, Roosevelt regularly declined face-to-face meetings, and the President responded only in limited ways to Churchill's insistent pleas for financial and military assistance. The exchange of fifty aged American destroyers for leasing rights to some British bases, to which FDR agreed in the late summer of 1940, was about as far as he felt he could go under the constraints of the Neutrality Act and the more potent parameter of American opinion.

Roosevelt watched with great concern as the Battle of Britain unfolded over the English landscape in September and October 1940. But his eyes were focused even more clearly on the presidential election that was occurring almost simultaneously at home.

The theory of democratic elections is that they afford periodic opportunities for expressions of popular sentiment, a plebiscite on the performance of incumbents, a guide to future directions. And here, as the world was catching the fire of war, was a brilliant opportunity for an American election to serve that purpose. But in the autumn of 1940, there was little possibility of this occurring. A Gallup poll in the month before the election had asked the people whether they thought America should help England at the risk of war or whether it should stay out of the war. Fifty percent chose the first response, 50% the second.[16] With public opinion so deeply split, Roosevelt opted for caution.

Here's what he said in Boston a week before the election in Boston:

> . . . I have said this before, but I shall say it again and again and again: Your boys are not going to be sent into any foreign wars. They are going into training to form a force so strong that, by its very existence, it will keep the threat of war far away from our shores. The purpose of our defense is defense.[17]

The 1940 election failed to consolidate opinion on the war. Roosevelt won, of course, but not by offering any clear vision of his intentions for responding to the European crisis or the Japanese threat. The candidates avoided the real issue— should America get in the war or not—as they had in 1916 and would subsequently in 1964. If elections were capable of providing crystalline expression of public opinion, they could drive national security policy. But they rarely do. And their substantive ambiguity thus leaves it to presidents, after the election, to do the driving themselves.

With the election over and British prospects growing dimmer, Roosevelt did begin to assume the role of national conscience and aggressive mobilizer that popular histories have awarded him. The draft law was extended (by a single vote in the House), mobilization plans were implemented, and new appropriations were extracted from the Congress. In March 1941, the Congress enacted Roosevelt's Lend-Lease program for providing arms to the British. And Roosevelt finally met with Churchill, in a secret, shipboard rendezvous off the coast of Newfoundland in August 1941.

With new money and new recruits now flowing, the armed forces grew rapidly. By mid-1941, the Army reached a strength of 1.5 million men and 34 divisions. By the end of 1942, troop strength reached 5.4 million. And the flow of weapons and materiel kept pace. Even before the Japanese struck Pearl Harbor, more had been spent for military procurement than during all of World War I.[18]

Especially worth noting in the run-up to World War II is the central role played by the president. When the president was cautious, the government was cautious. Preparation for war and engagement with allies moved slowly. These were choices that may have been shaped by the conditioning effect of congressional reluctance, but they were the president's choices. There was no congressional policy of preparedness or international engagement, save what the president initiated.

Once the election of 1940 was out of the way and the deteriorating international situation loomed larger, Roosevelt's opportunities for bolder initiatives improved. Lend-Lease effectively ended all pretense of neutrality. And the mobilization that took place between the election and Pearl Harbor, while hardly adequate in terms of all future needs, certainly left the country much better prepared for war than it had been in 1917.

Aftermath

The two great wars of the twentieth century left little unchanged in their path. When World War II ended, there was no complete demobilization. American troops and ships stayed on station around the world. For the first time in its history, America maintained a large standing armed force. Abandoning George Washington's ancient warning about "entangling alliances," America engaged in an orgy of treaty-making. Two superpowers survived the war and soon both possessed the ultimate weapon of mass destruction. The national security state was born.

In recognition of that, and of the president's key role in it, Congress in 1947 passed the National Security Act, broadly reorganizing institutional arrangements that had existed since the beginning of the republic. And in this new structure all lines pointed to the president.

MAKING WAR: THE EVOLVING PRESIDENTIAL ROLE

That America's twentieth century wars affected the role and operations of the presidency must be one of the least surprising deductions of political science. When one contemplates the tasks involved in deciding to go to war, in making war, and in winning a war, it is instantly clear that all of these contribute to the magnification of executive responsibilities and capacities. At the same time, they minimize the value of many of the qualities that are characteristic of legislatures. Since wars are national activities, they also elevate the role of national governments and shine a bright light on national leaders. The contemporary American presidency, for all of these reasons, is in many ways an institution forged in war.

Contemplate the tasks of war making. Each demands sturdy executive skills: speed and agility in decision making, the ability to define goals, to marshal resources, to build broad support, and to delegate wisely. That, we can suppose, is why countries are usually led to war, and led in war, by their executives not their legislatures. The recent phenomenon in Britain and America of executives pushing their countries to war with Iraq, in the face of significant legislative resistance, was not at all anomalous. It was simply history repeating itself.

Among the tasks most common to war making in democracies are the following.

Define Real Threats to National Security

Someone has to define the threat, draw lines against it, determine the form of protection necessary to keep it at bay or defeat it. Citizens in most countries pay little attention to foreign affairs. They may regard the brutality of foreign governments against their own people or their neighbors as regrettable, even tragic, but not as a direct or immediate concern—rather as someone else's problem. Only when leaders in government begin to argue that American interests are engaged do most citizens become aware of the possible need for military action.

When the French were defeated at Dienbienphu in 1954, the Eisenhower administration briefly contemplated the option of intervention, then rejected it. A decade later, a different president decided that Vietnam posed a considerable threat to American national security and defined a response that called for deployment of hundreds of thousands of American troops. Better, Lyndon Johnson had said, to fight the communists in Vietnam than on the shores of San Francisco.[19] In neither instance was the definition of the threat or of the proper response simply a matter of political pressure. Presidents played the decisive role.

Rally and Retain Popular Support for the War

Since countries and their citizens are rarely predisposed to go to war nor enamored of the prospect, public support must usually be constructed. This responsibility often falls to those with a capacity or willingness to march ahead of public opinion—often in the past against long pacifist or isolationist traditions. The need is especially prominent when there has been no attack nor overt threat, when leaders must encourage preparedness for a war that many citizens do not regard as inevitable or desirable.

One could argue that the Spanish-American War was an exception to this norm, that the commitment of forces by President McKinley was a response to a public opinion that had been whipped to a war frenzy by vivid journalism and sloganeering. But, if so, the pattern did not repeat in the twentieth century. In each of America's wars in that century, threat definition and response definition were top-down, not bottom-up activities. Even in the case of World War II, the attack on Pearl Harbor came only after several years in which President Franklin Roosevelt had sought persistently to define serious threats to national security and to prepare the country to meet them. Pearl Harbor only simplified his task.

Construct a Powerful Armed Force

It takes armies to fight wars. Until recently, most democratic countries did not maintain significant standing armies. So the onset of war required a major commitment of resources and an enormous logistical operation to raise, equip, train, and deploy armed forces. And, of course, to pay for all that.

Standing armies are more common now, but few of them are on anything resembling war footing. A war of any duration or consequence will require: (1) augmentations of troops, first from reserves and then perhaps from conscripts; (2) additional weaponry and ordnance; (3) deployment to the war zone; and (4) additional and substantial appropriations of funds to pay for all this. Putting an effective fighting force in the field and convincing the controllers of the purse strings to pay for it are principal components of war making.

Construct Alliances to Fight and Direct the War

Wars usually occur after diplomacy between the future combatants has failed. Americans negotiated furiously with Germany before entering World War I and with the Japanese before the outbreak of World War II. In the second half of the twentieth century, much pre-war diplomacy now occurs through international organizations, especially the UN. The failure rate is not noticeably diminished as a result.

As negotiations with adversaries break down, negotiations with allies become more critical. Finding allies to share the burden of war is, of course, one of the purposes of these negotiations. Retaining some semblance of balance of power, even among non-combatants, is another. All of the normal channels of diplomacy flow at full capacity in times of war. New channels are constantly under construction.

Direct National Resources to the War Effort

Wars are national priorities. The broader and longer the war, the greater its impact on national economies and life on the home front. The redirection of resources to the war effort doesn't just happen, as Americans learned painfully at the outset of both world wars. Economic planning, new agencies of economic control, and often new laws that deeply regulate economic markets are all commonplaces of war.

But neither do these just happen. They only follow exercises of leadership aimed at directing the war effort. And those exercises often result in centralizations of authority that the citizenry would not abide in peacetime. Wage and price regulation, rationing, shortages and scarcities—anathema to free markets in peacetime—must be imposed in wartime to ensure that the fighting forces have the material they need to succeed. Because national governments must direct and enforce these economic dislocations, their authority is elevated in war and popular opposition to those elevations is muted.

Secrecy and Domestic Security

Civil liberties are luxuries of peace that rarely survive intact during wars. Wars place demands on leaders to impose and justify limits on personal freedom that democracies would not tolerate in peacetime. Travel is restricted. Censorship and propaganda thrive. Dissent is stifled, even punished.

During World War I, the government conducted "slacker raids," rounding up and detaining young men on the assumption that they had failed to register for the draft. In World War II, the federal government deported tens of thousands of its citizens, who happened to be Japanese-Americans, to detention camps hundreds of miles from their homes. Prominent leaders initiate, endorse, or acquiesce in such encroachments, deeming them essential to the war effort. Public opposition is minimal, as citizens play follow-the-leader.

Even a cursory review of these essentials of war making yields an obvious conclusion. These are tasks far more fitted to the characteristics of executive institutions than to legislatures. It can hardly be a surprise, therefore, that in the American wars of the twentieth century presidents have taken on the bulk of these responsibilities and have dominated the war-making effort.

THE WAR ON TERRORISM

Now America finds itself at the dawn of a new century, confronting a new kind of war. The threat of that war, at least in its magnified state, is only recently realized. Analyses of it, of likely responses to it, and of its consequences for government operations are necessarily speculative. So let the speculation begin.

Characteristics of the War on Terrorism

Like much else in our lives, war has evolved over the centuries. The impacts of mechanization and of technological sophistication, especially, have made modern warfare very different from its antecedents. But the character of conventional warfare has probably changed more dramatically in the past quarter century than in any other similar period in history. Precision-guided weaponry, widespread use of lasers, computerization of the battlefield, unmanned drones: these and so many other recent developments have profound effects on the way modern wars are fought.

But it is not just the science of war that has changed. The war on terrorism is vastly different in a geopolitical sense as well. Who Americans are fighting is as different as how they are fighting. The combination of these two profound changes has some significant effects on the character and impact of the new war.

The war on terrorism is not a war against a state.   The enemy in this war is much more amorphous than in previous American wars. It is a nest of sometimes interwoven, sometimes independent organizations that use non-traditional methods of attack. The enemy is hard to define and assess and hard to confront. As a consequence, it is hard to measure success in the war or to know when it is over. A clear goal guided the United States through World War II, the "unconditional surrender" of enemy states. Such a goal has little meaning, and little capacity to guide American efforts, in a war where the enemy is far more evanescent than ever before.

The war on terrorism is not a war against an enemy army.   While the popular dialogue sometimes treats Al Qaeda and Hamas and other terrorist entities as if they were trained armies, such a notion is more misleading than helpful. None of the terrorist forces contemplates a direct confrontation, nothing resembling a pitched battle, with American armed forces. The armed forces, as in Lebanon and Yemen and even at the Pentagon, are sometimes targets of terrorists. But these are probes at vulnerabilities, suicide attacks, not battles. In asymmetrical warfare of this sort, the value of powerful armed forces is diminished. It does little good to have the strongest army, when the enemy doesn't come into the field to fight.

In the war on terrorism, military manpower needs will be much smaller than in previous wars.   Because the enemy rarely enters the battlefield and because modern warfare now often substitutes technology for human cannon fodder, there is little need for armies and navies of millions. Real warfare, in the traditional meaning of that term, will likely be a small component of the war on terrorism. Even when armed forces enter the fray, they will be lean and nimble. In all likelihood, this will obviate the need for conscription or even significant call-ups of reserves. A small standing army, with well-trained troops and advanced equipment, will probably be satisfactory to meet the military demands of this war.

The costs of the war on terrorism will be large but widespread over time and many agency budgets.   Shooting wars are frightfully expensive. Recruiting, training, equipping, and maintaining millions of combatants eats though federal budgets like a swarm of termites. The recent engagement in Iraq reminds us that even with smaller armies, costs are huge because of the daunting price tag on the modern technology of warfare. But most of the war on terrorism will not be fought on the battlefield. It will be fought in airports and at immigration stations and in the back rooms of the FBI and the CIA. These efforts, too, will impose real costs, but their impact should be neither as sudden nor dramatic as in earlier wars. It is hard, for example, to imagine the sale of war bonds to fund the war on terrorism. The costs will be spread across the federal budget and much of the cost will be borne by consumers through higher costs for travel, for passports, for use of ports and other facilities requiring elevated security.

Because the costs of the war on terrorism will be more elongated and more diluted than in previous wars, they will be less apparent to the naked eye of the typical American—and thus less likely to be a source of opposition or constraint on the conduct of the war.

Much of the action in the war on terrorism will take place on American soil. Nothing more distinguishes this war from its twentieth century predecessors than its location. Sure there are soldiers and spies in Afghanistan and Iraq and other foreign sources of terrorist threats. But the real mobilization for this new war has taken place at home. A new cabinet department was created to manage the homeland defense. A terrorist threat warning system is now in place. Americans have been instructed in how to make their own family emergency plans.

Defense has been a significant part of previous American wars and rose in prominence during the Cold War. But all of America's twentieth-century wars were built around offensive capabilities, the capacity to take the war to the enemy and to defeat him with overwhelming force. The war on terrorism will have a significant offensive component—some military, some covert, some diplomatic. But it will be primarily a defensive war, designed to protect American domestic security from lethal, but ill-defined threats.

An important consequence will be a deeply altered balance between civil liberties and domestic security. In the period since September 11, 2001, the Congress has enacted or the administration has ordered more restraints on civil liberties than Americans have experienced since the beginning of the Cold War. Abridgements of civil liberties are a concomitant of every war, but in a war where much of the threat is in the homeland, Americans should expect bolder government efforts to restrict civil liberties than they have experienced in other wars. The USA Patriot Act of 2001 may bear a name that's a semantic improvement over the Sedition Act of 1918, but the objective is the same, and the means and authorities that support it are broad and deep.

A second consequence of the location of the terrorist threat seems to show up in public support for a war on terrorism. Americans who watched large jets fly into Manhattan skyscrapers or saw the panic that ensued when anthrax was discovered in congressional mail need little convincing that this is their war, that the threat is real and imminent, and that a vigorous response is essential. Incubation of public support for the war has not been required as in previous wars, nor has there been much need for a political leadership role in building such support. The Congress, which participated actively and often as a constraint in the run-up to the world wars, has been largely neutralized—some would say disappeared—by the suddenness and dominance of the war on terrorism on the political landscape.

THE WAR ON TERRORISM AND THE PRESIDENCY

It is hard to imagine a set of circumstances more conducive to a reinvigoration of presidential power than the war on terrorism. It has been less than a decade since President Clinton was forced at a press conference in 1995 to defend the relevance of the presidency. The first eight months of the Bush presidency seemed to mirror that concern. Policy initiatives languished in Congress, appointments were filled at the slowest pace ever, the president's job approval ratings in the last measurement before September 11, 2001 had fallen to 51%.[20]

Then, in a flash, America was under attack, and the President called the country to war. The president sought new authorities, the Congress acquiesced. Other leaders in the administration, notably the attorney general and the secretary of defense, aggressively asserted their own authorities, often dismissing congressional calls for information along the way. New government agencies took shape and new appropriations poured forth. The president's job approval ratings soared.

Presidential power has always been more charismatic than constitutional. It's what presidents are able to make of it. Wars have magnified presidential opportunities for leadership, "nourishing the presidency" in Arthur Schlesinger's svelte phrase.[21] In some cases, the light has dimmed when the war was over and presidential authority contracted. But there has also been a discernable, long-term ratchet effect. Wars generate institution-building, financial support, and public and congressional expectations that accumulate over time and accrete to presidents, if not genuine power, then greater opportunity to exercise power.

The new war on terrorism promises to continue that trend, perhaps even with longer-term effects than earlier wars. In some important ways, it has been easier than before to get this war up and running. President Bush has not been burdened with the need to convince the American people of the threat they faced nor of its imminence. He has not had to lead an expensive and logistically complicated mobilization of armed forces. No program of conscription has been imposed, nor is one likely. And the costs of the conflict have been borne mostly by debt-financing, not by frontal assaults on citizens' wallets.

The character of the war, especially the reality that the "battleground" is very close to home, has enlarged the benefit of the doubt that presidents always get in wartime, perhaps significantly. For nearly a half century, American presidents justified growing foreign aid budgets, covert operations, and repeated military adventurism as essential to contain the spread of communism. Terrorism is the new "ism." It may well come to serve a function similar to the one that communism provided through the Cold War, a justification for presidentially determined acts of war and abridgements of domestic civil liberties in the name of some overbearing but largely amorphous threat.

As long as enough Americans agreed that their way of life was endangered by the "Communist threat," presidents could make war and the FBI could spy on American citizens almost at will. The threat of terrorism is in many ways more apparent and more imminent than communism ever was—save perhaps during the early McCarthy hysteria. The opportunities it presents as justification for the use of military force, for extensive expenditure in the name of anti-terrorism, and for abridgements of civil liberties may in the end—if there ever is an end—be even greater than what Americans experienced during the Cold War. Even a conventional war against a conventional enemy, like the recent war in Iraq, can be mounted with less resistance as part of a war on terror than standing alone.

And, if that is the case, scholars of the future will look back on the war on terrorism as the frame and the rationalization for the greatest enlargement of presidential power in American history.

But, of course, it may not be the case at all. History is quite compelling in demonstrating the cyclical nature of presidential power, especially during or after wartime inflations. It is not hard to imagine two possible scenarios in which a high-flying presidency descends rapidly. In one, the effects of September 11th begin to peter out, no new and consequential terrorist attacks occur, and the public tires of the game of "Wolf!" The critics of presidential foreign and domestic security policies would then be back in the game.

Another possibility is a continuance of terrorist attacks on American soil or on American facilities or personnel abroad. An accumulation of these, or even a single dreadful event of magnitude similar to September 11th, could lead to criticisms that the president has failed to defend American interests, that the war on terror is not succeeding. That, too, could energize political opposition and awaken the Congress.

It's an interesting moment in the history of the American presidency, but presidency watchers have much watching still to do.

NOTES

1. Quoted in Arthur S. Link, *Wilson*, Vol. 4 (Princeton, NJ: Princeton University Press, 1947–1965), p. 111.
2. Patrick Devlin, *Too Proud To Fight: Woodrow Wilson's Neutrality* (New York: Oxford University Press, 1975), p. 359.

3. John Patrick Finnegan, *Against the Specter of a Dragon: The Campaign for American Military Preparedness, 1914–1917* (Westport, CT: Greenwood Press, 1974), p. 8.

4. Robert H. Ferrell, *Woodrow Wilson And World War I, 1917–1921* (New York: Harper & Row, 1985), p. 14.

5. Quoted in *ibid.*, 25.

6. Finnegan, *Against the Specter of a Dragon*, p. 189.

7. U.S. Department of War, "Report of the Secretary of War," *War Department Annual Reports, 1913* (Washington, DC: GPO, 1914), p. 13.

8. Ferrell, *Woodrow Wilson And World War I, 1917–1921*, p. 18.

9. Recently, for example, the report of the National Commission on the Public Service recommended that "The President should be given expedited authority to recommend structural reorganization of federal departments and agencies." National Commission on the Public Service, *Urgent Business for America: Revitalizing the Federal Government for the 21st Century* (January, 2003), p. 17.

10. Ferrell, *Woodrow Wilson And World War I, 1917–1921*, p. 87.

11. Charles Gilbert, *American Financing of World War I* (Westport, CT: Greenwood Press, 1970), pp. 220–234.

12. Finnegan, *Against the Specter of a Dragon*, p. 195.

13. Edwin S. Corwin, *Total War and the Constitution* (New York: Alfred A. Knopf, 1947), p. 47.

14. Sean Dennis Cashman, *America, Roosevelt, And World War II* (New York: New York University Press, 1989), pp. 39–40.

15. U.S. Department of the Army, *Mobilization: The U.S. Army in World War II, The 50th Anniversary* (CMH Pub 72–32) [http://www.army.mil/cmh-pg/documents/mobpam.htm], pp.10–11.

16. Reported in Walter Phelps Hall, *Iron Out of Cavalry: An Interpretive History of the Second World War* (New York: Appleton-Century, 1946), p. 189.

17. Speech on October 30, 1940, *Public Papers and Addresses of President Franklin D. Roosevelt*, Volume IX, p. 514.

18. U.S. Department of the Army, *Mobilization: The U.S. Army in World War II, The 50th Anniversary*, pp. 11, 16–17.

19. Quoted at http://www.juntosociety.com/uspresidents/lbjohnson.html.

20. Gallup Poll for September 7–10, 2001 (http://www.pollingreport.com/BushJob.htm)

21. Quoted in James L. Abrahamson, *The American Home Front* (Washington, DC: National Defense University Press, 1983), p. 165.

CHAPTER 12

Constitutional Prerogatives and Presidential Power

◆◆◆

Richard M. Pious
Barnard College

In the 1960s, presidential power involved persuasion more than command. New Deal incumbents won congressional majorities to build the welfare state; Republican counterparts consolidated or trimmed it. Both led a Free World coalition of the willing in high-stakes crises. Between then and now presidents have expanded their claims of prerogative power: the power to unilaterally determine a course of action by relying on constitutional powers—and have evaded framework laws instituted by Congress to promote inter-branch policy co-determination. All this has come to a head post-September 11, as White House counsel have taken claims of prerogative where no claims have gone before in prosecuting its war on terrorism and in the invasion of Iraq and its military and diplomatic aftermath.

This chapter discusses some of these claims to "high prerogatives" in diplomatic, military, intelligence, and domestic security affairs. These claims include the power to make commitments aside from treaties; the power to make pre-emptive war without congressional declaration; the power to evade both funding cut-offs and statutory controls on intelligence operations; the indefinite detention of enemy combatants; and the use of military tribunals outside the framework of statutory law. My purpose is to describe the sweeping nature of these claims and their sometimes dubious constitutional or legal footing. I also suggest that governing with prerogative power is ultimately unsustainable unless it is once again accompanied by an increase in both presidential authority (the sense that a policy is viable) and legitimacy (the sense that a decision is constitutional and lawful) at home and abroad. In other words, the presidential power of persuasion must be a complement to prerogative governance.

211

THE EXPANSION OF PREROGATIVE POWERS

Presidents have always claimed the inherent and implied powers of a "chief executive," arguing that they may take actions "necessary and proper" to implement their executive powers. They combine statute law with executive orders, memoranda, and signing statements to create their own reading of statutes. They claim the dispensing power, refusing to execute the law if doing so might be harmful to the nation, and instead implementing policy by referring to a "mass of legislation."[1] They invoke sovereign powers and concomitants of nationality to make unilateral commitments to foreign nations, and the commander in chief clause to commit the military to combat or peacekeeping. In domestic security they preserve the "peace of the United States" in ways that go beyond statute law.[2] They exercise a Lockean Prerogative: the power of the Executive "to act according to discretion, for the publick good, without the prescription of the Law, and sometimes even against it."[3]

They assert these prerogatives for four reasons: first, to initiate new policies, particularly in the first years of their administration when they claim a mandate; second, to secure control of the departments and centralize decisionmaking; third, to use checks and balances against Congress, particularly when they face anti-administration majorities; and finally, to protect themselves against checks and balances, particularly congressional investigations, the impeachment process, or legal process directed against them or their administration.

Presidents who institute prerogative governance leave themselves open to two lines of attack: critics challenge their authority (claiming that they don't know what they are doing) and their legitimacy (claiming that they are going beyond the constitutional powers of the office, or the government as a whole, or are violating private rights). These criticisms are often partisan and evoke a predictable response of "situational constitutionalism" in which the White House will be defended by its own partisans: Franklin Roosevelt won support of most Northern Democrats but only a small percent of Republicans on votes involving presidential powers, a pattern holding also for Truman and Kennedy; Nixon, Ford, Reagan and both Bushes gained far more support from Republicans than Democrats in Congress on issues of presidential power; only Lyndon Johnson and Eisenhower won bipartisan majorities.[4]

"Frontlash" occurs when the presidential policy is successful.[5] Congress legitimizes White House decisions through authorizations and appropriations (sometimes immunizing or indemnifying officials). The president's party unites and the opposition splits. Courts legitimize the presidential action (or use procedural issues to avoid decision) and the "living presidency" of historical precedent assimilates the prerogative.

When policy fails, the president loses authority, and a "backlash" against the legitimacy of the action is likely to occur. The president's party splits while the opposition unites. Congress puts new limits on the president's ability to make policy unilaterally. Courts may overturn the constitutionality or legality of a presidential act, although they usually couch it in ways that show "respect for a coordinate branch" by characterizing the issue not as one of presidential prerogative, but rather as involving the legality of actions of subordinates.

In a few cases the presidency "overshoots and collapses" in a constitutional or legal crisis resulting in White House reorganization after the resignation of key officials, along with adverse judicial rulings and congressional investigation or initiation of a censure or impeachment process. In two such cases secretaries of state (Henry "Super-K" Kissinger and George Shultz) temporarily held things together in quasi-parliamentary interludes while the incumbents were psychologically and politically paralyzed.

For the most part the Cold War and post-Cold War presidents have benefited from a remarkable string of judicial victories, as well as equally remarkable congressional acquiescence when they have made their claims of prerogative power. Some of the key developments in constitutional law are outlined below in an attempt to indicate how little remains of judicial and congressional checks on presidential prerogative power.

Commitment Powers

Presidents have expanded their powers to commit the U.S. by using executive agreements, department-to-department agreements, and PUPDs (parallel unilateral policy declarations.) They have also been able to reinterpret commitments or even abrogate them—all unilaterally without judicial review or congressional participation in decisions.

Eliminating a role for the judiciary, for example, was an important part of the *Iran Hostage Agreement of 1980*. To secure the release of American diplomats held hostage in Teheran, the U.S. government concluded an executive agreement with Iran that included the establishment of an international claims tribunal. Treasury Secretary Donald Regan subsequently ordered the transfer of hitherto blocked Iranian funds to London banks. The American construction company Dames and Moore sued Regan, claiming that there was no statutory or diplomatic power that could override attachments of funds already ordered by a federal court.

In a breathtaking feat of legal virtuosity, the Supreme Court first read the *International Economic Emergency Powers Act* in ways that contradicted the plain letter of the law in order to uphold the power of the Reagan administration to order the transfer.[6] Justice Rehnquist referred to "the general tenor" of emergency powers acts, holding that it may invite the executive to perfect the intent of Congress. He held that the court was "not prepared to say the President lacks the power to settle such claims," hardly a ringing endorsement. Rehnquist denied the plaintiff's premise that its access to federal courts had been taken away by the International Claims Tribunal, holding that the executive agreement had only *changed* the rules by which federal courts would resolve the issue, since cases not accepted by the Tribunal would revive, and therefore court jurisdiction had not been eliminated. Finally, he invited the plaintiffs to go to the Court of Claims, where they could argue that a "taking" had been unconstitutionally mandated by the executive agreement, a tacit acknowledgment of its "reasons of state" basis.

Reinterpretation of treaties provides an example of a presidential claim resulting in a reduced role for the Senate's commitment powers. Is the treaty power a blended power or is the role of the Senate merely to consent? If the former, interpretation might be a blended power as well. The question arose when the Reagan administration decided to reinterpret provisions of the ABM treaty involving the development and testing of space-based laser and particle beam weapons. Up to that point, the agreed interpretation had been that only ground research on these weapons was permitted. Reagan argued that laser and particle beam weapons did not fall into weapons categories under Article II of the treaty (ABM systems involving interceptor missiles). He argued that "Agreed Statement D of the Treaty" referred to "ABM systems based on "other physical principles" and stated that "their components would be subject to discussion . . ." Reagan interpreted this language to mean that testing and creating these weapons was permitted, but deployment would need to be negotiated later. Critics argued that Article II did cover weapons other than missiles, that the treaty bans the *function* of missile defense, not just particular kinds of ABM systems, and that Agreed Statement D referred only to future land-based weapons, and did not have to do with other prohibitions in the treaty in Article V against testing or deploying space-based systems.

The Reagan administration argued that it alone could determine the "entrenched meaning" of treaties, based not only on plain text, but also on version of the negotiating history. It also argued that the legislative history could be superseded by presidential responsibility to interpret the treaty obligations in the national interest, because a treaty's "legislative history" differs from that of Congress when it passes a law: in the former case, the president "makes" the treaty and the only role of the Senate is to consent, not to participate in the actual making of the law.

The White House view is that when the president ratifies a treaty, it is according to *his* interpretation; the Senate's view is that *its* understandings and conditions are binding. The Senate mandated in the *Fiscal Year 1988–89 National Defense Authorization Act* that no funds could be used for SDI tests other than those Congress had concluded would not violate the treaty; bowing to political realities, Reagan limited himself to tests in accordance with the "shared understanding" of the treaty.

In dealing with a related treaty involving limits on intermediate range missiles, Congress passed the *Biden Condition* to reaffirm its view that the *shared* understanding of the executive and the Senate is fully binding. Reagan promptly sent a letter to the Senate denying the constitutionality of the *Biden Condition*, and there the issue remained.[7] It surfaced once again, albeit in somewhat different form, during the Second Gulf War, when the question arose as to whether the Allied Coalition could employ tear gas in the event it had to disperse crowds of civilians marshaled by the enemy as part of an "unconventional" attack. The United States had ratified the *Chemical Weapons Convention* in 1997, but had reserved the right, based on an executive order issued in 1975, to utilize tear gas against civilian screens. In the run-up to the 2003 hostilities in Iraq the Bush administration argued that it would not violate the Convention's provision that riot control agents are prohibited as a method of warfare, since the purpose would be to save lives, not take them. But the Senate, anticipating such an argument, had already tried to handcuff the president from any reinterpretation: in its 1997 resolution of consent it not only put in a provision upholding the 1975 executive order as its interpretation of the treaty, but it also *barred* the president from altering the policy that had been set forth in the 1975 executive order; the Senate did so in order to align *its* understanding of the treaty with the general consensus of other signatories.

Still another expansion of the commitment power at the expense of both Senate and Congress as a whole involves abrogation of treaties. The Constitution is silent as to where the power is vested. Past precedents have involved unilateral presidential prerogative; advice and consent of the Senate by a two-thirds vote on a resolution of abrogation; passage of legislation inconsistent with the treaty; by joint resolution of Congress in the case of issues involving peace or war and other issues confided to Congress; or means specified in the treaty itself.

The issue arose when President Carter abrogated the *Mutual Defense Treaty of 1954* with Taiwan. Senator Barry Goldwater, armed with a Senate vote declaring the sense of the Senate that abrogation is a shared power, petitioned a district court for declaratory and injunctive relief. The district court held that creation of the treaty was shared lawmaking, and therefore that abrogation was a shared power as well, to be exercised either by the Senate or by Congress as a whole. The Court of Appeals, criticizing this reasoning as "sterile symmetry," used the *Myers* case recognizing a presidential removal power as an analogy (presidents appoint with Senate consent but remove unilaterally). Abrogating a treaty is not the same as repealing statutory law, nor is the Senate role to be part of a process of lawmaking; instead, the Senate is merely a check on presidential treatymaking, with a role that is not ongoing, either for interpretation or for abrogation. The Supreme Court neither affirmed nor denied the decision of the Court of Appeals: it dismissed the case *per curium*, with the practical effect that President Carter retained a power to abrogate not mentioned in the Constitution, though Congress retained its abrogation powers as well—though not a power to check the president's assertions of such powers.[8] Subsequently President George W. Bush unilaterally abrogated the *ABM Treaty of 1972* without a constitutional crisis, the issue of abrogation having been settled—or to be more precise, left unsettled to the president's advantage.[9]

War Powers

Presidents have used the military without congressional assent more than 200 times, to put down piracy, protect American lives and property, guarantee freedom of the seas, pacify and colonize territory, and defeat guerilla movements. But not until after World War II (the Civil War excepted) did they engage in large-scale war-making without formal congressional declarations. They have legitimized their postwar use of force by cobbling together congressional resolutions or appropriations, treaty obligations and other international commitments.

At the start of the Korean War, Harry Truman claimed the power as commander in chief to engage in "police actions" to enforce Article 51 of the UN Charter and a UN resolution authorizing force. But Truman ignored the *UN Participation Act of 1946* that required congressional approval for U.S. collective security efforts conducted under UN authority, and also bypassed the Military Committee in the UN that was supposed to coordinate such efforts.[10]

Subsequent crises involving "mutual assured destruction" were not to involve Congress: during the Cuban Missile Crisis John Kennedy's warning that "any attack by Cuba on any nation in the Western Hemisphere will be taken as an attack by the Soviet Union on the United States, requiring a full retaliatory response" was not followed by any request for an authorization from Congress. Nor did Kennedy try to win UN Security Council backing, instead relying on a resolution from the Organization of American States and on the *Rio Treaty*, as well as Article 53 of the UN Charter permitting regional organizations to repel aggression.

During the Vietnam War Johnson claimed that South Vietnam was a state that had been attacked by another state, and that it was covered by the Protocol to the *SEATO Treaty* that required the U.S. to defend it. He also claimed UN obligations to resist aggression under Article 53. Finally, he claimed that Congress had authorized hostilities when it passed the Gulf of Tonkin Resolution stating "That the Congress approves and supports the determination of the President, as Commander-in-Chief, to take all measures necessary to repel any armed attack against the forces of the United States and to prevent further aggression," continuing with "the United States is, therefore, prepared, as the President determines, to take all necessary steps, including the use of Armed Forces."[11] But these were problematic justifications: South Vietnam was a military regroupment zone and not a state; and the fighting involved a civil war in Vietnam, not one state's aggression against another.

The SEATO protocol did not require a presidential response to such a condition with armed forces, but did require the U.S. "to consult immediately" with other SEATO members to agree on measures to be taken for the common defense, though no such consultations ever took place. Nothing in the *SEATO Treaty* was self-executing or required the use of force, particularly to defend a non-signatory "state" covered only under its protocol. Finally, the *Gulf of Tonkin Resolution* authorized only limited retaliatory response to a naval incident, and not full-scale war, and eventually it was repealed during the conflict.

Throughout the war federal courts either ruled to uphold presidential warmaking or used the doctrine of "political question" to avoid rendering decisions.[12] It was not until after the *Paris Peace Accords of 1973* that Congress acted to end further hostilities in Indo-China by instituting a ban on the bombing of Cambodia, followed by passage of seven statutes banning other military actions on land, sea or air in the area—bans justifiably ignored by President Gerald Ford in 1975 when American armed forces were used to evacuate personnel from South Vietnam after Congress refused his request to repeal these laws and provide him with authority to use the military for the evacuations.

Presidents since have continued to use a patchwork of international commitments and prerogative powers to substitute for congressional collaboration in peacemaking as well as warmaking. After Congress put language in the fiscal 1994 defense appropriation stating that funds should not be expended for peacekeeping in Bosnia "unless previously authorized by Congress," Clinton indicated that he would ignore any restrictions on his prerogatives as commander-in-chief.[13] When Clinton ordered bombing in Bosnia he did not ask for congressional authorization, but relied instead on the commander-in-chief prerogative and NATO's enforcement of a no-fly zone as authorized by the United Nations Security Council.[14] In the bombings of Serbia and Kosovo in 1999, the Clinton administration also refashioned its justifications under international law (relying on NATO authority when it lacked authorization from the UN). Assistant attorney general Walter Dellinger went so far as to argue in the district court in *Campbell v. Clinton* that the ambiguities in the Constitution left unclear the responsibility to "declare" war, and that the president has the final word on the decision to make war.[15]

Congress engages in symbolic position taking: providing authorization to use force (which then satisfies the formal requirements of the almost defunct WPR), but leaving the final decision to the president, as it did in the Gulf War, or providing authorization well in advance, as it did in the Four-Week War. Presidents pocket these authorizations without conceding they need them: in the First Gulf War Bush initially indicated that he did not need congressional authorization, but with the American public split on the question, he eventually agreed to work for passage of authorization, though without giving up his claim, as he pointed out in his signing statement. Meanwhile the judiciary upheld Bush's prerogative claims even before Congress acted.[16]

In the run-up to the Second Gulf War, the president used a "soft" prerogative, obtaining an open-ended resolution from Congress, and relying on an earlier law declaring that it was a goal of the U.S. to replace the Iraqi regime.[17] In this way he could claim "joint concord" in enforcing congressional will as well as his own policy.

Bush *fils* also relied on a combination of UN resolutions requiring the Iraqi regime to enforce the terms of the 1991 cease-fire and to comply with requirements to eliminate its weapons of mass destruction or be in "material breach" of its commitments, to press its claim that the war was legal under international law.[18] But the UN resolutions state that a breach by itself does not re-activate the 1990 UN resolution authorizing the use of force, which must be done by the Security Council. The *UN Charter* states that "All members shall refrain . . . from the threat or use of force against the territorial integrity or political independence of any state." Except in cases self-defense against an armed attack,[19] no state may use force without Security Council approval—though it should be noted that since the creation of the UN more than 100 instances exist of force being used without such approval (which include, one might add, some French interventions, let alone Soviet and Russian). The Security Council itself is supposed to limit the use of force under its sanction to "maintain or restore international peace and security."

Failure to obtain Security Council authorization for the use of force led the administration back to the president's irreducible core of prerogative power: "The United States of America has the sovereign authority to use force in assuring its own national security" President Bush asserted, adding "That duty falls to me, as Commander-in-Chief, by the oath I have sworn, by the oath I will keep."[20] The White House report to Congress made the point that "The President has full authority" as commander-in-chief," and that other statutory authorizations "support" his prerogative.[21] The final decision was made unilaterally by Bush, who took the congressional vote passed months before as a functional equivalent of a declaration of war.

Once the fighting began Congress (by overwhelming bipartisan votes) passed a resolution supporting the troops, and within three weeks appropriated some $80 billion to replenish defense funds depleted by the wars in Iraq and Afghanistan.[22] The federal courts, relying on the passage of the congressional resolution, ruled against challenges, declaring once again that use of war powers was a political question.[23] Had they needed to reach the issue, they could have ruled for the president on the basis of joint concord to press for regime change.

THE FAILURE OF INTER-BRANCH CO-DETERMINATION

When Congress responds to what it views as excessive claims of presidential prerogative, particularly after a policy failure, it passes framework statutes requiring inter-branch co-determination and balanced institutional participation. Co-determination deals with new policies rather than past performance and emphasizes collaboration rather than checks and balances. Action-forcing "report and wait" deadlines are incentives for informal consultations between executive officials and legislators, as are committee clearances and concurrences, legislative vetoes by joint or concurrent resolution, and requirements for annual presentation of policy options to congressional committees. Presidents have objected to (and sometimes vetoed) these framework laws, claiming they infringe on presidential prerogatives. Their passage (sometimes over the veto) has been followed by minimal presidential compliance: provision brief and misleading reports, failure to consult legislative leaders, and use of loopholes to evade the intent of the law.

The War Powers Resolution

Consider the sorry fate of the *War Powers Resolution of 1973 (WPR)*. Congress passed it *after* hostilities had ended in Southeast Asia, right in the midst of the "Saturday Night Massacre" period of Watergate and during the first week of the Yom Kippur War. It was re-passed over Nixon's veto the day of a nuclear showdown with the Soviet Union. To re-pass it over Nixon's veto a bipartisan coalition was required, which meant sponsors had to weaken key provisions, enabling the White House to exploit its loopholes.

The WPR purportedly specified the conditions under which the president could use the armed forces, but a compromise placed this provision in the "purpose and policy" section 2(a)—not a judicially enforceable part of the law. Section 3 required the president to consult with Congress before introducing forces into hostilities, and to consult "regularly" thereafter, but did not specify committees or leaders, or what "regularly" meant, leaving all to the president's discretion, along with an "in every possible instance" loophole. Provision 4(c) required the president to report to Congress within 48 hours of use of armed forces in hostilities or if they had been placed in a situation in which hostilities were imminent (language which presidents interpreted to mean that the U.S. forces had to be inserted into a situation with an intent to fight, and that merely being fired upon would not define the situation as "hostilities").

The only meaningful provision was that the reporting requirement would set off a 60-day "clock" under 5(b) in which the president would have to obtain one of three things to continue hostilities: a declaration of war; specific statutory authorization, or a time extension. This meant that Congress would have to put itself on record within sixty days for a war begun by a president to continue; legislative paralysis, or buckpassing, no longer favored the White House. Provision 5(c) enabled Congress at any time to order withdrawal of forces by concurrent resolution, once a report had been issued or had been required.[24]

Presidents have done what they could to make this law meaningless. Ford established the precedent in the *Mayaguez* incident that reports would be one or two paragraphs and there would be no meaningful prior consultation with legislators. Carter parsed the language in Yemen and Zaire in 1979 to make reporting that triggered the 60-day clock highly unlikely. Reagan won a resolution from Congress in 1982 extending the use of armed forces in Lebanon, then issued a "signing statement" reasserting his position that the president was not bound by the WPR.

In *Crockett v. Reagan*, a case brought by a member of Congress claiming that Reagan had not submitted a required report about American forces in El Salvador, a federal judge denied the motion that the court retroactively start the clock from the time the report should have been issued, and then, sixty days already having elapsed, order forces withdrawn. Judge Joyce Green ruled that the issues presented a "political question" that the court was not competent to determine.[25] In dicta Green indicated that even if the issues had been justiciable, she would not have started the clock retroactively, because doing so would deny Congress the right to vote to authorize hostilities or extend the deadline. Green's decision cut the heart out of the WPR's main check on presidential warmaking, which was the provision that prevented a president from continuing hostilities in the event Congress did not authorize them within sixty days.

After *Crockett*, it was clear that Congress would have to take affirmative action to end hostilities. With Reagan's reflagging of Kuwaiti ships in the Persian Gulf in 1987, Congress itself gave up on the *War Powers Act*, passing a separate resolution authorizing the use of force and specifying various reporting conditions, and requiring an affirmative vote by Congress to remove the Navy from hostilities in the Gulf.[26] A court challenge at that time, insisting that the WPR be enforced, was dismissed on technical grounds (issues of remedial equity), but resulted in a signal from the federal judge that if a case could surmount various procedural hurdles, the court would then consider the question of the constitutionality of the WPR itself.[27]

Intelligence Oversight

When Congress created the Central Intelligence Agency (CIA) in 1947 the so-called "fifth function" allowed it to engage in covert operations. High-risk operations were taken to a committee of the NSC, consisting of deputy and undersecretaries, for approval, which gave the president "plausible deniability" if needed. Financial control was given up by Congress and a "black box" budget system agreed upon, with funds hidden in appropriations to other agencies and then transferred to the CIA with the approval of ranking members of Appropriations. Oversight of operations consisted of informal relationships between the Director of Central Intelligence (DCI) and sixteen legislators designated by the leadership from the Armed Services and Appropriations committees.

With the revelations by the Church Committee in the 1970s that most covert operations, including attempted assassinations of foreign leaders,[28] had not involved prior or subsequent briefings given to the overseers, Congress moved to institute better oversight. The *Hughes-Ryan Amendment of 1974* barred operations without a presidential finding and report to the Committee on Foreign Relations and Foreign Affairs.[29] When Congress passed the *Intelligence Oversight Act of 1980*, it required a presidential finding for covert operations, provided for advance briefing procedures to the Intelligence Committees (created in 1975) by the DCI (or alternatively to selected congressional leaders), or in emergency situations, allowed for "after the fact" briefing by the President.[30]

The Iran-Contra affair, in which Hawk and Tow missiles were traded for the release of several American hostages in Lebanon, and some of the "residuals" were transferred to the Nicaraguan Contras, demonstrated the toothlessness of these oversight provisions. These arms sales were illegal under U.S. law, violating the *Arms Export Control Act of 1976* and the *Anti-Terrorism Act of 1986* and several executive orders barring sales to nations sponsoring terrorism.[31] The Reagan administration claimed that since this was an intelligence operation it would not have to follow these laws. But the administration did not follow the framework law either: Reagan was supposed to issue "findings" but in some instances did so verbally and in others retroactively; the DCI must keep members of the intelligence committees fully and currently informed, but legislators were not briefed, as the administration interpreted the provision that "the President shall fully inform the intelligence committees in a timely fashion" to mean that he could wait until the very last day of his term.

The transfer of funds to the Contras violated the Boland Amendment prohibition against "any agency or entity of the United States" involved in intelligence activities from expending funds on their behalf.[32] The President's Intelligence Oversight Board had ruled that the N.S.C. was not an "entity" under the meaning of the law, but *Executive Order 12333*, issued by Reagan at the start of his term, had specifically stated that "the N.S.C. shall act as the highest executive branch entity that provides review of, guidance for, and direction to the conduct of all national foreign intelligence, counterintelligence, and special activities, and attendant policies and programs."

In the aftermath of the Iran-Contra Affair, the Tower Commission steered matters away from law breaking and into a discussion of improving supposedly flawed National Security Council decisionmaking processes, by characterizing Reagan as too disengaged and detached, though there was substantial evidence on the record that Reagan was fully engaged in the key decisions. Cosmetic reforms were instituted, none of which addressed the fact that Reagan and his subordinates had knowingly and deliberately ignored substantive and framework laws—and that his subordinates in the N.S.C. had used a system of plausible deniability to conduct the operations, even after such deniability had supposedly been ended with the "findings" provisions of framework law. Congressional investigating committees made a deliberate decision not to focus on Reagan or move toward censure or impeachment.[33] Lesson learned: illegal operations based on policy inversion could hollow out framework laws; privatization could make irrelevant the appropriations powers of Congress; if things went awry, congressional oversight would focus on operatives but spare the president.

MILITARY LAW

The Bush administration has fused statutory and prerogative powers to a breathtaking degree against suspected terrorists or non-state belligerents. Some of these involve statutory delegations under the *USA Patriot Act* and subsequent guidelines by the Attorney General regarding surveillance and investigation, and detention of security risks, but they do not involve expansion of prerogative power and will not be discussed here. There are, however, some developments involving enemy combatants and military law that do represent expansions of presidential prerogative and limitation of the role of statutory military courts. It remains to be seen whether this extension of presidential powers will be sustained by courts or Congress.

Indefinite Detentions of Enemy Combatants

President Bush applied the Geneva Conventions to Taliban prisoners captured in Afghanistan, but not to the al Qaeda detainees (because the al Qaeda is not a sovereign state and is not a party to the conventions), and neither group was granted prisoner-of-war status, but were considered "unlawful combatants." Under the *Geneva Conventions* only lawful combatants are granted significant due process of law guarantees. If captured, they are entitled to defense by a qualified advocate or counsel of their own choice (Article 105), right of appeal of conviction to civilian courts (Article 106), and right to same sentence as U.S. personnel, which would limit the death penalty (Article 87).

Each *unlawful* combatant's status is supposed to be determined, according to the *Geneva Convention*, by a competent tribunal: President Bush, without using the civilian courts or military courts, made the determination unilaterally for a whole class of detainees. The due process rights of these unlawful combatants are set forth in the *1977 First Additional Protocol to the Geneva Conventions.*[34] But the U.S. is not a signatory, and though the U.S. does claim to accept as binding the norms of customary international law, the administration reserves the right not to accept as binding any terms of a convention to which the U.S. does not adhere, irrespective of how many other nations are signatories.

As of the September 11, 2002 anniversary of the attacks, 598 Taliban and Al Qaeda enemy combatants from 43 nations had been flown in from Afghanistan, where they were housed in prison facilities known as Camp X-Ray. On November 13, 2001, President Bush ordered that the detainees were not to be accorded the status and protections of prisoners of war. No treaty or U.S. law grants the detainees access to a lawyer, though they would have such a right if they were charged with a crime. None were allowed access to families or their lawyers, and none told of charges against them.

Lawyers representing some foreign nationals held at the base have sued in U.S. courts, claiming that the bases are functionally the equivalent of U.S. territory, and that therefore those detained there must have access to the U.S. courts. In the first wave of detentions federal judges ruled in favor of the government. A federal judge ruled in one case that he lacked jurisdiction because the base detainees were being held—Guantánamo—was on Cuban soil, the detainees were aliens who had been captured abroad and "have not stepped foot on American soil," and because the plaintiffs (ministers, lawyers and professors) lacked standing. In another early case a federal district judge dismissed petitions for habeas corpus brought by lawyers for two Britons and an Australian.

Military Tribunals

The outer reaches of presidential prerogative power were reached on November 13th, 2001, when President Bush issued a military order creating military commissions based on his power as commander in chief.[35] The order mandated the establishment of military commissions (either inside or outside the territory of the U.S.).[36] The substance of the military order involved the suspension of the writ of habeas corpus and the establishment of military commissions presided over by military judges appointed by the president.[37] Under its terms, any *non-citizen*, including aliens residing in the U.S., could be subject to these tribunals at the discretion of the president, but U.S. citizens would not be subject to their jurisdiction. The president would determine who would be tried by such commissions, and if defendants were found guilty, would determine the sentence. Those subject to the commission would be members of al Qaeda, persons involved in "acts of international terrorism," or persons who had "knowingly harbored" others in the first two categories. Some or all of the detainees in the high-security camp at Guantánamo could be subject to these proceedings.

There were some elements of due process in the tribunal proceedings. Defendants would be presumed innocent, would be given notice of charges before trial, and would not have to testify against themselves, with no presumption being drawn from their refusal. They could choose their own counsel (if they could afford them) or military counsel would be provided for them. The burden of proof would remain with the government. Defendants could call witnesses in their defense. They could see the evidence presented by the government. Trials might be opened to the media. Two-thirds of the three to seven-member panel would have to vote to convict. According to DOD rules, the death penalty would be recommended only with a unanimous verdict of seven members required in death penalty cases. Guilty verdicts could be appealed to an independent appeals board on which civilians might serve.

But in many respects due process protections were wanting. No definition of "international terrorism" was provided in the order or in subsequent regulations. Group association and membership, rather than commission of concrete acts, could be the basis for detention and trial, and there was no requirement of "probable cause" that a crime has been committed.[38] A person could be charged and tried solely at the discretion of the president, without any judicial review of that decision. (In civilian criminal proceedings, the Fourth Amendment requires a prompt judicial determination of probable cause after an arrest has been made, usually defined as 48 hours.) Anyone charged could be held indefinitely at any location in the world, a provision that went far beyond congressional intent in the USA Patriot Act, which specified only a limited seven-day detention period, after which a person held must be charged with a crime or immigration violation, and which provided for judicial review in habeas corpus proceedings.

The president would appoint the judges, prosecutors, and military defense lawyers all. The accused would be permitted a civilian lawyer of his choosing, but the attorney would have to be cleared for "secret" information under Defense Department guidelines.[39] There would be no right to confront witnesses, proceedings would be secret, and illegally and unconstitutionally obtained evidence would be permissible if it had "probative value to a reasonable person." (This stands in sharp contrast to courts-martial, in which strict rules of evidence similar to civilian courts apply.) There would be no exclusionary rule for evidence illegally obtained, particularly by unreasonable search and seizure, or for illegally obtained confessions or other statements made by an accused or by witnesses. Evidence would not have to be authenticated, nor a "chain of custody of incriminating evidence" demonstrated. There would be no jury.

A two-thirds vote of the judges would be sufficient to convict, and the verdict would be based not "beyond a reasonable doubt" but on "probative value to a reasonable person." The appeals board could only examine the evidence, and could not apply the Constitution or federal laws. There would be no right of appeal to the civilian courts. The penalties would set by the president (though he could not change a not guilty verdict to guilty), and could include the death penalty, with the penalty being carried out in secret. Finally, the Pentagon intimated that even if a tribunal acquitted a defendant, he might still be kept in custody if thought to be dangerous.[40]

Under the terms of the military order, the decisions could not be reviewed by any civilian court, or by any foreign nation or international tribunal.[41] This stands in contrast to Section 412 of the USA Patriot Act, which provides for habeas corpus proceedings to review any detentions of non-citizens "reasonably believed" to be involved in terrorism and detained under the act. It also stands in contrast to the Constitution, which provides that the privilege of obtaining the writ of habeas corpus may not be suspended, except in cases of invasion and rebellion.

Through this military order President Bush had created a parallel court system not based on congressional action, nor confined to the statutory codes enacted for courts martial. The right to do so has been a longstanding administration position:

as early as 1912 Judge Advocate General Enoch Crowder argued in a Senate hearing that irrespective of congressional establishment of courts-martial, presidential war courts would have concurrent jurisdiction.[42] The executive may rely on "the law of war" as much as it does any statutory code, and such "law of war" is even acknowledged in the *Uniform Code of Military Justice of 1950* itself.[43] The presidential establishment and concurrent jurisdiction of parallel military courts has been recognized in subsequent congressional legislation as well.[44] Nevertheless, Congress specifically stated in the Code that military tribunals "may not be contrary to or inconsistent with the UCMJ."[45]

The administration claimed the president had constitutional authority to establish such commissions by fusing his power as commander in chief with his oath of office to defend the Constitution, creating resulting powers of investigation and military justice, and it also based his authority on a reading of international law that emphasized concomitants of nationality, and that used *Curtiss-Wright* to claim that the presidency was the instrument of sovereignty in these matters.[46] It pointed to past precedents, including the Civil War, in the Second World War, and in the Korean War (though in the last instance they were never used). The White House claimed that these tribunals had already been upheld by the Supreme Court in *Ex Parte Quirin* (in which some of the saboteurs even held double citizenship), as well as in *Eisentrager v. Johnson*, a case in which Germans had been tried by military tribunals in China for passing military secrets to the Japanese, even after the German surrender.[47]

This was not the only choice open to the Bush administration. A second and less rigid approach—"close adherence"—might have been adopted. It is a maxim in international law that a state is obligated to adhere to the norms of international law, even when it has not formally adhered to a particular convention. The Bush administration could have used this maxim creatively, in order to claim a close adherence to the fundamental principles, while drawing enough distinctions to maintain its commissions. Likewise, according to the USCMJ, military tribunals are supposed to conform as close as practicable to the courts martial. Again, the Bush administration could have claimed that it had met the "close as practicable" standard. This approach might have inoculated the Bush administration from any close scrutiny it might subsequently receive from federal courts.

CONCLUSION

Richard Neustadt's insight that the presidential power to command is usually associated with a prior failure to persuade, and Richard Rose's warning that presidential policies, absent this persuasive power, can lead to "global failure," seemed particularly apt as the crisis over Iraq unfolded in 2003.[48] In the aftermath of the Soviet collapse, neither the development of unilateralist international policies (particularly those repudiating former commitments) nor the projection of American military power abroad had led to a strengthening of national security. The Garrison State under construction by the White House would not protect America completely. The normalization of risk (brinksmanship with North Korea, for example), and risk homeostasis (the Bush doctrine of preemption) might in the future lead to an institutional crisis: expanded formal powers of presidential prerogative could conceivably be counterbalanced by shrinking political support and congressional backlash. This did not occur in the immediate aftermath of the Four-Weeks War, but might occur with a future military engagement or intelligence operation, or domestic security program.

Presidential authority is often corroded rather than enhanced by excessive reliance on prerogative power. Prerogative governance magnifies the impact of "groupthink" boosterism, and other dysfunctions of the advisory system. It removes the need to consult others, and thus reduces the flow of information upward in the executive or laterally across from other institutions or other governments. The advantage of separated institutions sharing power, and of inter-branch policy co-determination required by framework statutes, is that it requires executive officials to remain in a consultative and collaborative frame of mind, to explain their reasoning to others, and to be prepared to face up to problems within their line of argument. It may well reduce the likelihood of a presidential decision leading to a policy fiasco.

The contradictions of increased prerogative power and decreased authority (at least for now in the international arena) embodied in this "presidency for a new century" cannot continue indefinitely. If the White House continues to expand its claims of prerogative, and ignore and evade framework statutes, either incumbents will increase their authority through a "frontlash" effect (much as Lincoln and Franklin Roosevelt were able to do), or the presidential office will be subject to yet another overshoot and collapse amidst the wreckage of yet another failed "imperial presidency." Adherence to framework statutes and renewed attempts to work within the structures of the international community may be frustrating to those charged with making and implementing policy, but they may also represent in the long run a sustainable approach to the projection of presidential power.

NOTES

1. For mass of legislation arguments see *In re Debs*, 158 U.S. 564 (1895) and *NTEU v. Nixon* 492 F. 2d 587 (1974).

2. *In re Neagle*, 135 U.S. 1 (1880); *In re Debs*, 158 U.S. 564 (1895).

3. Thomas Langston, and Michael Lind, "John Locke and the Limits of Presidential Prerogative," *Polity*, Vol. 24, No. 1, Fall 1991, pp. 49–68.

4. J. Richard Piper, "'Situational Constitutionalism' and Presidential Power," *Presidential Studies Quarterly* 24 (Summer 1994), p. 584.

5. Richard Pious, *The American Presidency*, (New York: Basic Books, 1979), pp. 51–78.

6. *Dames and Moore v. Regan*, 452 U.S. 654 (1981).

7. *Weekly Compilation of Presidential Documents*, Vol. 24, June 10, 1988.

8. *Goldwater v. Carter* 481 F. Supp. 949; reversed 617 F. 2d 697; dismissed 444 U.S. 996 (1979).

9. There was, however, joint concord involved, since the Republican majority in Congress had passed H.R. 4, S. 257, the *National Missile Defense Act of 1999*, which President Clinton signed into law on July 22, 1999, stating that: "It is the policy of the United States to deploy

as soon as technologically possible an effective National Missile Defense system capable of defending the territory of the United States against limited ballistic missile attack (whether accidental, unauthorized or deliberate) with funding subject to the annual authorization of appropriations and the annual appropriation of funds for National Missile Defense."

10. *United Nations Participation Act*, 22 U.S.C. Secs. 287a, 287d.

11. Leonard Meeker, "The Legality of the United States Participation in the Defense of Vietnam," *Department of State Bulletin*, Vol. 54, (1966).

12. *Berk v. Laird* 317 F. Supp. 715 (E.D.N.Y. 1970); *Orlando v. Laird* 317 F. Supp. 1013 (1970), 443 F. 2d. 1039 (2-nd cir. 1971); *Massachusetts v. Laird* 451 F. 2d 26 (1971); *Mitchell v. Laird* 448 F. 2d. 611 (D.C. Cir. 1973); *Da Costa v. Nixon* 55 F.R.D.145 (1972).

13. P.L. No. 103-139, sec. 8146, 107 Stat. 1476 (1993).

14. *Weekly Compilation of Presidential Documents*, Vol. 30, February 6, 1994, p. 406.

15. See the discussion in David Gray Adler, "The Law: The Clinton Theory of the War Power," *Presidential Studies Quarterly* 30 (March 2000), pp. 155–268.

16. In *Dellums v. Bush*, 752 F. Supp. 1141 (D.D.C. 1990) (aff'd D.C. Cir Ct. of Appeals, 203 F. 3d 19, 2000) a suit brought by 53 members of the House and one Senator to obtain a preliminary injunction prohibiting Bush from using the troops of Desert Shield for war, the court ruled that the claims of the president were far too broad, and denied that the case presented a political question—but then determined that the issue was not "ripe" for judicial resolution because Congress had not passed legislation barring such use of troops or insisting on a declaration of war. In *Ange v. Bush*, 752 F. Supp. 509 (D.D.C. 1990), the courts denied relief to national guardsmen deployed in the field on the grounds that the deployment was a political question.

17. H.R. 4655 sec. 3 (1996) "It should be the policy of the United States to support efforts to remove the regime headed by Saddam Hussein from power in Iraq and to promote the emergence of a democratic government to replace that regime."

18. These include Resolutions 678 and 686 passed in the aftermath of the Gulf War, and Resolution 1441 passed before the Second Gulf War. Reasons given to the Security Council were that Iraq was in material breach of the cease-fire of 1991, and that authority to act under 678 to restore peace and security in the region then revived under terms of resolution 1441. But this reasoning, also adopted in the Goldsmith Opinion in the UK, was not fully convincing. Paragraph 6 of Resolution 687 lays down in precise terms when the conditions would be established for the allies, in accordance with resolution 678 (1990), to bring their military presence in Iraq to an end: a UN observer force was to confirm the re-establishment of the international border between Iraq and Kuwait. The "cease-fire" provision itself says that upon official notification by Iraq of its acceptance of the above provisions, a formal cease-fire would become effective between Iraq and Kuwait and the Member States co-operating with Kuwait in accordance with resolution 678 (1990). Resolutions 678 and 687 authorized the invasion of Iraq only in so far as it was necessary to restore the territorial integrity of Kuwait. Subsequent resolutions indicated that Iraq's disarmament obligations were to be enforced by sanctions, not by an end to the cease-fire or through invasion. Resolution 1441 added nothing, since it only "recalled" the previous resolutions. In any event, Resolution 687 contained a final paragraph that said the Security Council would decide on further measures but provided no authorization for the use of force, nor did it specify that authority to use force automatically would be revived in the event Iraq did not comply. The Bush administration argued that 1441 warned Iraq of "serious consequences" if it did not comply and disarm, and that nations understood that the wording would allow the United

States to act preemptively if necessary, and that if further Security Council authorization were necessary it would have been included in the language. But upon its adoption, France Russia and China all issued a declaration stating that the resolution excluded such automaticity, and that new Security Council authorization would be required.

19. The White House, in its Report to Congress on the rationale for the war, cited Article 51's ground of self-defense, using the conditional "may proceed" in order to reserve this right, irrespective of Security Council authorization.

20. "Address to the Nation on Iraq" *Weekly Compilation of Presidential Documents*, Vol. 39, March 17, 2003, p. 339.

21. *Authorization for Use of Military Force Against Iraq Resolution* (1991) P.L. 102-1; *Authorization for Use of Military Force Against Iraq Resolution of 2002*, P.L. 107-243.

22. S. Res. 95.

23. *Doe v. Bush,* 2003 US App. Lexis 4477 (2003).

24. In the aftermath of *Chadha v. INS* 462 U.S. 919 (1983), a case striking down one-house and concurrent resolutions, Congress passed measure stating that if the court struck down Section 3c, a joint resolution would be substituted for the concurrent resolution.

25. *Crockett v. Reagan,* 558 F. Supp. 893 (D.D.C. 1982).

26. Richard M. Pious "Presidential War Powers, The War Powers Resolution, and the Persian Gulf" in *The Constitution and the American Presidency*, eds. Harold Fausold and Alan Shank, (New York: SUNY Press, 1991) pp. 195-210.

27. *Lowry v. Reagan,* 676 F. Supp. 333 (D.D.C. 1987).

28. Loch K. Johnson, *America's Secret War: The CIA in a Democratic Society*, Oxford University Press, 1989, pp. 27-29; Senate. Select Committee to Study Governmental Operations with Respect to Intelligence Activities. *Final Report.* 94th Cong. 2nd Sess. Senate Report No. 94-755. Six Volumes. Washington, D.C.: General Printing Office, 1975.

29. 88 *Stat* 1804 (1974); P.L. 93–559 (1974).

30. P.L. 96-450 (1980)

31. 22 USC secs. 2751-2796c (1976); P.L. 99-399, 100 Stat. 853, sec. 509 (a) (1986).

32. P.L. 98-473 (1984).

33. Cohen and Mitchell, *Men of Zeal* (New York: Viking, 1988), p. 45.

34. Article 75 rights include trial by impartial and regularly conducted court, means of defense, presumption of innocence, the right to examine witnesses and not to testify.

35. "Military Order on Detention, Treatment and Trial of Certain Non-Citizens in the War Against Terrorism," 66 *Fed. Reg.* 57831 (2001).

36. *Procedures for Trials by Military Commissions of Certain Non-United States Citizens in the War Against Terrorism*, Department of Defense Military Commission Order No. 1, March 21, 2002.

37. Sec. 7(b)(2)(i).

38. There are precedents for this approach, notably the *Nuremberg Charter*, which criminalized the SS, SA and Gestapo. In the U.S., First Amendment law was broadened when *Dennis v. US, 341 U.S.* 494 (1951) was overturned by *Noto v. United States 367 U.S. 290 (1961), Scales v. United States 367 U.S. 203 (1961), and Yates v. United States 354 U.S. 298 (1957)*, and the Supreme Court held that only a knowing affiliation with an organization intending to take illegal actions, and intention of furthering such goals, could sustain a prosecution.

39. This clearance requirement under provisions of CIPA had already been upheld by a federal court in *US v. Osama bin Laden,* 58 F. Supp. 2d 113 (1999).

40. See comments by William J. Hayes, II, in Katharine Q. Seelye, "Pentagon Says Acquittals May Not Free Detainees," *The New York Times*, March 22, p. 13

41. Sec. 7(B)(2)

42. *Hearings before the Committee on Military Affairs*, U.S. Senate, 62nd Congress, 2nd Session, 1912, p. 35.

43. 10 U.S.C. 361.

44. 10 U.S.C. Sec. 821 (1994).

45. Sec. 36

46. *U.S. v. Curtiss-Wright*, 299 U.S. 304 (1936).

47. *Ex Parte Quirin* 317 U.S. 1 (1941); *Johnson v. Eisentrager* 339 U.S. 763 (1950)

48. Richard Neustadt, *Presidential Power* (New York: John Wiley, 1960); Richard Rose, *The Postmodern Presidency* (Chatham: Chatham Publishers, 1988).

CHAPTER 13

The Bush Doctrine

♦♦♦

John Dumbrell
University of Leicester

General Charles de Gaulle once observed that "the United States brings to great affairs elementary feelings and a complicated policy."[1] His meaning appeared to be that foreign policy statements by American leaders tend to exhibit a directness of emotion, couched often in moral language—"elemental," perhaps, rather than "elementary"—whereas policy is invariably affected by the fragmented nature of the American political process, as well as by the complex uncertainties of international politics. At least when shorn of its strong air of condescension, De Gaulle's observation seems to fit the Bush Doctrine, as expressed in President George W. Bush's West Point graduation speech of June 2002 and the National Security Strategy issued in September 2002.[2]

The following discussion examines and contextualizes the Bush Doctrine, drawing out some of its complexities. The 11 September 2001 terrorist attacks, and ensuing war on terrorism, brought with them major new challenges for the declaratory and rhetorical aspects of presidential foreign policy, as well as for the substance of America's post-9/11 diplomatic and military conduct. This chapter considers the origins and development of President George W. Bush's doctrine of preemption and various reactions to it. As we will see, the Bush Doctrine on preemption constituted, in itself, a major assertion of discretionary presidential authority.

First, some remarks about presidential foreign policy doctrines in general. The issuance of such doctrine is an important, though frequently unrecognized, part of the president's repertoire of power in foreign policy. As Cecil V. Crabb put it:

> The major diplomatic doctrines of the United States have been issued by the chief executive; their meaning has repeatedly been interpreted by the president or his agents; and the provisions of these doctrines have in main been applied by decisions made in the White House, sometimes with participation by Congress. Consequently, America's foreign policy doctrines have strongly reinforced the position of the president as initiator and manager of foreign policy.[3]

It is far from clear what exactly constitutes a "doctrine." Presidents virtually never describe certain statements of policy, intent or modality as a "doctrine." The 1985 Reagan Doctrine, committing the U.S. to aid anti-Communist forces in the developing world, was constituted by journalists as a presidential "doctrine" in the weeks following Reagan's slightly ambiguous verbal undertakings. The most celebrated doctrine of all—President James Monroe's 1823 warnings to European powers not to entertain Western hemispheric ambitions—was accepted as such only in the 1850s.[4] Nevertheless, once codified and constructed by contemporary opinion, presidential "doctrine" rapidly bequeaths an integrative and compelling force to executive foreign policy. Projection of doctrine is thus an important facet of presidential power.

Although serving an integrative and prioritizing function for presidential foreign policy, doctrines should not be confused with statements of grand strategy. The most famous doctrine of modern times, the Truman Doctrine of 1947 (on anti-Communist containment in Europe in the context of aid to Greece and Turkey) certainly did give expression to grand strategy. Most Cold War doctrines, however, were, in effect, presidentially generated, unilateral warnings to enemies, usually issued in times of widely perceived crisis with one eye on the need to mobilize domestic opinion behind controversial policy stands. The Eisenhower Doctrine of 1957 and the 1980 Carter Doctrine were such unilateral warnings to the Soviet Union, in relation to the Middle East and Persian Gulf regions.[5]

BUSH DOCTRINES

Perhaps strangely, President George Bush Senior's "New World Order" is rarely, if ever, described as "the Bush Doctrine." A broad vision for the post-Cold War era, the New World Order would seem to lack the necessary admonitory and unilateralist thrust of the majority of recognized presidential doctrines.[6] As if to compensate, Bush *fils*, within two years of his inauguration in 2001, had been accorded at least two doctrines.

The first form of words to be described as the Bush Doctrine was contained in the speech, written by Michael Gerson and delivered by President Bush on the evening of September 11, 2001. The key sentence was: "We will make no distinction between those who planned these attacks and those who harbor them."[7] Delivered after consultation with National Security adviser Condoleezza Rice—though not apparently with Secretary of State Powell, Secretary of Defense Rumsfeld, or Vice President Cheney, this statement was glossed by Michael Hirsh a year later: "Either you stand with civilization and good (us), or with barbarism and evil (them). Choose. And to those nations that choose wrongly, beware."[8]

During 2002, a second Bush Doctrine was identified by some commentators in the concept of "regime change," the stated administration goal for policy towards Iraq. However, the more widely accepted version became the preemption doctrine. Implicit in the January 2002 ("axis of evil") State of the Union Address, and in some earlier statements, the doctrine of preemption was made explicit in the 2002 West Point speech and in the National Security Strategy. George Bush Senior had also chosen West Point, in January 1993, to deliver a major foreign policy address. Bush *pere* warned that the U.S. was now entering a "complex world" with "no single or simple set of fixed rules for using force."

The 1993 speech envisaged the need, at presidential discretion, for flexible resort to force, "where its application can be limited in scope and time, and where the potential benefits justify the potential costs and sacrifice."[9] The younger Bush's opening West Point tone was less circumspect. A world of irrational dictators, armed with weapons of mass destruction, could not—so argued George W. Bush in 2002—be managed through doctrines of containment. The war on terror would "not be won on the defensive." The U.S. must "confront the worst threats before they emerge." Americans must "be ready for preemptive action when necessary to defend our liberty and to defend our lives." The U.S. "has, and intends to keep, military strengths beyond challenge." The days of "destabilizing arms races" were over.

The tenor of the first part of the speech was distinctly combative and unilateralist, despite a denial of imperial ambition: "America has no empire to extend or utopia to establish." The latter part of the speech, however, was more in accord with Bush Senior's words. The graduation class of 2002 was told that "American needs partners to preserve the peace." The U.S. was also not simply preoccupied with security. America "stands for more than the absence of war," and "will promote moderation and tolerance and human rights," as well as battling against global poverty.

The National Security Strategy reaffirmed the September 11 undertaking to make no distinction "between terrorists and those who . . . harbor or provide aid to them." Cold War strategies of containment and deterrence were described as inappropriate to the world of "rogue states," and "terrorist enemies" whose "avowed tactics are wanton destruction and the targeting of innocents." In such a world, "to forestall or prevent such hostile acts by our adversaries, the United States will, if necessary, act preemptively." The U.S. would "act against . . . emerging threats" with "anticipatory action." As in the West Point speech, American military superiority was emphasized and declared essential to the strategy: "Our forces will be strong enough to dissuade potential adversaries from surpassing or equaling the power of the United States."

Yet, again, as in the West Point graduation address, the preemption doctrine and affirmation of U.S. military power sat alongside less security-oriented, more traditional, and even multilateralist passages. The U.S. was committed, according to President Bush's preamble, to the "advancement of democracy and economic openness." The Strategy document laid stress on values just as much as on security. The U.S., "a great multi-ethnic democracy," would promote "a balance of power that favors freedom." The U.S. would "implement its strategies by organizing coalitions," but was also firmly committed to working with the North Atlantic Treaty Organization, "the fulcrum of transatlantic and inter-European security," as well as with the European Union, America's "partner in opening world trade." Several pages were devoted to issues of aid and development. The developmental and free trade sections of the Strategy caused *The Economist* to comment: "In some respects, the document has reassuring continuities with President Clinton's world view, though the Bush White House would hate any such comparison."[10]

PREEMPTION

The doctrine of presidentially adjudicated preemption seemed to many commentators part of a wider program. To Senator Chuck Hagel, Republican member of the Senate Foreign Relations Committee, this wider program involved the Administration "preemptively and arbitrarily trying to impose our views and standards on the rest of the world."[11] To Todd Lindberg and Michael McFaul of the Hoover Institution, preemption was a welcome aspect of a wider "liberty doctrine," geared both to U.S. security and to "'the protection and spread of liberty across the globe." Several commentators also noted the apparent conflation in Bush's statements of "preemption" and "prevention."[12] This point was made on the Senate floor by Edward Kennedy in October 2002. According to Kennedy, "preemption" related properly to demonstrated, imminent threats. The expansive Bush Doctrine on preemption, however, seemed to embrace "prevention" of remoter threats, involving strikes on "a country before it has developed a capability that could someday become threatening."[13]

A majority of commentators, on either side of the debate, considered preemption a novel doctrine. Speaking in February 2003, Democratic Senator Dianne Feinstein of California portrayed the White House as articulating "a new, and in many ways, revolutionary approach to U.S. foreign policy." She pointed out that in 2000, in the second presidential campaign debate, candidate Bush had promised a "humble" foreign policy. As developed after September 11, 2001, argued Feinstein, the policy was anything but humble. A "new" Bush Doctrine of unilateralism and repudiation of the "successful bipartisan tradition born out of the Second World War" had emerged. The key operational feature of the new approach was the "doctrine of preemption." Feinstein also referred to the Nuclear Posture Review of January 2002, with its acceptance of the possibility that certain events might compel the U.S. to be the first to launch a nuclear attack, even against a non-nuclear state.[14]

Many Bush supporters actually revelled in the putative novelty of the administration's approach and in its courageous rejection of outdated concepts of deterrence and containment. Speaking shortly after the issuance of the Nuclear Posture Review, William Kristol, chairman of the Project for the New American Century, told the Senate Foreign Relations Committee: "The president has chosen to build a new world, not to rebuild the old one that existed before September 11, 2001." The Bush Doctrine included, according to Kristol, a willingness "to act preemptively and, if need be, unilaterally." It was part of a wider departure "from the pseudo-sophisticated *realism* of the first Bush administration or the evasive *multilateralism* of the Clinton years. The Bush Doctrine rests in a revived commitment to the principles of liberal democracy and the restoration of American military power."[15]

At least on the narrow issue of preemption, Feinstein and Kristol exaggerated the novelty of the Bush Doctrine. As the National Security Strategy document itself stated, the U.S. "has long maintained the option of preemptive actions." Such actions were frequently contemplated, and indeed committed, during the Cold War.

The notion of a "preventive war" against the Soviet Union, designed to prevent Moscow acquiring a major nuclear capability, was widely discussed in the late 1940s. In 1947, George Kennan acknowledged that such a war might be justified, though by 1949 he was arguing that a "democratic society cannot plan a preventive war."[16] (Rather extraordinarily, in the mid-1940s, British philosopher and peace campaigner Bertrand Russell had toyed with the idea of an American preventive war).[17] Such a war was explicitly ruled out in NSC-68 in 1950, though an American "first blow" was there held to be justified if it was "demonstrably in the nature of a counter-attack to a blow which is on its way or about to be delivered."[18] Yet American leaders in the 1950s did not entirely rule out a broader "preventive war," involving nuclear first use. In 1953, President Eisenhower wrote to Secretary of State Dulles, envisaging circumstances—essentially if the U.S. were presented with a choice between virtually inevitable war or "some form of dictatorial government"—when "our duty to future generations" might "require us to *initiate* war at the most propitious moment that we could designate."[19]

Famously, a preemptive strike on Cuba was rejected by President Kennedy's Executive Committee during the 1962 missile crisis. According to Robert Kennedy a preemptive "attack by a very large nation against a very small one" would be contrary to "our heritage and our ideals."[20] Under both Presidents Kennedy and Johnson, suggestions for preventive war against China were considered. A June 1963 Presidential briefing paper, prepared for an upcoming conference on the Limited Nuclear Test ban, raised the possibility of "possibly joint US-USSR" military action to prevent Chinese development of nuclear weapons.[21] The case for "direct action against Chinese Communist nuclear facilities" was considered in 1964 by President Johnson's Committee on Nuclear Proliferation, chaired by Roswell Gilpatric.[22] The Johnson Administration did not countenance nuclear first-use, though Llewellyn Thompson, Soviet adviser to LBJ, stated in 1964 that, in the event of a conventional Soviet "grab for Europe," the U.S. would consider immediate, first use of nuclear weapons.[23]

U.S. interventions in Central America and the Caribbean have had a strong element of preemption in their motivation. (Several critics of the Bush Doctrine actually saw it as an attempt to extend the Monroe Doctrine, underpinning U.S. military intervention in the Western hemisphere, to the entire globe.) In his memoirs, Lyndon Johnson made clear that the Dominican Republic invasion of 1965 was intended to head off Castroite influence as well as to protect American lives.[24] President Reagan attempted to justify the 1983 invasion of Grenada in words which might have come from the lips of G. W. Bush: "The world has changed. Today, our national security can be threatened in faraway places. It is up to all of us to be aware of the strategic importance of such places and to be able to identify them."[25] The Panamanian invasion of 1989-90, often cited as the first post-Cold War U.S. military intervention, was multifaceted in its motives and objectives. At least in so far as it was linked to the desire to protect access to the Canal, it may be judged to have had important preemptive aspects.

Looking beyond the Western hemisphere, the 1986 air raids on Libya had even stronger parallels to problems faced in the post-Cold War, post-9/11 era. Addressing the nation on 14 April 1986, President Reagan justified the air strikes as efforts to prevent Colonel Qadhafi from repeating the bombing of a West Berlin nightclub, frequented by U.S. servicemen. "We believe," stated Reagan, "that this preemptive action against his terrorist installations will not only damage Colonel Qadhafi's capacity to export terror, it will provide him with incentive and reason to alter his criminal behavior."[26] The Clinton doctrine of "rogue states" also provided a backdrop to preemptive action. In August 1998, President Clinton announced: "Today I ordered our Armed Forces to strike at terrorist-related facilities in Afghanistan and Sudan because of the imminent threat they presented to our national security." There was an "immediate threat from the bin Laden network."[27]

Clearly, the U.S. had, indeed, long maintained the option of preemption. In a sense, most military interventions have a preemptive (or preventive) dimension; the 1991 Gulf conflict, for example, was, at one level, an effort to preempt a move by Iraq against Saudi Arabia. It should also be appreciated that unilateralism and extreme presidentialism in military decision-making are hardly new. Most recent military interventions have, despite the provisions of the 1973 War Powers Resolution, flowed from exclusively White House—or at least executive branch—decisions, with little, if any, prior consultation with Congress, much less with allies. In the case of Grenada, an independent country in the British Commonwealth, London was informed of the invasion decision after it had been taken. In 1986, President Reagan informed congressional leaders of the impending Libyan air strikes when the U.S. bombers were actually airborne.[28]

Much of the controversy attending the 2002 articulation of the Bush preemption doctrine derived simply from the starkness of its expression, set amid a wider, putatively unilateralist, even imperialist, philosophy of American power-projection. More specifically, the doctrine attracted controversy due to its apparent status as a replacement for traditional concepts of deterrence, containment, and even national sovereignty under the United Nations Charter. Anthony Lewis wrote in the *New York Review of Books* that the preemption doctrine overthrew "the commitment that the United States and all other members" of the UN "have made . . .to eschew attacks across international frontiers except in response to armed aggression."[29] For good or ill, traditional notions of sovereignty had already been weakened by legal principles of humanitarian intervention developed in the 1990s. The new doctrine of preemption at presidential discretion, for many critics, pointed in the direction of international anarchy. Might the doctrine not encourage other nations, such as India or Pakistan, to take preemptive action against their neighbors? How likely was it that other nations would accept the idea that only the U.S., the world's order-guarantor of last resort, could practice discretionary preemption?

The 2002 expressions of the preemption doctrine also appeared, again at the discretion of the U.S. president, to lower the threshold which might trigger preemptive intervention. The doctrine seemed to make the U.S. president judge and jury of where and when to intervene. As G. John Ikenberry argued, it appeared that preemptive action was now permissible even without the demonstrated presence of a "clear threat" or "imminent threat," such as Clinton had asserted in connection with the 1998 raids on Sudan and Afghanistan. The route was open, according to Ikenberry, to "national security by hunch or inference, leaving the world without clear-cut norms for justifying force."[30] Outlining the policy of "proactive counter-proliferation" (rather than "non-proliferation") of weapons of mass destruction

(WMD), Defense Secretary Donald Rumsfeld declared that the "absence of evidence is not evidence of absence" of WMD.[31] As asserted by the president, and defended by leading members of his administration, the preemption doctrine—a doctrine of "strike first"[32]—certainly encompassed attacks, made at presidential discretion, without any necessarily convincing demonstration of imminent threat.

ROOTS OF THE BUSH DOCTRINE

President George W. Bush's major foreign policy statements of 2002—the State of the Union and West Point addresses, as well as the Nuclear Posture Review and National Security Strategy—provoked a debate about American imperialism not seen since the era of the Vietnam War, possibly not since the debates about imperialism which flourished in the U.S. around a century ago. Preemption was widely linked to the kind of neoconservative, putatively neoimperialist, foreign policy positions associated with the Project for the New American Century and with Assistant Secretary of Defense, Paul Wolfowitz. To many, an optimistic, crusading neoconservatism seemed to have taken over the whole administration. As Mary Kaldor wrote in 2003: "The Bushites believe, or appear to believe, that America is a cause, not a nation, with a mission to convert the rest of the world to the American dream and to rid the world of terrorists and tyrants."[33]

The neoconservative roots of the Bush Doctrine will be discussed shortly. It is worth pointing out, however, that the views expressed in the 2002 foreign policy addresses had important pre-echoes in the first Bush presidency, and even in policies associated with President Clinton. President George H. W. Bush's West Point address of January 1993—the elder Bush's valedictory foreign policy statement—was, as already been noted, set within a more cautious and multilateralist framework than George W's statement. Yet it was, essentially, a defense of presidentially directed, flexible U.S. power-projection. Bush Senior saw it as a major task of his presidency to eliminate "Vietnam syndrome" inhibitions on the use of American military power. He was also, notably in his preference for leading foreign policy through the issuance of largely unaccountable presidentialist National Security Directives, a staunch proponent of presidential authority.[34]

Bill Clinton's foreign policy, of course, was regularly condemned by Republicans in the 1990s as fuzzy, inchoate and incompetent. Yet in a number of respects, Clinton's policies pointed forward to the second Bush era. First, there was the doctrine of "rogue states," enthusiastically embraced by the Bush administration—with a view to destroying rather than containing their power—as a basis for the doctrine of preemption. The National Security Strategy identified "deadly challenges" from "rogue states and terrorists," reviving a phrase which the Clinton administration had, to hoots of Republican derision, abandoned in favor of "states of concern." The notion of "rogue states" was central to Clinton's efforts to resist proliferation of WMD. It was also linked to the Clintonite notion of a growing "family" of democratizing, globalizing nations, joined in free trade.[35] (Bush's National Security Strategy trumpeted "free trade" as a "moral principle.")

Second, it was the Clinton administration, in its, admittedly patchy, commitment to "assertive humanitarianism" and "liberal hawkism," which called into question traditional notions of sovereignty, notably in connection with the conflicts in the former Yugoslavia. Third, it should not be forgotten that, especially in its second term, the Clinton administration moved quite a way towards unilateralist foreign policy positions: opposition (reversed in Clinton's final days in the White House) to the International Criminal Court, unilateral attacks on Sudan and Afghanistan, the 1999 bombing of Kosovo without UN Security Council sanction, and so on. The unilateralist thrust of the second Clinton administration was associated with a perceived need to compromise with the Republican-dominated Congress, elected in 1994, and with a new confidence in American power which accompanied the supercession, especially in the context of U.S. economic success in the 1990s, of notions of American "decline."

Last, and less obviously, President G. W. Bush was able to inherit from his predecessor continued presidential dominance of the leadership of and agenda-setting in foreign policy. As just noted, this was achieved partly by means of second-guessing, and compromising with, the post-1994 Republican Congress. However, Clinton was clearly successful at resisting the widely predicted possibility that post-Cold War foreign policy would veer out of presidential control.[36]

The neoconservative roots of the Bush Doctrine, of course, were far more obvious than any debt to the first Bush or to the two Clinton administrations. To many commentators, in the U.S. as well as Europe, the neoconservatives were simply imperialists. According to Ikenberry, Bush's "neo-imperial grand strategy"' was bound to lead to extreme international resentment and to "imperial overstretch."[37] Ivo Daalder spoke of "democratic imperialism," involving the use of American power to remake the world in America's image.[38] To columnist Jay Brookman, war with Iraq "is intended to mark the official emergence of the United States as a full-fledged global empire, seizing sole responsibility and authority as planetary policeman."[39] Norman Mailer saw "empire" as President Bush's way of refreshing American purpose. Bush, in Mailer's words, "believes this country is the only hope of the world. He also fears that the country is rapidly growing more dissolute, and the only solution may be . . . to strive for World Empire."[40] The National Security Strategy provoked attacks on the putative imperialism of the Bush administration not only from Democrats and the left, but from Republicans like Chuck Hagel, and from the libertarian Cato Institute. Although the administration generally disavowed any imperial intent—"We don't seek an empire," announced Bush on Veterans' Day, 2002,[41] some critics noted that words and concepts associated with empire were regaining respectability.[42]

The Pentagon's "no rivals" plan, leaked in 1992 and principally authored by Lewis Libby and Paul Wolfowitz, was commonly seen as a founding document for the new neoconservative imperialism. The tone of the plan, a "defense guidance" for fiscal years 1994 to 1999, was primarily realist and unilateralist, rather than messianic. The U.S., according to the 1992 plan, "should be postured to act independently when collective action cannot be orchestrated." Future coalitions—coalitions of the willing—were likely "to be ad hoc assemblies often not lasting beyond the crisis being confronted." The U.S. would maintain military primacy and "retain the preeminent responsibility for addressing selectively those wrongs" which threatened US interests; it would, however, also address threats to "our allies or friends."[43]

Neoconservatism, as organized, after 1996, in the Project for the New American Century, had both realist and values-promotion aspects. It drew on the view that, following the presidency of Ronald Reagan, the American right had withdrawn into an irresponsible neo-isolationism. The Republicans' Contract with America, the basis of GOP congressional policy, following the 1994 elections, had concentrated on the supposed need to cut funds for international peace-keeping, to prevent U.S. troops from serving under UN or foreign command, and on the need for strong defense. On October 24, 1995, the UN's fiftieth anniversary, one of the "Republican revolutionaries," Representative Joe Scarborough of Florida, introduced legislation, providing for America's exit from the United Nations. On the balance of power between president and Congress on foreign policy, the congressional Republicans of the 1990s were rather schizophrenic. Formally committed to strong presidential leadership, and to repeal of the War Powers Resolution, they were also (as in 1995 votes against the Bosnian arms embargo) clearly challenging the executive's control of foreign policy. Their general tone was unilateralist, strongly nationalist, and suspicious of any foreign involvement that could not unequivocally be demonstrated as advancing rather narrowly conceived national interests.

By contrast, primacists within Republican ranks argued for a revived Reaganism: still largely unilateralist and hostile to the UN, but strongly presidentialist and confidently internationalist. Neo-Reaganites differed in the degree of emphasis placed on security interests as opposed to values-promotion. A common way of resolving this tension was to argue that values-promotion and security were interdependent: flip sides of the "Americanist" foreign policy coin.[44] Neo-Reaganite neoconservatives tended to be strong admirers of Israeli Likud foreign policy. (One source of the preemption doctrine is often deemed to be the 1981 raid on Iraq's Osirak nuclear reactor). The term "empire" also came, for proponents of Republican neoconservatism, indeed to lose many of its negative connotations. In the early 1990s, Charles Krauthammer wrote unapologetically of the attractions of a new Pax Americana—"Why be embarrassed by it?"[45]

Most assessments of the George W. Bush presidency identify primacist, unilateralist neoconservatism as just one element within the administration, albeit one which was immeasurably strengthened in the wake of the 9/11 attacks. Unusually early in the Bush presidency, the press put forward the view that the administration fell into two camps: unilateralist (centered around Donald Rumsfeld) and multilateralist (centered around Colin Powell). Initially, the press saw Vice President Richard Cheney and National Security Adviser Condoleezza Rice as adjudicating between the two camps, although it rapidly became evident that Cheney belonged firmly in the former. Rice's adherence to National Missile Defense also inclined journalists to placed her towards the right of the administration in its early days.[46] Various labels became attached to the key Bush personnel. Michael Hirsh, for example, identified a "lonely band of moderate multilateralists," headed by Colin Powell but also including (presumably) Deputy National Security Adviser Stephen

Hadley. Cheney and Rumsfeld constituted an "axis of realist unilateralists," with Wolfowitz leading "a third group of influential neoconservatives."[47] Ivo Daalder favored the term "imperialists" for the Wolfowitz group; "offensive realists" for Cheney and Rumsfeld; and "defensive realists" for the Powellites.[48]

The defining event for the Bush Doctrine, of course, was not the penning of the "no rivals" plan, nor the founding of the Project for the New American Century; rather it was the 9/11 assault on the US. Before 9/11, the administration had followed a policy of quasi-disengaged realism, an "American internationalism" proceeding, in Condoleezza Rice's words, "from the firm ground of the national interest and not from the interest of an illusory international community."[49] It was a foreign policy rooted in hostility to Clinton's pretensions to a globalized humanitarianism: a foreign policy geared to the perceived needs of a successful superpower in a unipolar world. The terrorist attacks did not so much push the administration on a multilateralist path, though in some respects (as in Bush's September 12, 2002, speech to the UN, requesting a resolution on Iraq) it did. Rather, it heightened and extended, to hitherto unimaginable proportions, American sensitivity to Reagan's 1983 perception that "our national security can be threatened in faraway places." It also pushed the administration back to the (also Reaganite) theme of values-promotion. Many commentators questioned the administration's commitment to the long haul of post-conflict nation-building, which would be required in countries such as Afghanistan and Iraq to effect democratic transition. However, at least at the level of rhetoric, there was a clear turn after 9/11 to talk of values. In the West Point speech and the National Security Strategy, the preemption doctrine was sufficiently enmeshed in statements of messianic purpose as indeed to justify its description as (depending on preference) an imperial, or as a "liberty" doctrine.

Finally, the Bush Doctrine was manifestly rooted in a commitment to, and recognition of, American international primacy. By the middle Bush years, U.S. military primacy had indeed advanced to a quite extraordinary extent. The preemption doctrine reflected both the extent and quality of this primacy. Envisaging a series of engagements with "rogue states," the Bush Doctrine aligned itself with the Rumsfeld preference for flexible, light and technologically developed warfare.[50] A large literature has proliferated on the roots of U.S. power—military, economic and "soft power"; on the prospects for successful military coercion in an era of asymmetric conflict; and on whether U.S. primacy will endure.[51] What can be asserted with confidence is that the Bush Doctrine was born from a unipolar reality. As so many realist commentators have pointed out, confident unilateralism is, at least at one level, merely a function of this unipolarity.

PRESIDENT, CONGRESS AND THE IRAQ WAR

In justifying the March 2003 invasion of Iraq, and in describing war aims, leading members of the administration tended not to invoke directly the Bush Doctrine of preemption. A Congressional Research Service study of March 2003 noted that, during much of 2002, such figures—especially Cheney, Rumsfeld and Wolfowitz—

tended to focus on the concept of "regime change." "Later in 2002," however, "WMD disarmament was emphasized as the primary objective."[52] Bush's September 12, 2002, speech to the UN called on the Iraqi government to disclose and destroy WMD, to end support for terrorism, to cease persecuting its civilian population, to release or account for all 1991 Gulf War missing personnel and to terminate all illicit trade outside the UN oil-for-food program. Bush's March 21, 2003, report to Congress described his goals as "to disarm Iraq in pursuit of peace, stability, and security both in the gulf region and in the United States."[53]

As in the 1990–91 Gulf crisis and conflict, the shifting of ground over military aims and justifications reflected the need to consider congressional objections to a war for "regime change."[54] In presenting its case for a use-of-force resolution in October 1992, the administration focused on the need to disarm Saddam. Like his father in 1990, the younger Bush apparently believed that no such resolution was strictly necessary.[55] In early September 2002, Congresswoman Eva Clayton (Democrat of North Carolina) read into the *Congressional Record* a series of statements from George W. Bush and Vice-President Cheney, seeming to indicate "that the President already has the authority to attack Iraq at wil."[56] Such authority supposedly derived, extremely controversially, from the constitutional commander-in-chief authority itself. Senator Russell Feingold (Democrat from Wisconsin) acknowledged in June 2002 that "few would disagree that the President must have the authority to launch a preemptive strike in advance of an imminent attack on the United States." However, according to Feingold, the "preemptive self defense argument" did not "necessarily fit squarely" with Iraq, where there was no demonstrated imminent threat.[57]

Where the Bush Doctrine, as delineated in the West Point address and in the National Security Strategy, did indeed appear to rest on some very broad construction of commander-in-chief powers, by the later months of 2002 the administration had virtually abandoned any hope that invocation of such powers would suffice to assuage Congress. Alternative sources of preemptive authority were the use-of-force authorization for the 1991 Gulf War (Public Law 102-1) and the post-9/11 congressional authorization of force (Senate Joint Resolution 23) in pursuance of the war on terror. As the debate on Iraq developed, however, it became evident that much congressional opinion would not be convinced that Public Law 102-1, geared to the liberation of Kuwait, might convincingly be expanded to cover an invasion of Iraq in 2002 or 2003. Whether Saddam's refusal to disarm constituted a reversion to conditions pertaining prior to the 1991 cease-fire, was a major issue in the legal debate surrounding the 2003 war. However, the White House did not seriously attempt to rest its invasion case, at least in terms of congressional authorization, on the 1991 measure.

As for the post-9/11 resolution, force authorization was closely tied to the 2001 terror attacks, albeit in the language of preemption. Under S.J. Res. 23, the president was authorized "to use all necessary and appropriate force" against "nations, organizations, or persons he determines planned, authorized, committed, or aided" the attacks in order to "prevent any future acts of international terrorism against the United States by any such nations, organizations or persons." Although the phrase, "he determines," opened up massive scope for presidential discretion, the 2001 resolution seemed to require a clear connection to be established between Baghdad and 9/11, if indeed S.J. Res 23 were to be used as the basis for invasion. A generalized invocation of preemption would certainly have involved stretching the post-9/11 use of force authority to breaking point.

The administration moved to secure a specific legislative authorization in September 2002. Bush's initial resolution invoked Iraq's "continuing hostility toward, and willingness to attack" the U.S. as a justification for preemptive action. Faced by some detailed Democratic objections to the expansive language, the White House accepted linguistic changes preferred by House Minority Leader Richard Gephardt of Missouri.[58] The final version omitted a phrase authorizing force to "restore peace and security to the region." Key Democrats saw the phrase as designed to justify attacks beyond Iraq. The version passed by both houses of Congress on October 10, 2002, also explicitly referred to the 1973 War Powers Resolution, and required an explicit presidential ruling that diplomatic channels had been exhausted, and that an attack on Iraq would not damage the wider war on terrorism. The authorization passed the House 296–133 and the Senate 77–23: these were considerably higher margins of support for the White House than Bush Senior had enjoyed in 1991. The final authority was very broad, giving George W. Bush permission to use force "as he determines to be necessary and appropriate" to defend U.S. security against Iraq's "continuing threat" and to enforce "all relevant" UN Security Council resolutions.

The September–October 2002 congressional debate on Iraq was perhaps not as intensive and wide-ranging as its January 1991 equivalent.[59] However, several radical lines of criticism of the Bush Doctrine were opened up by Democrats, and even by some Republicans. (Six House Republicans opposed the authorization on October10; in the Senate, the only dissenting Republican was Lincoln Chafee of Rhode Island.) For Representative Marcy Katpur (Democrat, Ohio), the "driving force of this potential war on Iraq is oil."[60] Much of the congressional criticism related directly to the degree of presidential discretion inherent in the preemptive doctrine. For Eva Clayton, preemption was "a radical departure from two centuries of U.S. defense and foreign policy."[61] Representative Pete Stark (Democrat, California) argued that the resolution gave Bush far too much discretionary leeway: "And so we are going to give an inexperienced, desperate young man in the White House the execution lever that kills thousands of Americans."[62] Vernon J. Ehlers (Republican, Michigan) declared: "I abhor the idea of the U.S. making a preemptive strike." Yet memories of 9/11 were still very fresh: "when the first punch" (continued Ehlers) "can destroy a city and kill hundreds and thousands of people, we must consider ways to stop that punch."[63]

One feature of the House response to the Bush Doctrine was the emergence of a group of anti-war libertarian (or, according to one's preferred terminology "neo-isolationist") Republicans. In March 2002, Congressman Ron Paul (Republican, Texas) put the case against discretionary preemption thus: "Arguing that someday in the future Saddam Hussein might pose a threat to us means that any nation any place in the world is subject to an invasion without cause."[64] In February 2003, Representative J. J. Duncan (Republican, Tennessee) outlined the basis of "conservative" opposition to war. It was "against every conservative tradition to support pre-emptive war." Such a war would turn the U.S. military into nation-builders and "international social workers," rather than upholders of national security.[65]

In the Senate, the principal upholder of congressional prerogatives, against the doctrine of discretionary preemption, was Democrat Robert C. Byrd of West Virginia. He argued that Congress was close utterly to surrendering its constitutional right to declare war. Byrd wrote that the resolution "would authorize the president to use the military forces of the nation, wherever, whenever and however he determines, and for as long as he determines, if he can somehow make a connection to Iraq." The Bush Doctrine was an "unprecedented doctrine of preventive war . . . against any nation that the president, and the president alone, determines to be a threat."[66] Carl Levin, Senate Armed Services Committee chairman, criticized the Bush administration's lowering the threshold of threat: "International law has never, never, gotten to the point where anything less than imminent threat was used as being sufficient."[67] Several anti-Bush Senators pointed out that Article 2(4) of the UN Charter prohibited preemptive attacks, certainly in the absence of any imminent need for self-defense. Comparisons were also made between the war resolution of October 2002 and the 1964 Gulf of Tonkin Resolution, giving President Johnson wide discretionary authority to wage war in Vietnam.

Senator Byrd's arguments, of course, did not win the day. His own opposition expired amid procedural issues and his unwillingness to mount a filibuster. Part of Byrd's case related to the timing of the resolution vote—less than one month before the midterm elections. *Congressional Quarterly* analysis did seem to indicate that members facing competitive races in November found it difficult to oppose the president.[68] However, the margin of victory for Bush's resolution was impressive, and cannot be explained away in terms of electoral pressures. Despite the White House's failure to establish any convincing case for linking Baghdad to the 2001 attacks, the specter of 9/11 hung over the legislative debate. Tom Lantos of California, ranking Democrat on the House International Relations Committee, even invoked the Munich analogy, describing anti-preemptionists as appeasers.[69] To many members, it was, ultimately, a matter of national solidarity.

CONCLUSION

The invocation of the need for national unity during the war on terror underscored the inherent weakness in such circumstances of congressional war powers. The Bush Doctrine of preemption involved both a major assertion of presidential authority and a potentially dangerous lowering of the threshold for war. One of the challenges for President George W. Bush in the wake of 9/11 undoubtedly was that of providing clarity in his declaratory foreign policy. Domestic audiences needed to be reassured. Enemies needed to be warned. However, excessively stark, excessively indiscriminate, excessively presidentialist declarations of intent were bound to provoke potentially damaging reactions, both at home and among America's allies. As we have seen, neither extreme presidentialism in war making, nor even the (uncodified) doctrine of preemption, constitute entirely new phenomena. The shock of 9/11, however, unquestionably threatened to weaken, even to destroy, important internal checks on presidential power, as well as to encourage the defense of policy by the rhetoric of exalted patriotism rather than reasoned, and constitutionally informed, persuasion.

All is not lost. Like most presidential doctrines, the Bush Doctrine on preemption embodied unilateral warning and, returning to the quotation from General de Gaulle, "elemental" feeling. In its development, it must, and no doubt will, also recognize complexity. Constraints on extreme discretionary presidential preemptionism emanate from the realities of international politics. The contrast between Bush administration policy towards Iraq and towards North Korea, an "evil" state capable of swiftly destroying its Southern neighbor, indicated that the doctrine would be implemented according to pragmatic dictates. History, and indeed the logic of democratic politics played out under the constitutional doctrine of separated powers, also indicates that extreme assertions of executive power soon provoke major challenges.

NOTES

1. Quoted in L. P. Bloomfield, *In Search of American Foreign Policy* (New York: Oxford University Press, 1974), p. 79.

2. Available at www.whitehouse.gov/news/releases/2002/06/20020601-3.html; www.whitehouse.gov/nssall.html

3. Cecil V. Crabb, *The Doctrines of American Foreign Policy* (Baton Rouge, LA: Louisiana State University Press, 1982), pp. 393–394.

4. See Richard Crockatt, *America Embattled: September 11, Anti-Americanism and the Global Order* (London: Routledge, 2003), pp. 136, 183.

5. Crabb, *The Doctrines*, lists also the following: two "Johnson Doctrines" (warnings to North Vietnam in 1964 and to Western hemispheric communists in 1965); and the 1969 Nixon Doctrine, on aid to international anti-communism. See also John Dumbrell, "Was There a Clinton Doctrine? President Clinton's Foreign Policy Reconsidered," *Diplomacy and Statecraft* 13 (No. 2, 2002): 43–56.

6. There are, of course, sub-presidential doctrines, such as the 1932 Stimson Doctrine on the non-recognition of Japanese aggression and the (Caspar) Weinberger and (Colin) Powell Doctrines on conditions for post-Vietnam War US military intervention.

7. Bob Woodward, *Bush At War* (New York: Simon and Schuster, 2002), p. 30. Michael Hirsh ("Bush and the World," *Foreign Affairs*, 81 (No. 5, 2002): 18–43), suggests that the president wrote crucial parts of the speech himself.

8. Hirsh, "Bush and the World," p. 19.

9. See John Dumbrell, *American Foreign Policy: Carter to Clinton* (Basingstoke, UK: Macmillan, 1997), p. 169.

10. "Unprecedented Power, Colliding Ambitions," *The Economist*, September 28, 2002, p. 53.

11. Quoted in James Kitfield, "The New New World Order," *National Journal*, November 2, 2002, pp. 3192–3198, 3195.

12. Todd Lindberg, "The war on terror: the Bush Doctrine," *Hoover Digest*, Fall 2002 (www.hoover.stanford.edu/publications/digest/024/lindberg, html).

13. www.truthout.org/docs_02/10.9A.kennedy.html.

14. Diane Feinstein, "The new Bush Doctrine," February 26, 2003, www.senate.gov/-feinstein/03speeches/nationalsecspeech2-6.html

15. William Kristol testimony, 7 Feb. 2002, www.newamericancentury.org/foreignrelations-020702.html

16. Quoted in John Lewis Gaddis, *Strategies of Containment* (Oxford: Oxford University Press, 1982), pp. 48–9.

17. See Ray Monk, *Bertrand Russell: The Ghost of Madness, 1921–1970* (London: Vintage, 2000), p. 298.

18. Gaddis, *Strategies of Containment*, p. 100.

19. Ibid., p. 149.

20. See Robert F. Kennedy, *13 Days* (London: Macmillan, 1969), p. 42.

21. See Gordon H. Chang, *Friends and Enemies: The United States, China and the Soviet Union, 1948–1972* (Stanford, CA: Stanford University Press, 1990), p. 245.

22. See Shane Maddock, "LBJ, China and the Bomb: New Archival Evidence," Society for Historians of American Foreign Relations *Newsletter* 27 (No. 1, 1996): 1–5.

23. See "US planning for war in Europe, 1963–1964," National Security Archive electronic briefing book 31 (ed. William Burr, 2000); Llewellyn Thompson to Seymour Weiss, December 29, 1964 (available on National Security Archive web site).

24. Lyndon B. Johnson. *The Vantage Point: Perspective of the Presidency, 1963–1969* (London: Weidenfeld and Nicolson, 1972), pp. 188, 195.

25. *Public Papers of the Presidents of the United States, 1983: Ronald Reagan, vol. 1* (Washington, DC: US Government Printing Office, 1985), p. 1521 (October 27, 1983).

26. Ibid., *1986: Ronald Reagan, vol. 1* (Washington, DC: US Government Printing Office, 1988), pp. 468–469 (April 14, 1986).

27. Ibid., *1998: William J. Clinton, vol. 2* (Washington DC: US Government Printing Office, 2000), p. 1460 (August 20, 1998).

28. See Louis Fisher, *Presidential War Power* (Lawrence, KS: University Press of Kansas, 1995), pp. 141–44.

29. Anthony Lewis, "Bush and Iraq," *New York Review of Books*, November 7, 2002, pp. 7–13, 8.

30. G. John Ikenberry, "America's Imperial Ambition," *Foreign Affairs*, 81 (No. 5, 2002): 44–60, 51.

31. Ibid.

32. See "Preempting Threats, Threatening Preemption," *The Economist*, September 28, 2002, pp. 14–15.

33. Mary Kaldor, "American Power: From 'Compellance' to Cosmopolitanism?" *International Affairs*, 79 (No. 1, 2003): 1–22, 12.

34. See Charles Tiefer, *The Semi-Sovereign Presidency: the Bush Administration's Strategy for Governing without Congress* (Boulder, CO: Westview, 1994).

35. See Anthony Lake, "Confronting Backlash States," *Foreign Affairs*, 73 (No. 2,1994): 44–55. The "rogue states" doctrine dated back at least as far as the later Carter presidential years. For a devastating critique of the concept, see Robert S. Litwak, *Rogue States and US Foreign Policy: Containment after the Cold War* (Baltimore, MD: Johns Hopkins University Press, 2000).

36. See Dumbrell, "Was There a Clinton Doctrine?"

37. "America's Imperial Ambition," pp. 56–7.

38. See Julie Kosterlitz, "Empire strikes back," *National Journal*, December 14, 2002, pp. 3640–3645, 3644.

39. Quoted in Norman Mailer, "Only in America," *New York Review of Books*, March 27, 2003, pp. 49–53, 51 (*The Atlanta Journal-Constitution*, September 29, 2002).

40. "Only in America," p. 50.

41. Kosterlitz, "Empire Strikes Back," p. 3641.

42. According to Andrew Bacevich, "empire" and "imperialism" are "no longer fightin' words," *ibid.*

43. See James Petras and Morris Morley, *Empire or Republic? American Global Power and Domestic Decay* (London: Routledge, 1995), pp. 15–16.

44. See Robert Kagan, "A Retreat from Power?" *Commentary*, July 1995, pp. 19-25; William Kristol and Robert Kagan, "Toward a Neo-Reaganite Foreign Policy," *Foreign Affairs*, 75 (No. 1, 1996): 8–32.

45. Kosterlitz, "Empire strikes back," p. 3643.

46. See John Dumbrell, "Unilateralism and 'America First'? President George W. Bush's Foreign Policy," *The Political Quarterly*, 73 (No. 3, 2002): 279–287.

47. Hirsh, "Bush and the World," p. 22.

48. See "Unprecedented Power, Colliding Ambitions."

49. Quoted in Hirsch, "Bush and the world," p. 32.

50. See Michael Cox, "American Power before and after 11 September: Dizzy with Success?" *International Affairs* 78 (No. 2, 2002): 261–76; Donald H. Rumsfeld, "Transforming the Military," *Foreign Affairs* 81 (No. 3, 2002): 20–32.

51. See Joseph S. Nye, "Limits of American power," *Political Science Quarterly* 117 (No. 4, 2002–3): 545–70; Kaldor, "American power"; Daniel Byman and Matthew Waxman, *The Dynamics of Coercion: American Foreign Policy and the Limits of Military Might* (Cambridge, UK: Cambridge University Press, 2002).

52. Steven Bowman, "Iraq: US Military Operations," Congressional Research Service report for Congress, updated 26 March 2003, p. 1.

53. Richard F. Grimmett, "War Powers Resolution: Presidential compliance," Congressional Research Service report for Congress, updated 24 March 2003, p. 2.

54. See Dumbrell, *American Foreign Policy: Carter to Clinton*, ch. 8.

55. See Bob Woodward, *The Commanders* (New York: Simon and Schuster, 1991), pp. 219–21; Miles A. Pomper, "Senate Democrats in Disarray After Gephardt's Deal on Iraq," *Congressional Quarterly Weekly Report*, October 5, 2002, p. 607.

56. *Congressional Record*, H6109, September 9, 2002.

57. Ibid., S5280-81, 10 June 10, 2002.

58. See Pomper, "Democrats in Disarray After Gephardt's Deal on Iraq," pp. 2607–2610.

59. See John Dumbrell, "The US Congress and the Gulf War," in J. Walsh, ed., *'The Gulf War Did Not Happen'* (Aldershot, UK: Arena, 1994), pp. 49–62.

60. David Nather, "'One Voice' Lost in Debate Over Iraq War Resolution," *Congressional Quarterly Weekly Report*, September 28, 2002, p. 2499.

61. *Congressional Record*, H6109, September 9, 2002.

62. Gebe Martinez, "Concerns Linger for Lawmakers Following Difficult Vote for War," *Congressional Quarterly Weekly Report*, October 12, 2002, pp. 2671–2675.

63. Ibid., p. 2678.

64. *Congressional Record*, H1075, March 20, 2002.

65. Ibid., H1359, February 26, 2003.

66. "Martinez, "Concerns Linger for Lawmakers Following Difficult Vote for War," p. 2675. See also Kirk Victor, "Congress in Eclipse," *National Journal*, 5 April 2003, pp. 1066–1070; James A. Chace, "Present at the Destruction: The Death of American Internationalism," *World Policy Journal* 20 (No. 1, 2003): 1–5.

67. "Martinez, "Concerns Linger for Lawmakers Following Difficult Vote for War," p. 2675.

68. Ibid., p. 2672.

69. Ibid., p. 2675.